T0301655

NATURE IN TRANSLATION

SHIHO SATSUKA

NATURE IN TRANSLATION

Japanese Tourism Encounters
the Canadian Rockies

DUKE UNIVERSITY PRESS   DURHAM AND LONDON   2015

Typeset in Chaparral Pro by Westchester Book Group

Library of Congress Cataloging-in-Publication Data
Satsuka, Shiho
Nature in translation : Japanese tourism encounters the
Canadian Rockies / Shiho Satsuka.
pages cm
Includes bibliographical references and index.
ISBN 978-0-8223-5867-1 (hardcover : alk. paper)
ISBN 978-0-8223-5880-0 (pbk. : alk. paper)
ISBN 978-0-8223-7560-9 (e-book)
1. Japanese—Alberta—Banff National Park. 2. Tour guides
(Persons)—Alberta—Banff National Park. 3. Tour guides
(Persons)—Japan. 4. Japanese—Travel—Alberta—Banff
National Park. 5. Ecotourism—Alberta—Banff National Park.
6. Banff National Park (Alta.)—Description and travel.
7. Japan—Civilization—21st century. I. Title.
F1080.J3S38 2015
971.23'32—dc23   2015004992

Cover art: Photo by Rebecca Lipes

Duke University Press gratefully acknowledges the Rachel Carson
Center for Environment and Society at LMU Munich, which
provided funds toward the publication of this book.

Printed and bound by CPI Group (UK) Ltd, Croydon, CR0 4YY

Contents

Notes on Transliteration

Japanese personal names are written in the Japanese fashion, with the surname preceding the given name, except for the names of authors whose works have been published primarily in English under their names in English order (e.g., Naoki Sakai, Miyako Inoue).

The modified Hepburn system (Hebon-shiki) is used to romanize the Japanese language. Macrons are used to indicate long vowels (ā, ī, ū, ē, ō) with the exception of names and terms commonly seen without macrons (e.g., Tokyo, Osaka).

Acknowledgments

Nature in Translation is a product of a long journey. Many people helped me to go through the process of completing this book by providing me with support, encouragement, and stimulation. My first and foremost thanks go to all the people whom I met during my fieldwork in the Canadian Rockies and follow-up research in Vancouver and Japan. While I would like to express my sincere thanks to each one of these wonderful individuals, I should refrain from identifying most of them by name in order to protect their privacy and maintain confidentiality. I am grateful for their generosity in sharing their experiences and insights, as well as their wit, humor, and sincerity. In Banff, I would like to thank Bill Fisher, then superintendent of Banff National Park, for allowing me to do fieldwork in the park. I also thank Mary Dalman, Heather Dempsey, Ann Morrow, and Kathy Rettie at Banff National Park, and Shauna Mc-Garvey and Gord Stermann at the Mountain Parks Heritage Interpretation Association for their kind support. Bob Sandford also helped me get oriented to the place and generously shared his insights about the area. Many thanks to Rebecca Lipes for allowing me to use her wonderful photo for the cover of this book. She also helped open my eyes to the delicate detail of the landscape. Ōhashi Kyosen generously spent time with me and answered my questions.

This book began as a doctoral dissertation in the Anthropology Department at the University of California, Santa Cruz. I was fortunate

to have Anna Tsing, Lisa Rofel, and Hugh Raffles as my core commit-
tee. Without their superb guidance and thoughtful encouragement, this
project would never have materialized. I cannot thank them enough for
their tireless support and brilliant advice. In Santa Cruz, I also learned
the joy of experimenting in new ways of thinking from Jim Clifford,
Donna Haraway, and Susan Harding. Their courage in exploring new
intellectual terrain provided tremendous inspiration. Noriko Aso, Don
Brenneis, and Alan Christy generously read parts of the manuscript
and offered extraordinarily insightful suggestions and comments. This
book also benefited from conversations with Timothy Choy, Bregje van
Eekelen, Lieba Faier, Cori Hayden, Hiroyuki Matsubara, Scott Mor-
gensen, Yen-ling Tsai, and Sasha Welland. I also would like to thank Ken
Little and Margaret Critchlow at York University in Toronto, who helped
me at a very early stage of this project. During my fieldwork in Banff,
Alan and Josie Smart, Pascale Sicotte, and Julia Murphy at the University
of Calgary, as well as Pamela Asquith at the University of Alberta, provided me with institutional, intellectual, or personal support.

A postdoctoral research fellowship in Japanese Studies from the Institute for International Studies and a visiting assistant professorship in
anthropology at Stanford University helped me to enlarge my perspective, especially regarding Japan's position in the world. I would like to
thank Harumi Befu, Paulla Ebron, Christine Guth, and Liisa Malkki, all
of whom helped me tremendously while I was there. I owe special thanks
to Miyako Inoue, Kären Wigen, and Sylvia Yanagisako, who read earlier
versions of the chapters and gave me extraordinarily helpful comments.
I completed most of the manuscript during my term as a Carson Fellow
at the Rachel Carson Center for Environment and Society in Munich,
Germany. I would like to thank the center's directors, Christof Mauch
and Helmuth Trischler, as well as Arielle Helmick, the managing director, for creating a wonderful intellectual community there. Bridget Love
and Sam Temple helped me by carefully reading the manuscript and
shared the pleasant time there as fellows. Along the way, many people
offered me generous support and inspiration for this project. I thank in
particular Andrea Arai, Bruce Braun, Michael Hathaway, Jean-Guy Goulet,
Etsuko Kato, Celia Lowe, Hideko Mitsui, Ayumi Miyazaki, Molly Mullin,
and Yuko Okubo for their helpful comments and suggestions.

At the University of Toronto, I would like to thank my colleagues who
have offered me intellectual stimulation and supported me in various
ways. In particular, the following colleagues read earlier portions of the

manuscript, discussed parts of the project, or provided specific institutional support: Sandra Bamford, Joshua Barker, Janice Boddy, Frank Cody, Girish Daswani, Naisargi Dave, Tak Fujitani, Chris Krupa, Michael Lambek, Tania Li, Hy Luong, Bonnie McElhinny, Lena Mortensen, Andrea Muehlebach, Michelle Murphy, Valentina Napolitano, Alejandro Paz, Todd Sanders, Atsuko Sakaki, Gavin Smith, Jesook Song, and Lisa Yoneyama. I am also grateful to many student assistants who helped at various stages of this project, especially Grant Otsuki and Johanna Pokorny, who not only assisted me in the editorial process but also carefully read and critically engaged with the manuscript.

Some parts of the book were presented at several conferences and workshops, including annual meetings of the American Anthropological Association and the Canadian Anthropological Society, the Tourism-Contact-Culture Research Network, and the Social Science Research Council's Japan Studies Dissertation Workshop. Earlier incarnations of some chapters were also presented at colloquiums and work-in-progress sessions, including those at the Japanese Studies Program and the Department of Anthropology at Stanford University, Asian Studies and Canadian Studies at the University of Washington, the Department of Anthropology at Trent University, and the Sociocultural Linguistic Discussion Series at the University of Toronto. I would like to thank everyone who participated in these events and provided insightful comments.

In addition to the fellowships already mentioned, this project became possible with the generous support of the Social Sciences and Humanities Research Council of Canada Doctoral Fellowship, University of Toronto Connaught Funds, University of California Pacific Rim Research Funds, and a Matsushita International Fellowship. The University of Toronto allowed me to take a nine-month research leave to accept a fellowship at the Rachel Carson Center in 2012. I also thank the Rachel Carson Center for help with the cost of publication. I am tremendously grateful to Ken Wissoker, Elizabeth Ault, and Sara Leone at Duke University Press for their patience and generous support. I would like to extend my gratitude to two anonymous reviewers whose careful reading improved this book. I also thank Kathy Chetkovich, Jessica Neely, and Pam Kido for their wonderful editorial help on earlier versions of the manuscript.

Finally, my parents, my sister, and my partner have supported me throughout the entire process of completing this book project. This book is dedicated to my late father, who is missed beyond words. I also would like to extend the dedication to people like him in Japan, Canada, and elsewhere; he was simply one of many humble "ordinary" citizens, yet his presence made a huge difference to the family he supported through his everyday hard work.

Parts of chapter 2 appeared in an earlier form as "Populist Cosmopolitanism: The Predicament of Subjectivity and the Japanese Fascination with Overseas," in *Inter-Asia Cultural Studies* 10, no. 1 (2009): 67–82.

Prologue A Journey to Magnificent Nature . . .
or Why Nature Needs to Be
Understood in Translation

This is an ethnography of nature in translation. In particular, the book focuses on Japanese tour guides living in Banff—Canada's iconic national park—and examines how they translated various notions of nature for tourists from Japan.

The experiences of the Japanese tour guides elucidate how translation of nature is not only about the superficial differences of cultural aesthetics, such as the idea that the Japanese love manicured gardens with bonsai-like trees, whereas North Americans like rugged landscapes of untouched wilderness. Translation of nature concerns what counts as human, what kind of society is envisioned, and who is included in the society as a legitimate subject.

The backdrop of this ethnography is the heightened sense of crisis about the Japanese economy since the 1990s: The so-called Japanese-style corporate system and work relations developed and praised as the source of Japan's post–World War II economic success were severely challenged and became targets of harsh neoliberal reform. In this social environment, quite a number of young Japanese "escaped" from Japan to go overseas for self-searching travel.

In particular, the "magnificent nature" (*daishizen*) of North America had a strong allure in attracting some of these Japanese, many of whom projected a vision of a utopian space for freedom onto the vast natural landscape in North America. A journey to magnificent nature has been

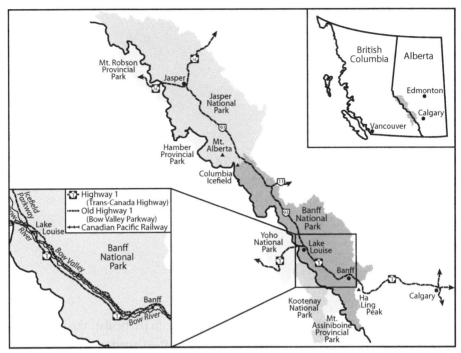

Banff National Park and Canadian Rocky Mountain Parks World Heritage Site.
Created by Johanna Pokorny.

one of the most popular themes in Japanese tourist representations.
Invitations to magnificent nature can be found in many places: books,
magazines, and abundant displays of colorful, glossy travel brochures
found at any major train station in urban Japan. Among many destinations, North America, particularly Canada, has a long history of being
marketed as the "dreamed of" place for Japanese tourists to experience
magnificent nature. What is the appeal of magnificent nature to Japanese travelers? How has the vast scale of nature in Canada served as a
site for young Japanese to transform their subjectivities at this critical
historical moment? What do their experiences tell us about the subjectivity of flexible workers who were pushed into transnational labor markets? How are the guides' experiences shaped by the larger historical
context of cultural encounters in asymmetrical global power relations?
This book aims to explore these questions.

My interest in nature and tourism originated in the 1990s when I
moved to Toronto from Japan and began studying anthropology. During the 1980s and the 1990s, the influx of Japanese tourists to Banff

National Park was a recurrent topic in the popular media. The Japanese tourists, who were the first non-Western group to travel the world en masse, attracted curiosity and attention. Their presence stood out and disrupted the assumed hierarchical division between who has the power and privilege of travel and who does not. In casual conversations with friends, fellow students, and even strangers with whom I exchanged a few words while sharing a table in a busy lunchtime cafeteria or while waiting for transportation, I received comments and questions about the Japanese tourists. Most of the comments centered around observations of the peculiar behaviors of the tourists from Japan—they wear identical badges with the same tour logo, stop at sightseeing spots for only a few minutes, take photos—click, click—go back to the bus, and rush to the next spot. I was asked many times, "Do they really enjoy nature?"

With this question in mind, as I shared the same image of mass tourists, in the summer of 1999 I joined a Japanese bus tour as a tourist.

The tour started from the Calgary airport with about twenty Japanese tourists: several middle-aged and senior couples, families with young children, a couple of young women, a pair of elderly sisters, my mother, my sister, and me. The bus was heading to Lake Louise in Banff National Park, about 200 kilometers (about 124 miles) northwest of Calgary. It was the first day of a five-day tour that promised participants they would experience the magnificent nature of the Canadian Rockies. During the drive on the Trans-Canada Highway—through cattle ranches, a First Nation reserve, and the Rocky Mountain foothills—the guide, a Japanese man in his early thirties, captured the tourists' attention with his wit and the breadth of his knowledge, especially about the natural landscape. He pointed to the rocky face of the mountains and told us we were actually looking at the bottom of the ocean. As we looked at the guide quizzically, he described how a collision of continental plates tens of millions of years ago raised the ocean floor, and how the glaciers carved the mountains into their current shapes. He also highlighted the Canadian national parks' efforts to conserve biodiversity. After entering the park, he pointed out the two "animal overpasses," prominent stone bridges built for wild animals to cross the highway, and explained that the park had spent $1.5 million to construct each bridge. The overpasses, he claimed, represented Canada's world-leading efforts to live in harmony with nature: the purpose of building the bridges was to connect separate areas of the wildlife habitat, which were divided by the highway, and to compensate for the inconvenience that human presence imposed on the animals. He quickly added that at first the animals were too wary to use the expensive bridges; when a black bear used one of them for the first time, the people in town celebrated.

Many of the tourists, especially the senior citizens, vigorously took notes on the guide's stories. Sometimes they missed information while they laughed at his jokes, but soon after they checked each other's notes for the missing pieces. At photo-taking spots, the tourists rushed the guide, asking him to take their photos, and then helped each other take photos with him. By the end of the day, the tourists seemed to be fully enchanted by the guide's informative and entertaining presentation.

This was my first experience with a commercial Japanese packaged tour. I was surprised to see how attracted the tourists were to the tour guide, and how he played a significant role in shaping their experiences. In particular, I was struck by the way the guide translated the relationship between nature and humans. Among the many stories he offered, one that most impressed me was about pine forests. After going under the animal overpasses and near several scenic mountains, the bus passed through a long, wide stretch of valley covered with a lodgepole pine forest. The scenery was rather monotonous in this section, but he continued capturing the tourists' attention by explaining the area's natural history. He began the story by saying, "Look at those straight, tall trees. From afar, they look like cedar or *hinoki* cypress from Japanese forests, since their branches do not spread out vertically. You might think that these trees were planted by humans, and that somebody is taking care of them by cutting off their branches, so they grow beautifully straight. But in fact, this is a natural forest, not an artificial one. These trees grow naturally in that shape."

His narration was puzzling to me: Why did he compare the conserved forest in the Canadian national park with industrial forests in Japan? Up until then, he had spent much time in explaining the national park's efforts at environmental conservation. He emphasized that the basic policy of the park is to minimize the human impact and to "leave nature as is." According to this logic, it would be reasonable to assume the shape of the trees in the forest was "natural" and not being pruned by people. Assuming that North American national parks were built for the purpose of protecting the natural landscape from industrial resource extraction, it sounded odd to me that the guide introduced the wild pine forest by using cedars and cypress in cash-producing Japanese forests as a reference point.

Then, I heard tourists commenting, "Isn't it amazing that these beautiful straight trees are all natural?" Even though it was a small footnote in his story, this explanation seemed to have a strong impact on the tourists. Whenever they saw a similarly vast conifer forest, they asked the guide if that forest was also natural. The guide's anticipated answer, "yes," prompted the tourists to further express their astonishment. I heard several times from different people, "How magnificent Canada's nature is!" (*Kanada no shizen wa sugoine!*)

The tourists might have assumed that if such a vast space existed in Japan, nobody would leave it alone, without utilizing it for industrial resource extraction, whereas in Canada the natural resource was so abundant that such a large forest could be simply left as an object for people's appreciation and for conserving space for other species. While the guide was attentive to various assumptions about the conifer forest and the different practices in a Canadian national park versus Japanese industrial forests, he also tried to bridge the gap between these various approaches to nature. His translation work was effective as it enhanced the tourists' experience of astonishment at the magnificent nature. Obviously, on this tour, the tourists did enjoy nature. Even though the time they spent at each spot was short, in the bus, the guide filled them with information to maximize their appreciation of nature in the limited time assigned to each site.

This experience of joining the tour prompted me to reflect on a comment I received from a person with whom I had shared a table at a cafeteria in Toronto. He told me that Japanese tourists reminded him of a herd of lemmings suicidally marching en masse—a popular misconception about the animal—blindly following a leader to cross the water, with many being drowned. His comment was interesting because my impression on the bus tour was, rather, that the tourists were learning how to see nature like Americans and Canadians. From the guide, they learned about the history of European expeditions and Parks Canada's efforts to conserve the natural environment. More fundamentally, although there is a long tradition of traveling in Japan, organizing mass tours to see nature as an object of the individual's subjective gaze was a relatively new practice introduced in the twentieth century in the process of Western-modeled modernization.[1]

It seemed ironic that a sense of cultural difference emerged in the midst of the Japanese attempts to learn new practices and perspectives of engaging with nature. I was further intrigued to ask: What was happening in the process of cultural translation of nature? While the guides' work of cultural translation had a considerable impact on tourists, the significance of their work seemed to be underestimated in the popular perception. What kind of role does a tour guide play in nature tourism? The comment from the man in the cafeteria also raises more fundamental questions about the relationship between nature and subjectivity as I heard similar comments repeatedly. Why did the Japanese tourists give the impression that they were like rodents blindly following instincts controlled by nature, rather than humans who have their own unique subjectivities to see nature as an object of their appreciation? How does the notion of nature play a role in the politics of subjectivity? Who is considered to have a normative form of subjectivity and, therefore, to be a legitimate member of human community? How did the guides' work of nature translation shape the way they construct their subjectivities in their everyday lives in Canada? What do the Japanese guides' experiences tell us about the cultural politics of nature—how different knowledge and practices were negotiated, what kinds of power relations are at work in the encounters of people living with different epistemological traditions? In order to explore these questions, I decided to move to Banff.

This ethnography is based on my fieldwork in Banff, a town located in Banff National Park and the tourist center of the Canadian Rocky Mountain Parks World Heritage Site, from February 2000 to December 2001, as well as my follow-up research and ongoing conversations with the tour guides until 2014. In Banff, I worked with a Japanese guide service company as an apprentice guide and lived in the company's accommodations for the first seven months of my fieldwork. As I lived and worked with them, the tour guides also guided me through the rough and unfamiliar passages of tracing nature in translation.

The main argument of this book is that nature is always in translation. Nature offers a site for people with diverse backgrounds to engage with one another by evoking the idea that we live in the shared natural environment and, as human beings, have the same nature. Due to these imagined commonalities, we must constantly translate how others understand nature, despite the tremendous differences in understandings of nature in various knowledge traditions. The process of translation reveals that we are always attempting to grasp what others know about nature by using our own knowledge framework. Translation simultaneously creates the meeting ground and highlights differences, tensions, contradictions, and frictions. This leads to the second point of the book: the translation of "nature" is not only a philosophical question. Nature also shapes politics and economies. Tensions and frictions in the translation of nature have actual and serious consequences for people's everyday lives, livelihoods, and life trajectories. Competing notions of nature affect how people make decisions about constructing a sense of place and remaking landscapes. They influence our ideas about what is good for our health and well-being, and our decisions about whether to ally ourselves with imagined progress or tradition.

Through their work of translating nature, the guides tried to make sense of the wide range of social problems in Japan, including work situations, family obligations, and gender expectations. They also tried to understand these issues within a global and historical context, to locate themselves in the world, to articulate the types of relationship they wanted to build with other people, and to envision the kind of society they wanted to live in. From everyday casual chats in such places as the company office, an empty tour van before or after the tours, somebody's living room, and on hiking trails, as well as from formal, recorded interviews, I learned how nature—both as a concept and as a physical environment—had a significant impact on the lives of the tour guides. Conversations about nature not only helped me to know each guide as a person but also provided me with a window through which to see the larger social issues that shaped each guide's experiences and life trajectory. The guides helped me to realize the importance of what Felix Guattari calls "ecosophy," an ethico-political articulation of three ecological registers—the environment, social relations, and human subjectivity (2008, 19–20). Thus, the focus of this book is on the journey of the tour guides, not that of the tourists.

Introduction

The Invisible Work of Tour Guides

One block behind Banff's busy main street, the town showed a different face. There were fewer colorful restaurant and souvenir store signs competing to attract tourists. The street was calmer. The squishing sounds of winter boots marked time. Occasionally, the spray of snow slush, brown from car tires, disrupted the rhythm. It looked like an ordinary small town in western Canada, except that it had a strong cosmopolitan flavor. Along with a small movie theater and a few outdoor equipment stores, there was a quiet, down-to-earth coffee shop run by a Korean family, a convenience store whose shelves contained international foods—especially a variety of Asian groceries—and a Greek souvlaki eatery that also served hamburgers and poutine, Quebecois "soul food." The buildings on this street housed an office supply store, an accounting office, a real estate agency, the Canadian Automobile Association, and other basic services for the residents. If Banff Avenue was the center stage for tourist encounters, this street was the backstage, the space where the actors and staff gathered their equipment, took a good break, and did all the necessary preparation for their interactions with tourists.[1]

The office of the Rocky Mountain Tours (RMT) was nestled in one of the buildings on this street, along with several other Japanese guide service companies. I entered the office to speak to the senior operations manager, Ms. Asada Atsuko, or Atsuko-san;[2] I intended to propose that I would work as an apprentice guide for the RMT. At a round table in the rear corner of the office, a Japanese man and woman, appearing to be in their twenties, were vigorously writing something with dictionaries in their hands. As I walked farther into the small office, I noticed that the desks and tables were covered with English documents, notepads, and English-Japanese dictionaries. Although Atsuko-san explained to me that guiding was a seasonal job and that work was scarce in winter, on that particular day the office was busy. In addition to the administrative staff, several guides were in the office, absorbed in translating an English book manuscript into Japanese. The manuscript was divided into short sections and assigned to the guides, who, when finished, handed the translated texts back to two senior guides in charge of proofreading. Putting their labor together, they were trying to meet a tight deadline.

Atsuko-san explained that the RMT had volunteered to help prepare for the main event of the year in the Canadian Rockies, the seventy-fifth anniversary of the first ascent of Mount Alberta, scheduled for the coming summer. The manuscript that the guides were translating was for a book about the legendary ascent of the Japanese climber Maki Yūkō that would commemorate the event. The book, *Called by This Mountain*, was written by Robert Sandford, a local historian and the vice president of the Canadian Alpine Club, and was to be published by the club as an English-Japanese bilingual book. In this work, Sandford glorifies Maki's achievement and recounts the legend—known in the North American mountaineering community—of the emperor's silver ice axe that Maki supposedly left at the peak.

Sandford's book was an important document that represented the transnational spirit of the event; it celebrated the love of mountains supposedly shared by people across the globe. In the published book's acknowledgments, Sandford thanked many individuals, both Japanese and Canadian, for preparing for, sponsoring, and participating in the event including a Japanese tour company that subcontracted the work to the RMT. But there was no mention of the guides from the RMT who worked hard to translate the book. This invisibility of the guides' work was a structural problem. In the complex subcontracting system of the tourism industry, the presence of the subcontracted company was often obscured and the significance of guides' labor in producing the transnational cultural encounter was often underrepresented. But on actual tours and in related events like this celebration, it was the guides who furnished the means to satisfy tourists' curiosity and mediate communication among people of various linguistic and cultural backgrounds.

Nature in Translation examines the work of these Japanese tour guides living in Banff. The guides' work, and that of other mediators like them, has been assumed to be less significant than the work of stars such as Maki or Sandford, whose performances have been highlighted as the centerpiece of cultural encounters. However, in their everyday work practices, these tour guides have played a significant role in exposing Japanese tourists to the "universal love of the mountain" that Sandford tried to promote. This ethnography illustrates the lives and work of tour guides who make transnational communication about nature possible and examines the distinct ways in which they shaped cultural encounters in the Canadian Rockies. The majority of the Japanese guides who worked in Banff, most of whom were in their twenties and thirties, had voluntarily dropped out of the Japanese corporate system or "escaped" from Japan to pursue their dream of living in "magnificent nature." Many of the guides had projected contrasting ideas of society on natural landscapes: they saw the openness of society represented in the large-scale mountain ranges, forests, and wide-open physical spaces in North America; in contrast, the narrowness of people's minds, constraining customs, and tradition-bound, suffocating social rules and expectations were seen as reflections of the "small-scale" Japanese landscape. The Japanese guides themselves also felt "called" by the natural landscape of the North American mountains. The life trajectories of the guides, which I will describe in more detail later, elucidate how the vast scale of this landscape provided resources for them to construct imaginaries of a global space, as well as temporal sensibilities of modernity. Through these imaginaries and sensibilities, the Japanese guides tried to carve out new positions and subjectivities in a global context.

Central to this construction of social imaginaries and subjectivities is the translation of nature. Since the late nineteenth century, learning how to see nature from within the modern Western epistemological framework has been a key theme in the development of Japan as a sovereign nation-state. Maki's achievement as the first internationally acclaimed Japanese mountaineer was significant in this regard. As I elaborate below, the translation of nature has a larger social significance because "nature" is closely related to understandings of subjectivity and individual freedom—foundational concepts of modern Western democracy. Like human nature, natural rights, and natural law, the concept of nature is central to modern political and economic systems. Through an ethnographic examination of the Japanese tour guides in Banff, this book explores how these translated sensibilities of nature have played a significant role in shaping the lives of people in contemporary Japan. In particular, it examines how the guides' practice of nature translation reflects the recent social changes wrought by neoliberalism, or *shinjiyūshugi*. In contemporary debates regarding the neoliberal restructuring in Japan, the incommensurability entailed in translations of "nature," "subjectivity," and "freedom" resurfaces and influences the lives of many people.

The late 1990s and the first years of the twenty-first century witnessed a heightened sense of "crisis" about the Japanese economy (see Yoda and Harootunian 2006). Corporate systems and work relations developed in the post–World War II period were challenged from various points along the political spectrum and became the target of "reform." A series of neoliberal policy changes were implemented under the slogan of "liberalization" (*jiyūka*) or "structural reform" (*kōzō kaikaku*). It was a time when previous assumptions about work and the state-corporate-sponsored social welfare system were seriously questioned. Correspondingly, the role of family and gender relations that supported work relations also became the subject of public debates. Responding to these social changes, many people, especially those who were coming of age and forming their subjectivities as workers, were compelled to embark on a period of soul-searching.

In examining the work of these tour guides at translating nature, this book explores not only how they interpreted the Canadian natural landscape for Japanese tourists but also how their changing worldviews and subjectivities were taking shape at this critical historical moment when the meaning of "freedom" became a contentious issue. The aim of this book is also to analyze what kinds of ethical and social values were produced and communicated in the process, and how the production of these values was intertwined with the construction of the guides' subjectivities in the process of remaking themselves as flexible workers in transnational settings.

Nature in Translation contributes to the critical analysis of cultural politics in two ways. First, adding to previous discussions of cultural translation, this book provides a detailed ethnographic account of the ongoing, everyday process of cultural translation and transformation. Cultural translation is a continuous process, not one completed once and for all at the moment of initial encounter. The coexistence of incommensurable ideas in "nature," "subjectivity," and "freedom" still plays a significant role in shaping Japanese everyday life in the twenty-first century. Heated debates about neoliberalism reveal how the translation word *jiyū*, for the English term "freedom" or "liberation," entails a tension with *jiyū* in the term *jiyū jizai*, derived from the Buddhist notion of liberation as self-detachment. By paying close attention to the everyday translation processes, this book highlights the quotidian nature of cultural politics and the constant process of negotiation over how to locate one's self in relation to nature, and how this negotiation shapes people's understandings of what it means to be a liberated subject.

Second, in relation to the preceding point, but more concretely, this book explores how cultural translation is central to the production of "value" in contemporary capitalism. Many critics have pointed out that, in contemporary capitalism, the weight of the economy has shifted to the immaterial aspects of work, such as offering services, knowledge, and information, as well as influencing one's feelings, emotions, and well-being (e.g., Hardt and Negri 2000, 2004; Lazzarato 1996; Virno 2004). The guides' labor certainly provides these intangibles: in their communications with tourists, guides provide information and knowledge, and direct tourists' feelings and views of the world. In this regard, this book joins the analysis of immaterial work and affective labor. Of particular note, however, the construction of subjectivity and exploration of freedom—key analytic themes in the critical analysis of immaterial work—are explicitly foregrounded in the work of tour guides who performatively construct their subjectivity as cosmopolitans, liberated from the constraints of contemporary Japan. Thus, this ethnographic analysis of the Japanese tour guides elucidates how the workers themselves understand and negotiate the issue of subjectivity and freedom in a manner grounded in their lives. Their everyday activities highlight how the ways in which the workers construct their subjectivities and pursue freedom are conflated in the production of value in contemporary capitalism.[3]

Translation in Practice

The work of the Japanese tour guides living in Canada inevitably entailed various kinds of linguistic and cultural translation. The RMT provided a variety of guide services, mostly through its contracts with several major travel agencies in Japan. Its main work was supplying guides for packaged leisure tours.

The Japanese guiding business in Banff got its start in the 1980s—a period of rapid growth in mass overseas tourism—encouraged, in part, by Japanese government policies that were themselves a response to the strong US pressure to reduce the Japanese trade surplus (see Leheny 2003). The major Japanese travel agencies designed and sold leisure-travel packages to tourists, using local "land operators" to assemble the tours. These land operators made arrangements for accommodations, restaurant meals, and ground transportation, as well as placing guide service orders with local guide companies. Upon receipt of these orders, the guide companies provided Japanese-speaking guides for the contracted tours, hiring young Japanese and training them to become "local" tour guides of the Canadian Rockies. Many of these men and women had moved to Banff to pursue their dream of living in a "Mecca" of outdoor activities or in a world-class luxury nature resort.

In the early years, the Japanese guides gathered details about the area by translating information from English sources, such as popular guidebooks and national park publications. Among many sources, Brewster's bus tour from Banff to the Columbia Icefield, the most popular sightseeing route in the Canadian Rockies, had perhaps the greatest influence on the narratives of Japanese guides. The Japanese companies hired Brewster's buses for their tours; in turn, Brewster offered free rides to guide trainees so that they could learn the routes. In these early days, the Japanese guides studied the way English-speaking guides narrated their stories and simply translated them into Japanese.

Brewster's began in 1902 as an outfitting business serving explorers and adventurers. It expanded to automobile tours in 1915 and eventually became a major player in Canadian Rockies tourism (Pole 1997, 73). Reflecting the company's origin, the basic narrative of the bus tours was one of discovery and exploration from the point of view of European explorers and settlers. For example, the tour explained how Castle Mountain was "discovered" by the British surveyor James Hector, a member of the Palliser Expedition, who explored the area in 1858, and how Lake Louise was "found" in 1882 by Tom Wilson, an outfitter for the surveyors. The lake was named Emerald Lake by Wilson, but the name was later changed to honor Louise Caroline Alberta, the fourth daughter of Queen Victoria and the wife of the governor-general of Canada at that time. The story ties the origin of Banff National Park with Canada's nation-building project. In the standard narrative, the park was established in 1885 to settle an ownership dispute over the hot springs between the Canadian Pacific Railway and three construction workers who claimed that they "discovered" the hot springs; the Canadian state intervened and settled the dispute by creating the national reserve around the springs.

Over the years, Japanese guides elaborated on these scripts, adding more explicit explanations of the basic concept of the national park and covering specific rules and regulations that would not be obvious to Japanese visitors. They also inserted stories of Japanese adventurers, such as Maki and Uemura Naomi, another legendary figure, who was the first Japanese to reach the summit of Mount Everest in 1970 and disappeared after succeeding in the world's first solo winter ascent of Mount McKinley in Alaska in 1984. The guides also pointed out how the scenery of the Canadian Rockies had been used as the background for Japanese popular television commercial clips and advertisements. By adding such footnotes to the mainstream Canadian narrative, the Japanese guides forged a sense of connection and familiarity between Japanese tourists and the North American mountain landscape they were visiting. Their cultural interpretation encouraged tourists to become a momentary part of the admired scenes from advertisements and the scenes in which professional adventurers made their extraordinary achievements. Such additions helped construct the North American landscape as the normative place to experience nature and satisfied Japanese tourists' desires to experience the place themselves.

In addition to interpreting the landscape, the RMT's guides often worked as translators, facilitating conversations between Japanese travelers and their Canadian interlocutors. Yet even when the guide's role was to be a language interpreter, his or her work was not only linguistic translation but also cultural translation. When I accompanied the tours as an apprentice guide, I observed that a guide never simply provided a literal translation but instead added context or explained assumed knowledge and perspectives, the sociocultural detail of which the Canadian narrator remained oblivious.[4] In order for translingual conversation to be meaningful, the guide needed to insert notes that explained the background history, social systems, cultural practices, and viewpoints of narrators living in different social worlds and having divergent epistemological frameworks. For example, as mentioned in the prologue, the guides often had to explain to the tourists that the tall, straight conifers they were viewing from the highway grew "naturally" and were not planted by humans. The North American assumption that a national park is a wilderness shrine did not automatically fit the Japanese understanding of a national park, even though the concept of national park was introduced to Japan with the American system as an initial model. In addition, the guides often needed to explain the meanings of particular words that did not have equivalent terms in Japanese. The guide's skill and tact could be measured by how well he or she inserted these explanations subtly and quickly so that the conversation still flowed naturally.

Through such linguistic and cultural translation, the tour guides "moved" people, both physically and affectively. They invited tourists to move their bodies in certain ways, let them walk along a particular route, placed them in certain locations, and directed their seeing, hearing, smelling, and other senses to a specific experience. That disposition led the tourists to be affected by the environment and other people around them, and caused the tourists to embrace certain feelings. In turn, these actions and feelings were channeled back to the tourism business by various means, ranging from informal conversations with guides to formal surveys and studies. They were interpreted and analyzed by the national park, tourism businesses, and other stakeholders, reshaping national park policies, rules, and regulations, as well as material aspects of the park and the town. Beyond the guides' direct influence on the Japanese tourists, their work thus also indirectly moved people and things materially and affectively on the Canadian side. Their translation work was integral to making things happen: they turned the natural landscape into objects of tourist admiration and into something to be valued in the tourist economy; furthermore, by so doing, they also shaped social interactions.

The Politics of Translation

Translingual and transcultural encounters have been recognized as key aspects of the globalizing world. Scholarly debates abound about the possibility or impossibility, and the limitations or creative potentials of cultural translation in such encounters (e.g., Clifford 1997; Papastergiadis 2000; Rorty 1989; Tagore 2006). Translation has caught the growing attention of Anglophone scholarship, yet for people who are at the margins of the hegemonic epistemological regime, translation has always been a foundational issue, shaping their everyday lives. Since the expansion of Western colonial power, accompanied by universal claims of Western science and knowledge, translation has been an unavoidable reality of everyday life for non-Western people living under the hegemony of modern Euro-American scientific epistemology, regardless of whether cultural translation is impossible or possible, whether it has limitations or potentials (Bhabha 1994; Butler 2000). In other words, it is "impossible" but "necessary" work (Spivak 2000) for anyone living in the world with an epistemological framework transported from somewhere else.

"Translation" has been a key topic in the critical analysis of scientific knowledge in examining how scientists enroll various actors in constructing scientific facts, translate nonscientists' concerns, and weave them into their scientific knowledge (e.g., Callon 1986; Latour 1987, 2005; Star and Griesemer 1989). In dialogue with these studies, a new anthropological literature has emerged, which situates actors in a larger social context and examines how scientific knowledge has been interpreted and transformed in nonexpert knowledge through cultural and linguistic translation in non-Western contexts (e.g., Adams 2001; Pigg 2001). Also, a series of exciting works has emerged that focuses on how translation of scientific knowledge formulates and reformulates transnational connections from postcolonial perspectives (e.g., Choy 2011; Hayden 2003; Lowe 2006; Masco 2006; Zhan 2009). This book joins this discussion by placing the politics of cultural translation at the center of the discussion.

In East Asia, particularly in Japan, translation has been essential to making sense of and coping with the colonial expansion of the Western powers. These encounters occurred relatively late in East Asia compared with other parts of the world such as South Asia and Latin America. European and American colonial power did not achieve its full reach until the nineteenth century. The Opium War of 1839–1842 and the cession of Hong Kong to Britain in 1841 marked a power shift in the region, from a loose network of actual or symbolic tributary relationships centered on China to an area influenced by the logic of the modern governing technology of imperialism and the colonial nation-state (Morris-Suzuki 1998). Witnessing China's shocking defeat by Britain and their own country's acquiescence in a treaty of commerce backed by American steam battleships that arrived in 1853, Japanese intellectuals and political leaders vigorously began to translate Western knowledge in order to integrate it into their political, economic, and social systems. In further efforts to maintain sovereignty under the threat of Euro-American co-lonial expansion, Japanese leaders attempted to rapidly transform the country in accordance with this Western model and the logic of the in-dependent modern nation-state. The influential nation-building slogan "Datsua Nyūou," or "Leaving Asia and Entering Europe," epitomizes the Japanese elites' impossible dream: by translating and transplant-ing Western civilization, technology, and political-economic systems, they sought to attain parity with the European and American colonial powers.

Thus, since the late nineteenth century, an enormous number of new words, concepts, genres, and epistemological frameworks have been in-troduced in Japan. Although Japan was not officially colonized by Euro-pean and American powers, Japan's modern history is inseparable from the expansion of Euro-American colonial powers. In a way, the Japa-nese elites colonized their own territory and its people by translating Euro-American knowledge, political-economic systems, and sociocul-tural practices. In doing so, they forced people to change their modes of perception of the world as well as their daily practices radically, and thereby turned them into new subjects of the modern imperial nation-state. This technical transformation was so successful (due in part to historical contingencies) that Japan itself became a colonial power in Asia, occupying an ambivalent position in world politics as both an ob-ject and a subject of colonialism.

The Special Effects of Translation Words: Nature, Subjectivity, and Freedom

In this process of rapid modernization, many *hon'yakugo*, or transla-tion words, were created. Hon'yakugo are not loanwords, or *gairaigo*, borrowed foreign words that can maintain a feeling of foreignness for a given language community by keeping some elements of the original sound. Unlike loanwords that are obviously inserted in the host language context, translation words—part of a wider introduction of practices of knowledge production—work to transform the conceptual system of the host language community. Instead of pointing out the gap between the concepts of guest language and host language, these translation words are supposed to insist on the existence of commensurable concepts in the host language. Thus, as Talal Asad (1993) points out, this practice of translation entails a certain epistemological violence that inserts the desirable effects in the host language (also see Liu 1995). Transformation by translation, however, is never complete (Tsing 1997). Even though the forceful insertion of translation words creates strong effects, there are always haunting traces of difference under the gesture of submission to the inserted words (see Bhabha 1994; Derrida 1983; Sakai 1997). This coexistence of new and old epistemological frameworks creates a constant instability in cultural encounters.

Yanabu Akira (1982), a translator and critic, offers an interesting account of the history of Japanese translation words. He points out that in the late nineteenth and early twentieth centuries, when Japanese intellectuals imported many new concepts from Western literature, they did not apply similar Japanese words for the translation. Instead, they created new words either by borrowing from ancient Chinese words not commonly in use in Japanese at that time, or by combining Chinese characters to create a totally new word. These methods allowed Japanese intellectuals to avoid any confusion in meaning between imported Western concepts and the similar but different Japanese words.

Tracing the process of making a translation word highlights the Japanese intellectuals' attempts to adopt and incorporate alien concepts. Among many concepts translated during the middle to late nineteenth century, "nature," "subject," and "freedom" were the most enigmatic but important ones in transforming the country and its population.

"Nature" is a prime example of the first type of translation word, as it was re-formed from the Chinese classics. Translation from the English was challenging because no corollary concept in Japanese indicates an objective existence in the material world that stands in contrast to the human spirit. In their attempts at deciphering and interpreting, Japanese intellectuals applied such words as *tenchi banbutsu* (all things in the sky and on the earth), *uchū* (universe), *zōbutsusha* (the creator), *seishitsu* (characteristics), and *hinshu* (kinds of things) (Yanabu 1982, 135). Gradually, however, the word *shizen* gained consensus as the translation of "nature." Shizen is a Japanese pronunciation of the Taoist concept of *ziran*, drawn from Laozi. It describes the condition of artlessness or a situation happening without human intention (132). Japanese intellectuals found shizen suitable for "nature" because both nature and shizen stand in opposition to human intention. However, the ways these concepts contrast with human intention differ. As a translation of "nature," shizen works as a noun, as a material object of human perception or action based on the binary framework of human as subject and nature as object. In contrast, shizen, as a Japanese elaboration of ziran, works as an adjective or adverb, and the conceptual framework it relies on does not have the distinction between the objective external world and the internal human spirit (1982, 133–134).

As I discuss in the following chapters, the incommensurability of shizen as a translation of the English word "nature" and variant of the Taoist word continues to exist in the contemporary Japanese concept of nature. In this way, the tension inherent in shizen is still integral to understanding the lives of contemporary Japanese. Shizen is used for the material natural environment as an object of human subjective feeling, intentions, and interventions; at the same time, it is also used to express the sense of unbroken connectivity between humans and their surroundings that generates certain flows of energy. Ultimately, the coexistence of incommensurable notions of shizen provides the foundation for contemporary debates on human nature in relation to the changing visions of society.

Paying close analytic attention to the process of translation also elucidates how the English word "nature" is itself multivalent and has passed through an interesting trajectory to acquire its current meanings. According to Raymond Williams, "Nature is perhaps the most complex word in the language" (1976, 219). Williams suggests that even though "nature" as a noun was introduced as early as the thirteenth century, "nature" as an abstract singular (now conventional) was developed in relation to the emergence of God from a god or gods (220). The English term presents a strong tension between its association with the monotheistic religious tradition of God as a creator and with Reason, which frames nature as an object of human observation. Thus, tracing the translation process also highlights the instability and indeterminacy contained within the source language, under its powerful guise of stability and universal applicability.

Yanabu argues that a translation word has a "special effect" that creates a new meaning different from both the imported word and the indigenous word. He explains that, like a small jewelry box, a translation word attracts people with an aura of something new and important, even though the contents are unknown (Yanabu 1982, 36–37). The special effect of a translation word signals both the desire for and the difficulty of comparison between the imported word and the similar concepts in one's indigenous language. A translation word attempts to bridge the gap between different epistemological systems, while preserving the tension and incommensurability within the word. Through repeated use of the word, the awkwardness of this coexistence seems to be dissipated, yet the tension is never fully resolved and can occasionally resurface.

When a new translation word is needed because existing words cannot capture a concept, there is also no lived experience to anchor or fix the meaning of the word. Yanabu observes the strong tendency in Japanese history to accept the lived meaning of the translation word upon creation. That is, the very creation of a translation word leads to the perception that the existence of the word itself is right, and that what is wrong is Japanese reality, which lacks a referent (Yanabu 1982, 40).

Parallel to the idea of nature as object that represents the wholeness of concrete physical entities, its paired concepts of human as subject also posed a significant challenge for translation. As many critics have suggested, "subject" and "subjectivity" have been perhaps the most alien yet significant concepts in modern and contemporary Japanese intellectual history, shaping key debates in modern Japanese political thought (see Karatani 1993a; Koschmann 2006; Miyoshi 1991; Sakai 1997; Thomas 2001).

Masao Miyoshi, a scholar of literature, points out that the Japanese translation of "subjectivity," *shutaisei*, is a native invention (1991, 97). According to Miyoshi, shutaisei also includes the related concepts of independence, identity, and individuality; thus, this excess of meaning in a translation word indicates the incommensurability of the concept of "subject" or "subjectivity" in the existing Japanese epistemological system prior to the encounter with Western knowledge (1991, 123).[5] Similarly, Naoki Sakai points out that the English term "subject" has been translated into several different Japanese words—*shutai* ("subject" from which an action is generated), *shukan* (subjective perception), and *shugo* ("subject" as a linguistic term)—to reflect the different aspects of the English term (1997, 119). This surplus reveals how foreign the concept is to the existing Japanese epistemology. And, in fact, the translated word of shutai cannot be easily translated back to the English word "subject."

Sakai's account is also helpful for understanding how "subject" and "subjectivity" have been debated in Japanese scholarly and popular discourses. Debates about the problem of Japanese subjectivity (shutaisei) proliferated in the mid-twentieth century across the political spectrum at the height of nationalism as well as in the post–World War II critical reflection on wartime totalizing discourses.[6] For example, influential discourses in the 1930s were formulated by the Kyoto school scholars, such as Watsuji Tetsurō and Nishida Kitarō, who advocated overcoming the problems of Western-centered modernity by imagining alternative notions of subjectivity. Although these scholarly explorations were more complex and nuanced, the part of "overcoming modernity" (*kindai no chōkoku*) was appropriated in nationalist discourses to intensify the uniqueness of Japanese vis-à-vis the "West" and was used to rationalize fighting against the British and Americans (see also Goto-Jones 2005, 2009). At the other end of the spectrum were the 1940s and 1950s "progressive" criticisms of wartime Japanese nationalism, exemplified by the political scientist Maruyama Masao. According to Maruyama, the "lack" of subjectivity was the main problem of Japanese who did not clearly identify who was responsible for the war. Without a doubt, the issue of subjectivity was fundamental to the entire project of Western-modeled Japanese modernization, yet it raised difficult questions for translating basic modern assumptions regarding human nature and society.[7]

Further, Sakai's approach to "translation" is useful for critically examining how the terms of identity such as "Japan" and "the West" were constructed in the process of modernization. He points out that, because of the historical incidence of Japanese modernization that relied heavily on the translation of Western thoughts, it has been impossible to enunciate "Japanese" thoughts without posing "the West" as a general point of reference. Sakai calls the Japanese desire to see oneself from another's position "transferential desire" (1997, 59). With transferential desire, the particularity of Japan is always articulated in reference to the generality or universality of the West. Because speaking about Japan depends upon the West as a norm, and setting the West as a norm makes Japan, as "non-West," something different from the norm, the notion of Japan always entails an existential constraint of being distorted from or behind the norm. The intellectual practice of placing the West as a norm and trying to see oneself from another's position has powerful identity-making effects. Instead of assuming an identity of Japan that existed before encountering the other, Sakai's argument helps us to understand the process of simultaneous and mutual construction of identities through translation. In the process of translation, the idea that there should be a solid identity, symmetrical and translatable with "the West," has been fortified. "The West" is constructed as a normative interlocutor in Japanese imagination, while the diversity among the people in the place called "the West" is overlooked. In turn, to consolidate "Japan" as a solid identity comparable to "the West," heterogeneous populations, cultures, and thoughts that did not fall into any shared sense of identification are organized into "Japan," although the content of the identity, or what "Japan" means, is not yet known.

The notion of "freedom" also raises difficulty in translation, partly because as it is generally understood in contemporary English, "freedom" is constructed from the paradoxical configuration of subject and nature. That is, a subject in a modern society should be free from the constraints of natural forces, yet the subject's basic rights and conditions derive from the very idea of nature: they are naturally given to all human beings. As I will elaborate in the chapters that follow, incompatible notions of freedom also coexist in the contemporary Japanese usage of jiyū, both as a translation word for English "freedom" and as the older translation of a Buddhist concept, jiyū jizai. Here again, jiyū as a translation of "freedom" presupposes a normalized distance between human subjectivity and its surroundings, while the Buddhist translation of jiyū rather idealizes a seamless connectivity among people attained by letting go of an individual ego.

The conflicting notions contained in the translation word of jiyū stimulate the Japanese desire to traverse the gap between imported norms of freedom and the actual everyday lives of the Japanese that do not quite fit the norm. This desire has shaped tourist fantasies of casting the space of freedom as outside of Japan. It also led many young Japanese, including the guides with whom I worked, to drop out of or not participate in the Japanese corporate system in their pursuit of freedom. With their aspirations of becoming cosmopolitan, liberated from the perceived social constraints of Japan, they turned themselves into transnational, flexible laborers.

Although the economic conditions and the hardships of work are quite different, the way the Japanese guides were interpellated to participate in the global economy of nature tourism has some similarities with Sherry Ortner's (1999) observations of Sherpa mountain guides in the Himalayas. Ortner describes how Sherpas, in their pursuit of liberating themselves from the conceived constraints in "traditional" social relations, became involved with international mountaineering expeditions. She explains that although carrying loads was considered to be work of lower social status in the previous commercial practices in the area, some Sherpas started to do this work for foreign expeditions not only for the money but also to detach themselves from the bounds of old communal social relations. Moreover, Ortner's documentation also illustrates how, as Sherpas became involved in international expeditions, their perceptions of mountains have shifted as they translated Western mountaineers' desires, such as modernist aspirations to transcend the limits of self and romantic yearnings to communicate with the self, nature, or God, with the existing conceptual mold of sacred mountain and the Buddhist norms of discipline and compassion; through this process, Sherpas gradually constructed their own "modern" perception of mountains and themselves became climbers.[8] In this process, the Himalayan mountains become similar to what Star and Griesemer called "boundary objects," objects that bring people in different positions to engage with them, and that are "both plastic enough to adapt to local needs and the constraints of the several parties employing them, yet robust enough to maintain a common identity across sites" (1989, 393).

The allure of modernity, and its promise of liberation from the old tradition, attracts people to engage in new forms of practices, yet it does not mean that people are assimilated to share the same conceptualization of the world or to have the same sensibilities. The modern Japanese history of cultural translation in the context of colonial encounters with Euro-American powers illustrates that the epistemological difference and the incommensurability of concepts and practices became apparent in the very midst of the Japanese attempt to earnestly translate and incorporate those concepts imported from Europe and America. Instead of serving as the impetus for resistance against the epistemological violence of Western conceptions, this awkward encounter became something to overcome by transforming Japanese society and people. In the very process of learning the foreign language and epistemology, traces of indeterminacy between the foreign language and the host language constantly emerge. The obedient gesture to find a word that reflects the original meaning of the imported concept results in an irreconcilable tension between the foreign and host worldviews.

In the following chapters, I explore how nature became an important locus in the tour guides' construction of subjectivity. Specifically, I analyze how the "magnificent nature" of Canada provides a site for the performative construction of subjectivity. I further analyze the way these constructions reflect the larger geopolitical context of post–Cold War

Japanese-US relations, as well as the neoliberal transformation of Japanese corporate relations and work practices.

Before moving on to the lives and work of the Japanese tour guides, it is helpful to examine a little more closely the cultural translation of Japanese climber Maki Yūkō—both Robert Sandford's interpretation of Maki's legacy and Maki's own essays. An examination of the role Maki played in the history of mountaineering, as well as his role as the first Japanese cosmopolitan mountaineer, provides some historical context for the work of the Japanese tour guides in Banff.

Mountains in Translation

To celebrate Maki's achievement of seventy-five years earlier, in the summer of 2000 the alpine clubs of Canada and Japan organized joint mountaineering and trekking expeditions and a big ceremony in Jasper National Park. The significance of Maki's successful ascent and its commemoration extended beyond the mountaineering community. The myth of the emperor's ice axe, which Maki was believed to have left on the summit, was featured in the free magazine *Where*, available in almost every major hotel, restaurant, store, and public facility in town and well circulated among tourists. Banff and Jasper National Parks, Alberta Tourism, the chamber of commerce in Banff–Lake Louise, and museums in Banff and Jasper hosted related events. For example, Banff's Whyte Museum curated a special exhibition of *ukiyoe* woodblock prints, introducing Japanese culture to its visitors. Posters and flyers for the Mount Alberta commemoration were placed on the walls and the doors of public facilities throughout Banff and Jasper.

Mount Alberta is legendary in the history of mountaineering in North America. In the early twentieth century, after all major peaks in the Rockies had been climbed, Mount Alberta remained unsummited. Considered to be the last remaining challenge in the Canadian Rockies, the mountain was featured as the frontispiece of the influential book *A Climber's Guide to the Rocky Mountains of Canada*, accompanied by the caption "A Formidable Unclimbed Peak of the Range" (Palmer and Thorington 1921). The challenge had more to do with the mountain's "forbidden" character than its height (3,619 meters).[9] Tucked behind the massive ice of the Columbia Icefield and a series of high mountain ranges, Mount Alberta was remote and difficult to reach. Moreover, the unaccommodating weather, vertical rock walls, loose gravel, and falling rocks made the final section of the summit extremely difficult. Inspired by the photo on the book and encouraged by his sponsor, Marquis Hosokawa Moritatsu, Maki set out to climb the mountain in 1925. This also marked the first overseas expedition of the Japanese Alpine Club (Maki 1991a).

Maki arrived in Seattle by steamship on July 1, boarded the train to Vancouver, and from there traveled to Jasper. On July 11, Maki left Jasper with a team of five other Japanese climbers, two Swiss guides (hired by the Canadian National Railway to develop safe mountaineering in the area), another Swiss climber, four Canadian horse packers, two cooks, twenty-four horses, and enough supplies for a month-long expedition. A week after they left Jasper, the party reached the foothills of the mountain and set up a base camp. The climbing team—six Japanese and three Swiss—moved on. On July 21, after sixteen hours of struggle with overhangs and the steep rock wall at the final section, Maki and his team stood on the mountain's peak at around 7:30 PM (Maki 1991a, 83–106). According to Sandford, this ascent marked the end of an epoch in mountaineering: the Canadian Rockies were no longer "terra incognita" (2000, 17).

The celebration of Maki's first ascent of Mount Alberta provides an interesting case of cultural translation concerning Japanese involvement in modern Alpinism. Based on the Swiss climber Jean Weber's notes and Maki's essays, Sandford's story portrays Maki's act as an example of the universal love of mountains. His account highlights the cosmopolitan mountaineering connection with a flavor of exoticism. The centerpiece of this rendering of Maki's story is the myth of the emperor's silver ice axe. As mentioned earlier, after Maki's ascent, a rumor surfaced that the Japanese party had left the emperor's silver ice axe at the peak. When the second ascent was made by American climbers Fred Ayers and John Oberlin in 1948, they discovered that the ice axe was not silver but Swiss-made steel—good quality, but not extraordinary as imagined in the myth. (In fact, the ice axe had never belonged to the emperor; it was given to Maki by his sponsor, Marquis Hosokawa.) Ayers and Oberlin tried to remove it from the peak because they had lost their own ice axe and needed one for their descent. The axe broke when they tried to dislodge it, the bottom part of the shaft trapped by the solid ice. After the expedition, they brought the partial ice axe to the museum of the American Alpine Club in New York, where it was stored for nearly half a century. Even after it had been debunked, the myth of the emperor's ice axe remained alive and circulated among some climbers as the fulfillment of an exotic fantasy (Sandford 2000, 18–21).

Sandford's narrative also introduces another legend about the international effort to restore the broken pieces of the ice axe and conveys the primary role Canada played in promoting an international appreciation for mountaineering. In 1965, another Japanese party, five members of the Nagano High School Old Boys Alpine Club, succeeded in reaching the peak. There, the Nagano team found the broken bottom shaft of an ice axe with the weathered climbing registration of the American party. They assumed that the ice axe had belonged to Ayers and Oberlin, and brought these items back to Japan (Sandford 2000, 25). It was not until nearly half a century later, in 1992 that a Canadian park warden named Greg Horne happened to find the top part of the legendary ice axe in storage at the American Alpine Club in New York while doing library research (21). He requested that it be returned to Jasper to join the permanent Canadian mountaineering collection in the Jasper-Yellowhead Museum. At that time, no one was aware that the other half of Maki's ice axe had been brought down from the peak and transported back to Japan due to the lack of communication across the Pacific. A few years later, when the Alpine Club of Canada asked the Japanese Alpine Club to contribute anything related to Mount Alberta to the collection, they learned that a broken bottom had been stored in Nagano. The two pieces fit perfectly. In 1997, at a special ceremony sponsored by the Japanese Alpine Club in Tokyo, the legendary ice axe was rejoined in front of the prime minister, crown prince, and eight hundred Japanese mountaineers (27).

In Sandford's narrative, the myth of the emperor's ice axe serves as a testament to the worldwide appeal of modern Alpinism: love of the mountain had become a global phenomenon, reaching as far as exotic Japan, where people imagined that the emperor had ordered an ice axe made out of precious metal. The mythic narrative fits well with Canadian multiculturalism. As pieces of the cultural mosaic, exotics are rendered as something that can be integrated into the dominant framework as proof of its legitimacy, while the universality and the cultural neutrality of this ordering scheme are assumed and rarely questioned. The narrative also suits the tourism industry's identification and promotion of the Canadian Rockies as the world-class stage for experiencing the universal love of mountains.

In contrast to Sandford's rendition, Maki's own writings reveal a more complex process of translating the so-called love of the mountain. Maki himself played a significant role as a cultural translator. He became a cosmopolitan mountaineer and a promoter of Alpinism, but the process through which he became cosmopolitan elucidates the struggle of a person trying to make the incommensurable commensurable.

After the "golden age" of modern mountaineering, when the major peaks in the European Alps had been summited, in the early twentieth century climbers raced to take difficult "alternative" routes that required serious rock-climbing skills (Koizumi 2001, 61–64). The Eiger's Mittellegi Ridge route was considered to be the last remaining challenge in the Alps at that time. Coming of age at the end of this era, Maki achieved the feat in 1921, when he was twenty-seven. An instant national celebrity in Japan, he also became a local hero in the mountain village of Grindelwald, where he had stayed for two years[10] (Koizumi 2001, 183).

During this period, people's perceptions of mountains were still in transition. In the late nineteenth century, a circle of European and American missionaries and professionals living in Japan started to climb mountains as a leisure activity. They frequented the high range in central Japan, which they called the "Japanese Alps." Among these foreigners, the most influential was Walter Weston, a British missionary who lived in Japan for three separate periods between 1888 and 1915 and encouraged the establishment of the Japanese Alpine Club. Unlike foreigners and a few cosmopolitan elites like Maki, most Japanese did not consider mountains sites of leisure activity. Instead, high mountains such as Mount Fuji were climbed as part of a long tradition of religious pilgrimages, not as a sport or solely for recreation. For many, the mountains were the objects of religious worship; for others—*yamabito* or mountain folk, such as hunters and woodsmen—they were the sites of one's livelihood. Nor were people accustomed to the new way of looking at the mountain as a physical object or landscape. Many common folk thought that the mountain itself was a deity with its own spirit, whose will was independent from and uncontrollable by human beings (Koizumi 2001; Kuwabara 1997; Machida 2003; Miyake 2004).

As Karatani Kojin (1993b) points out, landscape had to be "discovered" by introducing a new perspective that rendered the mountain as a material object. Simultaneously, the modern subject (shutai), who has an "inner self" from which to perceive the landscape, had to be constructed in order to acquire this new perspective. Detached from the gazing subject, the objectified landscape, in turn, provided a site for the viewer to project his or her own individual feelings and thoughts. The "discovery" of the alpine landscape took place along with the introduction of the Western disciplines of geography and natural history, and contemporaneously with the literary, artistic, and intellectual movements of Romanticism. Shiga Shigetaka's *Nihon Fūkeiron* ([1894] 1995) was arguably the most influential work to translate the Western perspective and introduce the new perception of seeing the landscape as a geographic object. Shiga's translation of "landscape" also had a strong nationalist and Enlightenment tendency. By promoting the new Western geographic sensibility toward various types of landscape in Japan, Shiga introduced the perception that the varieties of natural landscape represent the nation and, thus, encouraged readers to imagine the bounded geographic space called "Japan." His text was a powerful educational tool for teaching readers how to see nature and nation together. And, as Kären Wigen (2005) points out, the alpine landscape commanded central attention in Shiga's work. Perhaps this was due to the fact that Shiga's work was heavily based on the translation of European guidebooks, such as *Handbook for Japan*, which themselves were strongly influenced by the European Alpinism of that time.

Yet, as a translated concept, this notion of "landscape" was still not fulfilled by people's actual experiences in Japan, for Shiga himself was not a mountaineer. It was Kojima Usui who began to fill the gap between the imported concept and the lived experience. Influenced by Shiga's work, Kojima climbed many mountains, especially in the Japanese Alps. He documented his findings, the beauty of the mountain landscapes seen from a climber's point of view, in a series of essays published in 1910–1915 entitled *Nihon Arupusu* (Japanese Alps). Stimulated by Shiga's and Kojima's work, mountain climbing became a popular sport among the elite bourgeois youth. In these ways, Maki's achievements can be analyzed as the further intensification of fulfilling the experiences of translated modern European Alpinism.

Maki Yūkō and the Struggle of Cultural Translation

Maki was born in 1894 to a former samurai family in Sendai, a regional center of Tōhoku, the northeastern region of Japan. His granduncle was a disciple of Fukuzawa Yukichi (1835–1901), the most influential Enlightenment thinker who introduced fundamental Western philosophical concepts, practices, and institutional systems to Japan and helped "modernize" the nation along Euro-American civilizational norms. Maki studied at Keio University, which had been founded by Fukuzawa (Maki 1991b).

After graduating from Keio in 1917, Maki moved to New York and enrolled in Columbia University in 1918.[11] His education was disrupted by wartime American nationalism, and he dropped out after only a few months. In addition to being disturbed by the shadow of World War I, he was also unimpressed by urban life in New York. Maki was frustrated at "not being able to step on the soil" and felt "choked by this big urban city, the crystallization of modern civilization" (Maki 1991b, 136). His peripatetic movements over the next few years illustrate this. He spent the summer near Lake George in upstate New York and visited Concord, Massachusetts, following in the footsteps of Emerson, Thoreau, and Hawthorne. In 1919, Maki moved to England to visit his brother, who was studying at Oxford. After spending the summer in the Lake District and Scotland, Maki traveled to London in the fall to visit Walter Weston. Encouraged by Weston, Maki then moved to Switzerland and eventually settled in Grindelwald. There, he befriended Swiss mountain guides with whom he enjoyed climbing some of the major peaks in the Swiss Alps. After acclimating to the environment, Maki succeeded in the first ascent of the Mittellegi Ridge route with four Swiss guides (1991b, 190).

When he returned to Japan in 1921, Maki brought the latest versions of mountaineering equipment, such as an ice axe, rucksack, and mountaineering boots, that he had asked Swiss craftsmen to make for his expeditions in the Alps. Some of these items proved to be the first of their kind. Japanese craftsmen used them as models to make their own. Along with the new equipment, Maki also introduced the latest climbing techniques from Europe, especially rock climbing. Maki thus "modernized" mountain climbing and contributed to the shift in the meaning of the mountain.

Before going to Switzerland, Maki had already enjoyed walking in the mountains in Japan. But he had worn traditional *waraji*, woven straw sandals, and used oiled paper to protect himself from the wind and rain. He hired "guides" for his mountain expeditions in Japan, but they were local hunters. Maki respected these *yama an'nainin* (hunter/guides) and learned the techniques of walking in the mountains from them. For example, he wrote of his respect for the famous yama an'nainin Kamonji of Kamikōchi, from whom he learned how to locate a bivouac to avoid

wind and rain, and how to "walk like a cat" on the mountain, to minimize the impact of his presence (1991b, 53). These examples illustrate the
fundamental difference between hunters who made their livelihoods in
the mountains and the mountain climbers who considered climbing a
sport. While hunters tried to erase their presence and to merge with the
natural environment, climbers used mountains to affirm their presence
as individual human beings. The Swiss guides Maki hired were trained
for mountaineering as a sport and leisure activity; they shared the sensibility and the excitement of reaching high peaks with their clients.
The Japanese yama an'nainin, in contrast, were primarily hunters, who
guided the mountaineers to the mountain simply because they knew how
to navigate the territory. There was an obvious gap between their sensibilities and understandings of the mountain and those of their mountaineering clients.

Compared with Shiga and Kojima, Maki's own sensibility was more
cosmopolitan than nationalist. Yet, in his very effort to translate European Alpinism in a way that remained loyal to its original, he encountered the incommensurability in translation. The gap was felt strongly
by Maki's European counterparts. For example, in his essay "Yama no
Kokoro" (Heart of the mountain), originally published in 1974, Maki reflected on his trip to the Alps half a century earlier and on Weston's
impression of a Japanese party: "In 1926, when Prince Chichibu came
to climb the Alps, Reverend Weston greeted us in Switzerland. He was
surprised to see us, the whole party, lively and pleasantly descending the
mountain. He commented that the way the Japanese climb the mountain looked different from that of Europeans. He had an impression that
we did not feel any hardship. He speculated that it might be the influence of *Zen*" (1991b, 57–58).

Maki did not think he and others in the party, including the prince,
were nearly at the stage of a Buddhist spiritual awakening. Puzzled
by his mentor's remark, he considered the source of difference and
identified two kinds of mountaineering "spirit" among Europeans. One
was exemplified by John Hunt, the leader of the world's first successful Everest expedition, who felt the urge to reach the highest point on
earth by overcoming the physical challenge posed by the mountain. The
other was epitomized by Pope Pius XI, who experienced the satisfaction
of being able to move closer to God by transcending worldly concerns
(Maki 1991b, 58). Both spirits presumed the joy of transcending physical
and worldly concerns. Maki might have found this assumed distinction

between spiritual and material elements foreign, since in his view, the two could not be so easily separated. While admiring the profundity of these two mountaineering spirits, Maki introduced a third kind: "However, I wonder if there were another kind of spirit in us. That is, to recognize that one's self and nature are not separate entities, and to feel the joy of living as one with nature. This feeling can be criticized as too sentimental, intuitive and irrational. But I wonder if this atmosphere [that we produce], which is nurtured by our spiritual *fūdo* [climate and environment specific to a particular location], might have become apparent in the way we climb the mountains" (58–59).

Maki's essays illustrate the unresolvable tension that resides in the translated concept of *tozan*, or mountain climbing. Moreover, his interaction with his European counterparts elucidates the process by which "culture" emerged and became reified in the very act of translation, even in the midst of his serious attempt to make the incommensurable commensurable.

Maki's work as a cultural translator had mixed effects. On the one hand, his loyal attempt at translation legitimized the modern European view of the mountain. By adopting a hegemonic epistemological framework, along with normative mountaineering practices, he succeeded in being included as a legitimate member of the cosmopolitan mountaineering community. On the other hand, by submitting himself to the "global standard" of mountaineering and performing the normative practices of engaging with nature, Maki also revealed something that could not be fully contained within the dominant framework. This sense of "difference" evades the complete control of normative standardization. This inherent tension—the incommensurability residing within the translated concepts—haunts and destabilizes the liberal dream of equivalence. And it is this "difference," produced in the interstitial space of translation, that produces "value"—that is, the uniqueness of Maki's work as a cultural translator and the singularity of his subjectivity.

Guide as Translator

In their everyday work practices, the Japanese tour guides in Banff translated the activities of walking in the mountains and seeing nature for tourists from Japan. Their work was similar to Maki's in the sense that they introduced new modes of engaging with nature developed in the Euro-American tradition to a Japanese audience. Like Maki, the tour guides played a significant role in the cultural translation of mountain and nature.

But unlike Maki, they were not privileged members of the leisure class. Nor was their social circle that of a selected few elites. They were part of what is often labeled the *chūkan sō* (middle layer) or *chūkan taishū* (middle mass), a social category that emerged in post–World War II Japan, and has recently been considered to be dissolving due to the expanding precariousness in Japanese society (see Allison 2012). Government surveys show that since the 1970s, about 90 percent of people identify themselves as "middle" in terms of their position in the social strata.[12] This "class" consciousness is often discussed as the product of rapid industrialization and the mobilization of populations from rural agricultural communities to urban industrial environments.[13] The development of the so-called Japanese corporate system in the postwar period—characterized by lifelong employment, the seniority-based wage system, and the company-based labor union—provided relatively high job security and thus transformed employees into productive workers and active consumers. The middle mass has been the effective agent of Japanese postwar economic development. Many of the Japanese tour guides in the RMT fell into this category, identifying themselves as from the *futsū*, or "ordinary," family background in terms of social class, although their life histories revealed that there was a wide range within the ordinary middle mass. In the following chapters, I examine how the sensibility toward nature and mountains introduced by cosmopolitan elites like Maki was taken up by the masses, and I explore how the translation of nature now plays a significant role in shaping the lives of ordinary people in contemporary Japan.

The issue of the cultural translation of nature, subjectivity, and freedom resurfaced in new ways at the turn of the twenty-first century, with concerns about the political, economic, and social movement called "neoliberalism." With the emergence of the middle mass backed by the development of the corporate system, and the recent growing concern over the economic decay of post–Cold War Japan, the main site of debates over subjectivity and freedom shifted from nation building to economy, specifically employment. The discourses of freedom, the individual's urge to find subjectivity independent from the workplace, and the paradoxical desire to see nature as the utopian space of individual freedom—even as the exploitation of nature intensified—all emerged as central issues that corresponded to debates around neoliberalism, as well as the uncertain future of the nation and the globe that was felt strongly in the early twenty-first century. To understand how these issues shape the lives of "ordinary" Japanese and how Japanese have negotiated their positions amid recent social change, it is necessary to contextualize their lives and work in the legacy of cultural encounters and the broader epistemological struggle in cultural translation.

Organization of the Book

By introducing some of the "arrival stories" of the Japanese tour guides, chapter 1 examines how the image of magnificent nature in Canada was tied to a proliferating discourse of freedom in contemporary Japan. Many of the guides' narratives corresponded to the powerful popular discourse of "escaping Japan" and "liberating" oneself from the Japanese corporate system, a discourse that had been in circulation since the late 1980s. By examining the guides' stories of coming to Canada, the chapter traces the process of cultural translation about work and company. Neoliberal corporate restructuring in Japan intensified throughout the 1990s and stimulated the debate over notions of work and company. The coexistence of competing notions of work—work as a simultaneous activity of personal satisfaction and social contribution, and work merely as a means to gain money so that one can experience personal satisfaction outside work—caused confusion for many workers and motivated some of them to leave both their company and Japan simultaneously. The chapter examines how those Japanese who "escaped" the corporate system turned themselves into transnational flexible laborers in pursuit of the dream of freeing themselves from the old communal ties and living in magnificent nature.

Chapter 2 examines how this spatial imaginary of Canada has been constructed in popular culture and how these images influenced tourist encounters in the Canadian Rockies. Interestingly, before their arrival, many of the guides had no specific knowledge of Canada beyond an image of vast-scale nature in North America. Rather, they were simply motivated to go abroad or overseas. Canada's nature was a convenient location onto which the guides could project a utopian space where they would be liberated from the social and cultural constraints they felt in Japan. The chapter specifically examines the work of influential television entertainer and former member of the National Diet, Ōhashi Kyosen, who promoted Canada as a Japanese travel destination. Ōhashi developed his career by introducing American-style popular culture to Japan. The chapter traces the trajectory of his work and discusses how he redirects Japanese fascination with overseas travel from American culture to Canadian nature. Central to his revision of the travel itinerary for Japanese tourists was a changing perception of "affluence" from material wealth to personal satisfaction. This shift reflects new debates around the translation of "subjectivity," since the concept of personal satisfaction affirms the idea that each individual has an independent subjectivity and knows what will fulfill his or her own desire. An examination of Ōhashi's work reveals how the Japanese desire for a space of freedom overseas is a product of specific US-Japan relations from the period of occupation through the Cold War, and how this desire was reformulated in the post–Cold War, postindustrialized social context.

Chapter 3 offers an ethnographic analysis of the making of a tour guide. The chapter traces the guide-training process in the RMT and examines how the Japanese who moved to Banff became "local" guides of this cosmopolitan mountain town. Specifically, the chapter explores the paradoxical process of transforming oneself into a commodity in an affective economy. While many of the guide trainees in the RMT felt they had escaped from a commercialized society and workplace in Japan, they interpreted the commodification of self in their new workplace as an opportunity to develop a unique individuality rather than as an expression of the alienation or decay of an authentic self. The chapter examines how the Canadian natural landscape plays a significant part in this conflation of commodification and performative construction of individual subjectivity. The smooth conflation of the economic and ethical "value" of the guide's personality was most evident in the guide trainer's narrative of his own life history. By juxtaposing the frustration experienced by the trainees and the trainer's proud story of becoming a guide, the chapter illustrates the tension inherent in the translation of "freedom," which the trainees expected to achieve by moving to Canada. Through this examination, the chapter also elucidates the complex process of the commodification of self in the service industry.

Chapter 4 explores how the tour guides' performance as cultural translators has been shaped by the negotiation of gender and family. Specifically, the chapter analyzes how the female outdoor tour guides were particularly idolized by tourists as the embodiment of Japanese cosmopolitan desire. While most tour guides fulfilled dominant gender expectations, some female guides strongly attracted tourists because of their androgynous character. This character was developed in and aided by a specific social space that was characterized by some guides as "Neverland in nature." In addition, the guides developed playful, fictive kinship terms and quasi–extended family relationships among themselves to form a social support network in order to survive in a foreign country. The chapter examines how ideas of nature stimulated the guides to translate gender differently and to negotiate their positions in the gendered societies of both Canada and Japan. The guides' gender performances and the social world simultaneously conformed with and challenged the "naturalness" of a normative family system and gender relations.

Chapter 5 analyzes how Japanese tour guides translated the ecological knowledge and nature-interpretation practices developed in North American national parks. This process was integral to the construction of the guides' subjectivity as cultural translators of nature. In particular, the chapter documents the ways in which Japanese tour guides engaged with the Banff National Park's newly inaugurated nature interpretation accreditation program. This program was the park's response to the outsourcing of nature interpretation to commercial businesses. The program urged the commercial guides to act as "environmental stewards" and to spread this philosophy to their clients. The Japanese guides' engagement with this program elucidates the complexity of and politics surrounding the cultural translation of nature. While an understanding of Parks Canada's notion of ecology was assumed to be universal, the Japanese guides' struggles brought the tour guides, accreditation instructors, examiners, and park officials to an acute realization that knowledge about nature is socially embedded much deeper than they assumed.

Chapter 6 extends the discussion in chapter 5 and examines how ecology, as vocabulary, works both to standardize knowledge and to provide a tool for critical reflection on the incommensurability among different engagements with nature. The chapter explores how the Japanese tour guides' engagements with the ecological knowledge offered by the instructors representing the official Parks Canada standpoint complicitly constructs the agency's authority while they were puzzled by the tension between the park's notion of "ecological integrity" and the "nonanthropocentric" approach. I discuss how the Japanese guides, despite their own experience of puzzlement and struggles in making sense of the fundamental assumptions in the park's conceptualization of nature, were subjected to work as agents of disseminating the park's knowledge.

I contextualize the guides' practice in relation to the legacy of Japanese adaptation of modern Western science and technology and discuss its political implications in the contemporary context.

Finally, the epilogue explores the larger social implications of the foregoing ethnographic examinations. A study of tourism—in particular, the lives of tourism workers who engage with cultural translation at the crossroads of diverse sensibilities and worldviews—can reveal the process and politics of cultural encounters of various kinds. In particular, the translation of nature is key to understanding how cultural encounters are shaped because it concerns not only natural landscape and resource management but also what it means to be a human who has "subjectivity" and is a "free" and "liberated" subject within a society. Tracing the process of the cultural translation of nature allows us to see the tension between the universalized assumption of the configuration between nature, subjectivity, and freedom, and its incommensurability with less dominant epistemological legacies.

Although discourses of globalization and neoliberal deregulation assume a smooth flow and movement of people across national boundaries, in the actual practices of tourism, the nation-state still plays an important role in controlling the flow of people by policing national boundaries through passport, visa, and other related regulations, often in accordance with the economic circumstances of the people on the move. The outgoing flow of tourists and travelers is often used as an indicator of the degree of freedom that the population of a particular country enjoys, of the extent of democracy that the country has achieved, and of the level of integration the country has within the global system. Yet this enactment of freedom is not without friction (Tsing 2004). The modern history of Japan offers an unparalleled case through which to examine this complex process of friction-laden cultural translation and the struggle for integration in the global community by people who are at the margins of Euro-American hegemony. Japan transformed itself from one of the most exotic destinations for European and American travelers in the late nineteenth century (Guth 2004) to one of the largest exporters of overseas tourists in the late twentieth and early twenty-first centuries. In the process, the Japanese desire for freedom emerged, as did the quest for the recognition of the Japanese as legitimate and equal members in a world of asymmetrical power relations. Japanese tour guides' work of cultural translation is, in part, the enactment of this desire, not to be in the world as objects of an exotic tourist gaze, but to achieve the position of subjects and to be recognized as actors with a unique set of perceptions and practices of engagement in the world. Responding to this legacy, the Japanese tour guides in Banff dealt with this desire and performatively constructed their subjectivities as Japanese cosmopolitans. In their practices of cultural translation, in their acts of rendering the incommensurable commensurable, they effectively produced the "value" upon which this affective economy of tourism operated.

Nature in Translation is an attempt to trace the indeterminacy of cultural translation and to explore the instability inherent in any such act of translation. The analytic mode I employ is not an attempt to reclaim what is "lost in translation," a lament of authentic culture; rather, it tries to discover what can be "found in translation," those traces of constant movement and instability that propel cultural formation.

1 | Narratives of Freedom

Freedom from a Company

Hamada Satomi had followed a life course that was considered to be ideal for women until the mid-1990s. In 1987, she graduated from a two-year junior college that had a good reputation for women's education. Right after graduating, she started to work full-time in one of the largest stock brokerage firms in Tokyo. She lived with her parents in a suburban city and commuted to Marunouchi, the central business district in Tokyo.

She chose the company not because she was interested in stock trading but because at the time she searched for a job, the large financial corporations were considered to be the most solid and stable among companies. She was attracted by the sense of stability and security. Furthermore, working in a highly ranked *katai kaisha* (a company with "solid" and "square" characteristics) would give her a reputation as a reliable person. There was still a normative expectation that a young woman from a good family should live with her parents until she married. Living under parental control and working in such a company would improve her chances of finding a future husband among elite *sararīman* (white-collar salaried men). Although Satomi herself was not particularly keen on finding her future husband, she was aware of this expectation, and her parents were satisfied with her position as an OL (*Ō-eru*, "office lady")[1] in Marunouchi.

During the time of the bubble economy, OLs, along with female university students, were considered consumer trendsetters, whose tastes and behaviors were extensively discussed in the media, and by advertisement agencies and developers of new products. OLs were seen to represent fulfilling, exciting, and youthful lifestyles, and their preferred products would gain many followers. While conservative educators and critics denounced and despised their excessive consumer activities, the lifestyles of the young women educated in prestigious colleges and working in large, reputable corporations attracted people's attention, just like a beautiful flower would intrigue people. Hence, the expression "*hana no OL*," which literally means, "flowery office ladies," was used in popular discourse. OLs, especially those living with their parents, could use a large portion of their salaries as disposable income. Satomi used the term for herself sarcastically when reflecting on her life before moving to Canada. While the mass media depicted and stimulated the OLs' lavish spending on dining, overseas travel, and the latest fashions, Satomi spent most of her leisure time and money on skiing.

She started to ski enthusiastically as a college student. During her four years working at the firm, she became increasingly frustrated because she could not ski as much as she wanted. Her stress level had risen so much that she dreamed of changing her job and moving to a place where she could ski more often. She envied friends in her skiing circle who lived at a ski resort in the winter to concentrate on skiing and moved back to the cities during the off-season to work as *furītā* (freelance part-time workers).[2] Although their job security was low and they did not have full employee benefits, they had much more flexible work schedules. To Satomi, furītā looked truly "free" from the company and the constraints that she experienced; her furītā friends were freely pursuing what they wanted to do (*yaritai koto*). In 1991, after contemplating her situation for a while, she asked her supervisor if she could take a leave of absence. When the supervisor asked why, Satomi explained that she wanted to spend some time improving her skiing. Her boss told her this was not acceptable and tried to convince her to stay, but Satomi eventually decided to leave her job and move to Canada.

Reflecting back on Satomi's story two decades later, her yearning for freedom from the company is striking. Although it was considered normal at that time, the position of a regular, full-time employee with full benefits, or a *seishain* (literally meaning "a true member of a company"), is scarcer in today's Japan. After several steps of neoliberal change in corporate regulations and labor laws, many young Japanese today cannot assume the secure employment that Satomi had. In many companies, a noncareer track, assistant job is not that of a seishain anymore. These positions have been replaced with temporary workers sent from temporary staffing agencies. It is difficult to imagine that elite corporations would hire a good number of female junior college graduates every spring as seishain right after their graduation.

Accordingly, the meaning of furītā has changed drastically. As it was for Satomi, for many others, working as a furītā was an embodiment of freedom—someone who bravely freed oneself from the secure but constraining social pressures in the company and adventurously pursued one's own dream. The term was arguably coined in 1987 by Michishita Hiroshi, the editor in chief of *From A*, a magazine that posted listings for part-time jobs (Michishita 2001). Michishita explains that he wanted to support the young people who were pursuing their dreams—such as becoming a writer, film director, or photographer—while they worked part-time at an unrelated job. Now, in the 2010s, instead of having the positive connotation of an independent and creative pursuit of one's dream, furītā represents the instability of youth employment, and the precariousness that is gradually penetrating every corner of contemporary Japanese workers' lives. The youth who could not find regular full-time positions in a company became an object of social concern. The increase of furītā reveals the irony of the "freedom" of workers that Marx (1992) pointed out: workers in industrial society are "liberated" from the old communal ties and are "free" to sell their labor power in the market, as well as "free" from the means of production.

Satomi's story illustrates how, until the 1990s, a company had provided an important site for the construction of self for many workers. As many observers and analysts of Japanese work relations have pointed out (e.g., Dore 2000; Iwai 2003; Nakamaki et al. 2001), membership in a company as a community had played an integral part in people's lives. Her story also elucidates her ambivalence about being a part of the company as a community: on the one hand, she liked the sense of security and belonging that the company offered; on the other hand, she felt the company's communal bonds and obligations were too constraining. Interestingly, her desire to liberate herself from the company overlapped with her aspirations to leave Japan. Satomi simultaneously "escaped" from the company and the country. She looked to Canada as an ideal place for finding herself; with its vast natural landscape and its image as a frontier land, Canada seemed to be the place where she could free herself from these old social bonds and ties.

For Satomi, in addition to her desire to have more time to ski, what triggered her decision to leave the company was her disillusionment with its changing characteristics. Right after "Black Monday" in October 1987—six months after she was hired—to her surprise, she found that the company "revealed its aggressive side." She was pressured to sell stocks and bonds to customers even though she was not sure these products would be beneficial to them. She thought that the employees were the victims of the stock market industry, too. Employees were encouraged to buy the company's stocks, and as a result, she lost a large portion of her savings. This experience was an alarming sign of the changing nature of the company, which no longer was a place that would provide her with a sense of security, protection, pride in membership, and satisfaction in doing morally justified work.

Satomi was part of a generation of women who started to work soon after the Equal Employment Opportunity Law was implemented in 1986. With the implementation of this law, female workers in the noncareer track were given a choice of remaining in their present jobs or moving to the career track. Satomi was not interested in the career track. If she made this change, she would be expected to devote herself more to her work, but the work had lost its appeal. She started to wonder if she was helping customers improve their financial security or if she was merely being used by the company for its survival. Satomi was also stressed by her everyday life, which included spending nearly two hours commuting to her workplace from her parents' home. She wanted to free herself from the daily routine of getting up early in the morning, riding the crowded commuter train, being exhausted by work, and coming home late at night.

As experienced by Satomi, economic "liberalization" (*jiyūka*) and corporate restructuring since the late 1980s disrupted the notions of work and company in Japan. Like Satomi, many of the Japanese tour guides in Banff who narrated their life histories to me, suggested that they were struggling to interpret the meaning of company and work in their own ways in the midst of economic change. Their stories also elucidated that Canada, especially its vast natural landscape, had become a convenient site for them to reflect on their lives and establish their new subjectivities.

Around the year 2000, the Rocky Mountain Tours hired approximately fifty tour guides each season, with fairly equal numbers of men and women. Most of the guides left Japan when they were in their twenties. The majority of them had a postsecondary education, mostly university or junior college, and in some cases *senmon gakkō* (special vocational and professional training school). The length of their stay in Banff varied a great deal: some of them left Banff after one season and returned to Japan or moved to other cities in Canada; others stayed several years, received permanent resident status, bought houses, and raised families in Banff or the nearby area. Most of them considered guiding to be transitional work until they found *yaritai koto*, or what they really wanted to do with their lives, while some thought guiding was their dream job. The common theme among their life stories as narrated to me was their exploration of freedom and searching for self, or a desire to establish their own unique subjectivities.

Their narratives offer a glimpse of the changing work relations experienced by young Japanese workers in the late 1980s to 2000. This chapter examines how the tour guides narrated their life histories. Their stories elucidate how the idea of "magnificent nature" played a significant role in their pursuit of freedom and subjectivity. In many of the guides' narratives, Canada's spatial imaginary as a frontier dreamland served as a mirror to reflect on the frustrations, feelings of confusion, and dilemmas they experienced in Japan. The magnificent nature in Canada was imagined as a utopic space, in contrast to the culturally saturated space of Japan, where the weight of the "community" and the burden of following social rules and expectations put so much pressure on them that they felt they would not be able to pursue their own individual freedom.

The guides' stories also illustrate how the exploration of freedom and subjectivity in nature was experienced differently by those who entered the job market in the 1980s and 1990s. After discussing the spatial imaginary of Canada as a frontier dreamland, the following sections introduce the narratives of male guides who started to work as core full-time workers in the late 1980s, and the specific situation of women who entered the job market after the burst of the bubble economy in the 1990s. These women shared a similar fascination with living overseas with their male colleagues and tried to find a site for subjectivity construction outside of regular full-time work in Japan. This generation of women faced the challenging situation of being independent and establishing their own subjectivities, while also facing much slimmer job opportunities. Their narratives elucidate the predicament of freedom as it was translated and pursued in postindustrial, post–Cold War Japan under the ever stronger pressure to be integrated into the system of US-centered global capitalism.

FRONTIER DREAM

The way Satomi chose Canada was suggestive in understanding the guides' spatial imagination. When she looked for a location for her new life close to ski hills, she knew that she wanted to live either in Hokkaido, the northernmost prefecture in Japan, or in Canada. She explained, "It was because I wanted to go to an exotic but familiar place [*ikokuteki na kanji no mijikana basho*]." When she said to the tourists that it had been a tough decision between Hokkaido and Canada, her customers always laughed. It might have sounded ridiculous to them that she did not see much difference between simply moving to another prefecture in Japan and starting her new life in a foreign country. But in Satomi's mind, Hokkaido and Canada had an important commonality: both are frontier lands with a vast natural landscape, and this image provided her with a dream of detaching herself from the old social ties. Even though other ski areas on the main island (Honshu), such as Nagano and Niigata, also had beautiful mountains and good ski resorts, these places were not attractive for her because they did not have the appeal of the frontier, a space where she imagined freedom from a traditional community.[3]

It was not only Satomi who compared Canada with Hokkaido when explaining the desire to be liberated from the constraints of everyday life. Ogura Yoshiko, another guide, also said that Hokkaido was the only place in Japan she would consider living. After living in a ski resort in Nagano for two years, she thought that she would not fit in to rural Japanese villages because they were full of *shigarami*, ties that would bind her to the community's traditional social relations, old customs, and rules. Both Satomi and Yoshiko chose Canada over Hokkaido because of the strong allure of a foreign country. Satomi explained, "I have lived with my parents my entire life, so if I leave my parents' house, I wanted to go to a place as far away as possible." She wanted to be independent and to start her new life in a remote location, but that "remote place" should be familiar enough to provide the right mixture of adventure and comfort.

Canada was convenient for Satomi for several reasons. Perhaps the most important reason was that it has a working holiday program, a visa exchange program based on a bilateral agreement between countries that allows young people to work while they are traveling in the country. Japan established working holiday agreements with Australia in 1980, with New Zealand in 1985, and with Canada in 1986.[4]

All three of these countries were considered to be friendly for Japanese young people. Because English had been a mandatory subject from the first year of junior high school, living in these English-speaking countries was a realistic and manageable challenge. These countries also had reputations for being safe, with relatively low crime rates and strict gun control regulations. While the level of urban infrastructure was convenient and comfortable enough, Australia, New Zealand, and Canada also were known for their natural environments, accessible from their urban centers. With the widely circulated images of open, friendly people in a relaxed environment, these nations offered entry points for young people to experience life overseas. In particular, Canada's position is significant in constructing the guides' spatial imaginaries of the world because it is close to the United States, which has had a strong influence in shaping everyday life in Japan since the post–World War II occupation period. As presented in more detail in chapter 2, many of the tour guides described how their image of the world outside Japan had been constructed under the influence of "America."

WORK AS *SHUGYŌ*

Iwamoto Eita's story illustrates the dilemma that was experienced by a core full-time male worker. Like Satomi, he left his job in order to ski in Canada. After graduating from high school, Eita studied automobile repair skills in a vocational school. Since 1989, he had been working as a mechanic in a high-end car dealership in Osaka. Eita liked the job and worked very hard, but one day in 1993, his life changed when his friend showed him a brochure of a helicopter ski tour in Canada. Eita described how he was captured by the photo of a sole skier on the high-altitude mountain slope: "It was a landscape that we cannot find in Japan. A sharp-pointed mountain peak, the beautiful snow surface. . . . Skiing down the mountain where there is no trace at all. . . . It was beyond my imagination. The brochure looked like an invitation to a space flight . . . a trip to a world in a different dimension [*ijigen no sekai*]."

The cost of the one-week heli-skiing trip was nearly Can\$4,000. With a plane ticket from Japan to Canada, the total cost of the trip would be about 500,000 to 600,000 yen. It was not a small amount for Eita, the equivalent of about three months' salary, but he could not resist the allure of the brochure. Eita thought such a trip would be a "once-in-a-lifetime" experience. He convinced himself that the price was rather reasonable for such an extraordinary activity. Eita thought that the only way he could go to Canada for skiing was to leave his job. The day after he saw the brochure, Eita informed his boss of his intention to resign. His boss tried to persuade Eita to stay, but Eita's decision was firm.

Although he was considered a blue-collar worker, like Satomi, Eita was a salaried employee of a large, well-established corporation with a high reputation. He also had full health care and pension benefits like a sararīman. But he described his job as if it was that of a *shokunin*, or craftsman. He told me that he considered his work as *shugyō*, or ascetic practice.

I devoted myself to the work as if it was the whole stake of my entire life [*inochi gake to iukurai*]. I never thought of leaving work early nor having an extra day off. I had never used a paid vacation because it would be like admitting defeat in my struggle to improve myself [*jibun tono tatakai ni makeru*]. I never took a paid day off, never said I wanted to go home early, and never complained about any of the work practices at the company. I could not allow myself to do such frivolous things [*chara chara shita koto*] as requesting a vacation and going overseas for skiing. I could not imagine myself coming back to work after a weeklong ski trip to Canada, simply saying "it was fun."

Eita's narrative was puzzling to me. Why did he have to leave the company only to take a weeklong vacation? On the one hand, he was extremely serious about and proud of his work. If he was committed to work that much, how did he make sense of leaving the company just for the sake of going on a ski trip? On the other hand, he had a strong urge to go elsewhere, to see the world beyond his everyday life. If he felt an urgent need to refresh himself, why did he not just make use of the paid vacation that was legally guaranteed for salaried workers?

Eita explained that he decided to leave the company not because he had lost interest in his work but because the photo of the ski tour helped him recognize a feeling that had embraced him for a while. He said, "I did not quite fit in to the Japanese society [*Nihon no shakai ni sori ga awanai*]," even though he had never been abroad. He felt awkward in his everyday life in Japan. He said, "I felt that I was in adversity every day [*Mainichi ga gyakkyō*]." Interestingly, what made him think that he could not fit in was not the work culture that encourages employees to devote their lives to work, as might be concluded from the stereotypical idea of the problem of the Japanese work practice. Rather, it was the uneasy intrusion of modern industrial rationalization in his workplace.

The company required him to work like a shokunin, concentrating on his work seriously as if it represented his entire personality. In fact, Eita enjoyed this challenge. For Eita, work was not simply a means to earn money. He was proud of not giving up on a difficult task even when it looked like there was no solution. Repairing a car was not a mere mechanical task for Eita. By turning all his attention to the problem and by skillfully using his tools, he considered that he became a better person through the act of fixing the machines.

However, the company also pressured him to work effectively within a set time and cost, which forced him to compromise his work. He was frustrated that the company's pursuit of efficiency prevented him from achieving a quality of work that would satisfy him. Even though the working practices of the company were those of shokunin and demanded that employees work as if they were practicing shugyō, the company's nature as a profit-making capitalist entity did not allow employees to completely devote themselves to their work.

These conflicting principles of work created this conundrum and were a source of frustration for Eita. The photo of the heli-skiing sparked Eita's imagination about a world where he could be free from this kind of frustration. There seemed to be nothing that would disrupt him from devoting all his senses to engage with snow.[5] Eita told me that the heli-skiing turned out to be much more than he expected. He said, "I am not sure if this expression is right, but imagine you met a woman who seemed very charming. Once I started going out with her, I found she was much more attractive than I thought, far beyond my expectation. It was like that." He found that heli-skiing was such an ecstatic experience that his brain completely "blanked out" (*atama no naka ga masshiro ni natta*).

Before he left Japan, Eita took a working holiday visa, vaguely thinking that he would take this opportunity to see the world outside Japan. After the heli-skiing trip, Eita stayed in Vancouver and skied in nearby areas for several weeks. When the spring came, one day in late May, he decided to ride his bicycle across the country to Halifax, Nova Scotia, to see the ocean on the other side of the continent. Eita thought it might be ridiculous for a person with no experience overseas and limited English ability to cross the continent alone by bicycle. He thought the bicycle trip would give him time to reflect on what he wanted to do next at "the turning point of life." It was a chance to reset his life to *hakushi no jōtai*, or a blank slate.

During the four months of travel, he was strongly impressed by the kindness and open-mindedness of the people he met. Even though he was wearing worn-out, dirty clothes, many people spoke to him and showed a warm interest in his adventure. Several people offered him a place to stay or invited him to have dinner in their homes. By the time he arrived in Halifax in early October, he was confident about his ability to communicate in English. In addition to the generosity of people he met along the way, Eita was also impressed by their sense of independence and self-control. He imagined that North American workers had more autonomy than Japanese workers and thus could work in a way that satisfied them. He said, "The workers in North America work in the way that makes sense to them, don't they? [*hokubei dewa jibun ga nattoku suru yō ni shigoto suru desho?*]." During the bicycle trip, Eita reaffirmed that he liked his work as a mechanic and that he wanted to do what he liked in a place he enjoyed. He set a new goal of having his own motorcycle shop in Canada.

Eita learned that it was difficult to get an immigrant visa as a mechanic, but working as a tour guide was a good way to obtain a visa. He also heard that there was great demand for Japanese-speaking tour guides in Banff. He traveled back to Vancouver by hitchhiking and by bus and then headed to Banff. Once he started to work as a guide, he took the job as seriously as his work as a mechanic. He tried to find a meaning in guiding. For him, the guide's work was to maximize the tourists' opportunities to experience and appreciate the beauty of Canadian landscape and the good nature of people in Canada. It was "*ongaeshi*," or a demonstration of his gratitude to the people and the natural environment in Canada that had helped him realize what he wanted to do in his life.

Eita's narrative illustrates the conflicting idea of *shigoto*, or work, experienced in many Japanese workplaces in the 1980s and 1990s. On the one hand, work was idealized as an activity that would bring satisfaction and fulfillment. In Eita's case, shigoto should give him opportunities to challenge himself and be a means to better himself as a person. His engagement with shigoto could be endless (see Kondo 1990 for a similar discussion on the work aesthetics of artisans in Japan). On the other hand, work was also a business contract. In theory, Eita was simply selling his labor power based on the labor contract. The only thing he owed the company was a certain amount of labor time in exchange for his wages and employee benefits. The coexistence of these contrasting notions of shigoto created frustrating situations for Eita and many other guides.[6]

Eita's case was extreme because he clearly articulated that work was a shugyō. Other guides were not as explicit as Eita about such ethical aspects of their work, but many of them experienced a similar dilemma. Even Satomi, who worked as an assistant in a stock brokerage firm, had a strong desire to help customers by offering them financial security. In these guides' narratives, work was not merely a means to earn money but a way to connect to other people in society. Work offered a site to "polish" the self (*jibun o migaku*) and, by so doing, to find *ikigai*, a reason that makes one's life worth living (see Matthews 1996). As we saw with Eita and Satomi, when they started to have doubts that their work would provide them with a site for their moral pursuit of improving self (and society), they began to look for this site outside of their work. They often put pressure on themselves to choose either to devote themselves to their work in a company or to leave the company.

Others adopted different strategies to cope with this dilemma. Some convinced themselves that they were working merely to live. They tried to make a clear separation between time for work and time for personal enjoyment.

OVERSEAS FURĪTĀ: WORKING HOLIDAY

Noda Hiroshi was about the same age as Eita and Satomi, but Hiroshi did not feel at all guilty about using his paid vacation. Hiroshi graduated from a university in Kyoto in 1988 and found a full-time job in an administrative office at a large transportation company in Osaka.

Hiroshi could have been labeled as *shinjinrui* (literally "new Homo sapiens"), a term popularly used in the late 1980s to describe the emergent younger sararīman's sensibilities, which were different from those of the older generation. The shinjinrui generation was born in the 1960s and entered the job market in the 1980s. Its members grew up in a time when the Japanese economy had recovered from the devastation of World War II and was experiencing rapid growth. Unlike previous generations, who had a clearer awareness that their work served to rebuild the nation from the postwar rubble, these workers were fully absorbed in the consumer culture and their own leisure activities. The popular interpretation of shinjinrui was that they prioritize their own interests over their roles and obligations in the company. It was hard for the older generations to accept some of their practices, such as rejecting a senior coworker's or a manager's invitation to after-work drinks, not participating in the company's recreational events, or demanding to take paid vacations for leisure.

Unlike Eita, Hiroshi was clear that his work was simply a means to earn money so that he could travel on his time off. But like Eita and Satomi, Hiroshi also left his job because of a conflict between the company's expectation that he devote all his energy to work and his own desire to expand his perceptions by traveling. Soon, he found himself getting increasingly busy at work. Once he became part of the reliable workforce, it became difficult to balance his obligation to the company with his interests in backpacking and travel. He said, "I left the company because of the stress of not being able to travel [*tabi ga dekinai sutoresu de yameta*]."

Hiroshi started backpacking in rural Japan during his first year of university. In his second year, he traveled with his friend to Hokkaido. Hiroshi brought along a guitar and during their trip he sang songs at street corners and train stations. Hiroshi was fascinated by people's responses, which he found quite different from what he had observed in the cities in Honshu. He described the openness and the kindness of people in Hokkaido: "It [Hokkaido] looked like a wonderland to me. People gave money when I sang . . . not only coins, but even some 1,000- or 5,000-yen notes. We could treat ourselves and eat *yakiniku* [grilled meat] with that money. In some remote rural places, people invited us to stay at their homes. When we were hitchhiking, even a tour bus stopped and gave us a ride. In the bus, we sang songs, and the tourists cheered us so much." Since that first trip, Hiroshi had gone to Hokkaido every year. In his first year at the transportation company, he took ten days of paid vacation to go to Hokkaido. Thanks to an acquaintance in the northeastern sales office, he got a free ride on the company truck to travel to the north, but the following year, he encountered bigger obstacles to taking vacations because he was expected to assume more responsibility in the company. He decided to leave the company after working there for three and a half years.

After leaving his job in 1991, when he was twenty-six years old, Hiroshi decided to go to New Zealand on a working holiday visa. Of the three countries that had a working holiday exchange agreement with Japan, he thought New Zealand was most similar to Hokkaido because it was less populated and less urbanized. He was attracted by the images of people as pure and kind in a place less contaminated by urban civilization.

Hiroshi explained his motivation for going overseas: "I want to escape from a variety of social obligations and constraints [*iroirona shigarami ya seiyaku kara nogaretai*]." He liked Hokkaido because he felt the people there were less bound to shigarami, or the choking feeling of social rules and expectations, than in Honshu. He expected that, by moving farther away from his hometown of Osaka to New Zealand, he could free himself from these old communal ties and obligations. He thought that Japanese society had so many social obligations based on status and position—such as the oldest son being expected to take care of his parents, and a university graduate being expected to take certain kinds of jobs and to contribute to society—that it was hard to meet these expectations and be accepted as a decent person in the society. He said, "The bar is high in Japanese society [*nihon no shakai wa shikii ga takai*]."

In New Zealand, Hiroshi worked as a busboy in a hotel restaurant and traveled in the country during his days off. After nine months of this working holiday in New Zealand, as the day of his return to Japan approached, Hiroshi became anxious and worried about his future: After going back to Japan, what could he do to earn a living? Quitting a job as a sarariman was still a big deal, even for someone like Hiroshi who did not make a strong investment in his job. On the way back to Japan, he traveled to India and Nepal for three months via Singapore. Hiroshi said that the travel experience in India completely changed his perceptions. While wandering through poor city neighborhoods and seeing people who suffered from poverty and disease, he realized how trivial his problem was. He was moved by the people who were facing the fundamental challenge in life: simply to live.

Instead of going back to Japan and finding a new stable job, Hiroshi wanted to broaden his horizons by traveling even more. He was addicted to travel. He decided to take a working holiday again, this time to

Canada. Hiroshi was not interested in Canada itself because he thought it was too developed and too close to the United States, and thus also to mainstream Japanese society, but he thought Canada would be a convenient place to earn money for additional travel. In the fall of 1993, he flew to Vancouver, traveled to Jasper by Greyhound bus, and then hitchhiked to Banff. Since then, he had worked as a tour guide in Banff every summer, backpacking in many other countries during the off-season. The seasonal nature of the guide's work was convenient, allowing him to prolong his working holiday even after he turned thirty, the official age cap for the working holiday program.

Interpretation of Company

As we have seen in the stories of Satomi, Eita, and Hiroshi, their narratives of escaping from Japan and seeing the world overseas recounted their responses to the dominant idea of how a person should work in a company. The guides' narratives illustrate that they internalized the norm that working full-time as seishain required total devotion to the company, which was considered not only a profit-making institution but a community of workers. A responsible employee was expected to be concerned that taking a long vacation or demanding to leave work would disrupt the work relations in the company and impose extra burdens on coworkers. Like Satomi and Eita, many of the guides strongly internalized the work ethic of the company as community but also wanted to escape from the obligations and constraints of being a full member of the company, especially when they had doubts about the company as community. When they felt a strong drive to go somewhere else, instead of taking a vacation or separating their private time and their work, they left their jobs because it was too hard to balance their commitments to their companies and their own desires to pursue other activities.

Scholars of Japanese work relations have argued that post–World War II Japanese capitalism can be characterized by the unique development of the company as a community-like entity (e.g., Dore 2000, 2002; Inagami 2008; Iwai 2003, 2005; Nakamaki 2006; Nakamaki et al. 2001). For example, sociologist and longtime observer of Japanese work relations Ronald Dore compares the Japanese perception of firms with what he calls the "Anglo-Saxon model," or the dominant American and British views of firms, and argues that in the Japanese community model "the firm is seen as a kind of individual-transcending entity with a history, a personality, a reputation, and if everybody does his job properly, a future" (2002, 118). Accordingly, Dore suggests, in the community model, the managerial board is considered to be, and also acts as, "the elders of an enterprise community" instead of "agents of the shareholders" (118). Usually, each board member has worked for the same company throughout his career and, after a long time spent working with only a modest salary increase, is promoted to the board. The managers work for the long-term prosperity of the company, including all its employees, present and future (27).

This community-model firm, according to Dore is more or less "the employee-favoring firm," in contrast to the Anglo-American model of the "shareholder-favoring firm."[7] Unlike the shareholder-favoring model, which is characterized by its focus on high short-term profits and wide income disparities between top executives and other workers, the characteristics of the community model corporation are often described as structural stability and a relatively egalitarian distribution of profit. As a community, a company assumes long-term commitments to workers. The well-known practices of so-called lifetime employment, the age-grade wage system, and a closed, firm-specific union provide employees with a sense of security and, in turn, foster their loyalty to the company. Although Dore's observations are based on large corporations, small companies have also developed their own community-model work relations.[8] For example, Dorinne Kondo (1990) vividly illustrates how the idea of "company as family" was enacted in a small sweets factory in downtown Tokyo.

Economist Iwai Katsuhito (2002, 2003) observes similar characteristics in Japanese companies, but instead of emphasizing the ethnicized cultural difference,[9] he argues that these differences derive from the ambivalent constitution of the corporation as a legal person. He explains that the corporation as a legal person has characteristics of both subject (a person) and object (a thing). The corporation is simultaneously a subject of business transactions and an object of ownership by actual human beings ("natural person") as subjects. This dual quality of corporations allows different interpretations of the nature of the company and has opened up debates among economists. Iwai summarizes the debates as a dispute between "corporate nominalism" and "corporate realism"—that is, over whether a corporation is merely the name of a legal fiction or a real entity (2003, 117–119).

Corporate nominalism considers a corporation as a fictional tool that allows actual human owners to conduct their business efficiently. This position regards the subject of business transactions as the actual shareholders of the corporation. In this view, the corporation is merely an object of possession by the shareholders and can be sold or purchased like any other commodity in the market. The purpose of the corporation is to make as much profit as possible for the owners (shareholders). Like Dore, Iwai explains that many Anglo-American corporations operate under this idea (Iwai 2003, 122–132). (Both Dore and Iwai point out that there are many variations between the extreme poles of the Anglo-American and the Japanese model of corporations, and the continental European models of corporation stand between these poles).[10]

In contrast to corporate nominalism, which tries to minimize the corporation's characteristics as a subject, corporate realism takes a corporation as a subject to the full extent. Iwai argues that the post–World War II Japanese model of corporations embodies the far corporate realist end of this spectrum. Under this model, large Japanese corporations have developed the cross-shareholding system: most large firms consist of a group of stable shareholders, including banks, stock brokerage firms, and insurance companies that prevent hostile takeovers from outside the group. Through the mutual possession of stocks by a number of companies, there is no single majority stockholder; thus, the input of stockholders as owners of the corporation was not as strong or transparent as in corporate nominalism. The well-known development of keiretsu, a group corporation system, represents this practice (Iwai 2002). In many cases, the corporate group itself is the largest stockholder. Thus, in this system, the corporation becomes its owner and appears as a real entity; in this sense, the corporation itself becomes a subject. The purpose of the corporation as a real entity is to continue its existence, instead of being an object of business transaction that is sold and purchased, as in corporate nominalism (Iwai 2003, 138–148).

Not surprisingly, the worker's relationship with the corporation differs in these two models. In corporate nominalism, a worker is supposed to be an independent subject whose relationship with the corporation is based on the sale of his or her labor according to a rational contract entered into by his or her own free will. The corporation is merely a legal fiction that mediates a contractual relationship between actual human beings. Each actor, shareholder, manager, and worker pursues his or her own profit, and the model does not assume an ongoing relationship between these actors. Both managers and workers are stimulated to develop their own skills that they can sell to other corporations as general human assets.

In contrast, in corporate realism, the relationships between the corporation, managers, and workers are more organic. In order for a corporation to function as a subject, like a person, employees are needed to function as if they were organs of a corporation as a whole person. In this system, instead of general skills, the corporation places more value on what Iwai calls "organization-specific human assets," which skills that are developed to be particularly suitable for a specific corporation. The ideal worker in this context is not a person who has a general skill that may be sold to another company but a person who can cultivate a specific skill for the needs of a particular company. In this sense, what is happening in the workplace is the mutual cultivation of personality among workers and the corporation itself. Thus, instead of locating the place of true identity outside the company, workers are motivated to identify themselves as valuable organs of the corporation (Iwai 2003, 149–159).

Iwai (1997) suggests that this system was developed in Japan because of the combination of its particular history, cultural genealogy and the logic of capitalism itself. He explains that Japanese capitalism before World War II took the form of classic capitalism and corporate ownership relations in which the zaibatsu families owned their companies, and their companies owned their subsidiaries. During the war, in order to accelerate the growth of national productivity, the corporations' activities were strongly integrated into national economic plans by restricting the rights of the company owners. Also, cooperation between the workers and corporate operators was encouraged to enhance productivity and serve the wartime national economy. The postwar dissolution of zaibatsu ordered by the General Headquarters of the Allied Powers led to the expulsion of the corporate owners. What was left were the workers and production assets. It created a vacuum of strong corporate ownership by an actual person. The corporations within a former zaibatsu group started to own each other's stocks in order to stabilize their relationships. Especially during the 1960s, this practice accelerated in order to prevent the inflation of the stocks in the midst of the stock market recession and to protect the Japanese corporations from foreign takeovers following capital liberalization (84–85).

In addition, Iwai also points out that the Japanese *ie*, family system might have provided a mold to construct this postwar corporate system which positions a corporation as a subject. The characteristic of the Japanese ie system is that the actual blood relations are not central to the system. What is important is the continuity of the family through the generations, which is symbolized by the continuity of the family's name. Therefore, the adoption of an heir from among nonkin was a commonly used strategy to maintain an ie for the future. Accordingly, the househead is not the sole owner and controller of the family, but the househead's role is rather that of a chief executive operator of the family, who is responsible for passing the ie to the next generations. Ie existed as if it were itself a subject of economic activities, rather than an object to be controlled by a person (87–88).

Iwai argues that this corporate system functioned well when the Japanese economy was relatively weak in the global economic system and protected the corporations from foreign takeover while allowing their growth in the relatively large domestic market. However, once the Japanese economy grew stronger and the corporations were "liberated" from protection and open to the global capitalist market, it also unavoidably exposed them to a world whose philosophical ground was under the hegemony of the Anglo-American interpretation of the corporation based on the binary distinction between a person and a thing (89–92).[11]

The practices of the community-model firm (Dore 2000, 2002) or corporate realism (Iwai 2002, 2003) were praised in the 1980s as they were considered the source of the Japanese economy's strength. One of the advantages of the community model is that it allows companies to develop long-term perspectives and strategies because they are not pressured to produce short-term profit and to raise stock returns as in the shareholder model. Also, the assumed long-term engagement of employees mobilizes their self-training efforts to commit to innovation and improvement in their work.

Meanwhile, the problems of this form of company have long been addressed as the individual worker's strong identification with the company often leads to overwork. Since the 1980s, the phenomenon of *karōshi*, or death by overwork, has been widely recognized. Also, the merging of personal aspirations and the company's objectives sometimes clouds workers' judgment and encourages them to commit antisocial practices "for the sake of the company." The milder but more widespread social concern was for the phenomenon of burned-out retired workers, especially male white-collar employees who had been working as core members of a company's community. Corporate workers who feel no personal fulfillment outside the company have been mocked in the media with such words as *shachiku* (domesticated animal of a corporation), and retired workers who lost their sense of purpose have been caricatured as *sangyō haikibutsu* (industrial waste).

Another problem of the community-model company in Japan is that the core companies have been dominated by males and the Japanese ethnic majority. Women, ethnic minorities, and people from historically discriminated *hisabetsu buraku* (communities associated with the feudal outcast group) have been marginalized, although efforts have been made to improve legal and social conditions for these groups in the workplace. In other words, a company has been a specific kind of community that requires its male Japanese core employees to subject their selves to a larger entity, the corporation. Eita's narrative exemplifies how he ambivalently internalized this model's work ethic. If Dore's observation about the "employee-favored" company is accurate, the employees would be "favored" in exchange for their devotion to the company.

As the Japanese economy grew and social stability was reestablished, discourses that incite men to be independent from the corporation became popular. Simultaneously, the need to open up core full-time positions to more diverse populations, especially women, was addressed. Beginning in the 1990s, when Japan experienced an economic recession, the community-model company became the target of neoliberal reforms. The characteristics of this type of corporation, which favored long-term relationships with workers and practices that do not necessarily produce short-term profit, were considered to be sources of inefficiency from the point of view of the stockholder-favoring firm model.

This drastic change in work relations took place around 1995, when Nikkeiren, the Japan Federation of Employers' Associations (which was integrated into Keidanren, the Japan Business Federation, in 2002) published an employment strategy report titled *Japanese-Style Management in a New Era*. The main strategy addressed in this report was maintaining the strength of existing labor relations in large corporations while incorporating more flexible labor forces to reduce human resource costs. Nikkeiren's recommendation was to manage human resources by forming "employment portfolios" consisting of three kinds of labor force: (1) long-term core employees, who are supposed to maintain the strength of the existing Japanese corporate model and are paid a monthly or annual salary; (2) skilled technical specialists, who deal with specific issues that require special professional knowledge, such as IT;

and (3) flexible workers, who are hired temporarily to conduct simple routine tasks (Itō 2007, 234).

Responding to employers' demands, the employment law was revised step by step. *Haken*, or indirect employment of temporary staff, had been tightly restricted by the Employment Security Law (Shokugyō Anteihō) since 1947 in order to protect workers from being exploited by employment brokers. In 1986, the Worker Dispatch Law (Rōdō Hakenhō) was implemented to allow haken work for skilled specialists, such as software developers and language translators. The intention was to make haken work an exception, not to make it a regular form of work. In the 1996 revision of the law, the list of allowed short-term haken work was expanded from sixteen to twenty-six categories. In the 1999 revision, haken was allowed for all but seven categories of work (Wakita 2010).

Many corporations have implemented changes in corporate governance and revised their human resource management strategies. The number of seishain, or core full-time employees, drastically decreased. According to government statistics, the number of regular employees decreased by 4.5 million from 1995 to 2005, or from 80 percent to 68 percent of the working population. During the same period, the number of contracted, nonregular employees increased from 10 million (21 percent) to 16 million (32 percent). Moreover, nearly half of female employees in 2005 were contracted employees (Itō 2007, 240). However, many critics argue that the pressure to work for most nonregular employees is as intense as for regular employees (Itō 2007; Nakano 2006). Nakano Mami (2006) points out that instead of encouraging the life-work balance, the change in corporate structure and labor laws simply benefited employers by reducing their human resource costs.

Genda Yūji (2001) suggests that young people were most influenced by these corporate restructurings. Many companies made an effort to maintain good relations with their existing workers but refrained from hiring new graduates; instead, staff shortages were filled by flexible temporary workers. Mary Brinton (2008) argues that the younger generation was deprived of the site, or *ba*, to construct their social identity. The company had been an important site for young graduates to locate themselves in society, through work and long-term relations. With the reduction of long-term, full-time positions, young people were thrown into insecure labor relations and were unable to develop strong ties with the company as community.

Freedom in the "Ice Age"

Unlike the previous generation of guides who entered the job market in the 1980s, many of the guides who finished their schooling in the mid-1990s came to Canada not because they wanted to escape from a company but because they found that the door to a suitable seishain position was firmly closed.

The younger generation of guides experienced what they referred to as the "job seeker's ice age" (*shūshoku hyōgaki*). Even if they had good educational backgrounds, they did not have the same experience in obtaining secure full-time work. This was particularly evident for women. This generation of women with university degrees had a wider range of choices for their life courses. Like Satomi, for the earlier generation, the general expectation of a woman's role in a corporation was to be an office lady, who remains in an assisting position and retires within a few years to become a housewife and a caretaker for her husband and children. Women's position in society was assumed to be in the household. In some exceptional cases, a woman was expected to "work like a man" by sacrificing her personal life, which often meant being discouraged from marrying or having children. Following the implementation of legal guidelines for equal employment opportunity in 1986, women university graduates were given more socially recognized choices. On the surface, this move seemed to be a step toward the "liberation" of women from the household. Yet, as Miyako Inoue (2007) cautions, the effects of gender equity labor reforms need to be analyzed in the context of the neoliberal political and economic restructuring. Releasing women from the domestic realm entailed "freedom" in an ironic sense. As many companies revised their paternalistic corporate practices, many young men were no longer entitled to family allowances, unlike the previous generation of men. The younger generation of sararīman could not depend on the additional stipend given to heads of households to support a wife and children. Women were "free" from domestic obligations as well as from the husband's company benefit. Young women felt stronger pressure to work outside the home even after marriage in order to support themselves and their families. Being a housewife without an obligation to earn an income became a luxury for many young women.

In this context, Inoue (2007) describes how female workers at a Tokyo office were urged to reconstruct their subjectivity in accordance with the neoliberal principles of self-sufficiency, individual choice, and responsibility. Female workers were constantly asked, "What do you want?" Women were faced with this question when they were given the choice to remain on the noncareer assistant track or to switch to the career track, or when they were asked to identify problems of gender inequality. This question helped rediscipline them as agents responsible for challenging gender inequality in the workplace by themselves. Instead of framing the gender issue as a social and structural problem, this question turned gender inequality into a personal and individual matter. At the same time, being a house husband was still considered an anomaly, leaving men with less choice regarding their degree of involvement in the labor market, but women were suddenly given many choices and pressured to be responsible for their own life courses. Many women who entered the job market in the 1990s faced a stronger demand to establish their subjectivities as independent individuals in exchange for freedom. The women who attended university in the 1990s went through similar self-disciplining exercises as the female office workers depicted by Inoue (2007), which encouraged them to find what they really wanted to do in their lives. Many of the life stories of female guides were narrated in terms of seeking freedom and independence, searching for what they wanted to do (*yaritai koto o sagasu*).

SECURITY LOST

Among the guides I talked to, Yoshiko most drastically experienced the loss of security that had been given by the company. She grew up in Kobe and went to a competitive private university in the Kansai area. Because she wanted to be independent from her parents after graduating, she majored in legal studies, thinking it would give her an advantage in finding a job. To expand her potential job opportunities, she also earned certificates for teaching social studies in high school and junior high school. She graduated in March 1995, not long after the Great Hanshin-Awaji Earthquake that hit Kobe in January of that year. It was a difficult time for her to concentrate on her job search because the house where she lived with her parents had been severely damaged. She vividly remembered that the staff at her university job search office advised her to reflect deeply about what she had done so far and what she wanted to do in her life in order to find a suitable workplace. She felt guilty and strange pursuing her own aspirations while her parents and relatives were suffering from the devastation of the earthquake, yet she also felt increasing pressure to be economically independent as she lost the sense of security. Following her job search counselor's advice, Yoshiko reflected on what she wanted to do. She chose to apply for a job in a company rather than becoming a teacher because she wanted to expand her experiences outside of a school setting. Her preference was to work for a sports-related company, such as a sporting goods manufacturer or fitness club, because she liked sports activities, especially skiing. Given the tight job market, she also applied for sales positions in other industries that she thought actively hired women, such as interior design, housing, and insurance. Despite her serious efforts, Yoshiko did not receive any offers from companies she liked.

Yoshiko's sense of security and her experience with corporations stood in stark contrast to those of her parents. Yoshiko's father was a junior high school graduate who had been recruited as a "golden egg" (*kin no tamago*) by one of the largest shipbuilding companies in Japan. During the rapid economic growth in the 1960s, companies like these actively recruited many junior high school graduates in rural agricultural communities to fill labor shortages in manufacturing industries. The large corporations provided on-the-job training and, in some cases, even vocational schooling to turn their employees into skilled workers. They also provided employees with lodging and recreational facilities to provide for the entire lives of these young workers. Under this older corporate system, blue-collar workers without a high school education, like Yoshiko's father, could live comfortably. He supported his full-time homemaker wife, sent two children—Yoshiko and her brother—to private universities, and enjoyed golf as his hobby. When the earthquake hit their house, the company provided temporary housing for them until they could move to another home.

Yoshiko was thankful for her father's company, but she was also aware that her generation could not expect this same kind of security. If she could not expect to receive social security benefits in exchange for her devotion to work, she wanted to find work that was worth spending her time on. After graduation, until she found her "real" job, she worked part-time as an office receptionist. In the winter, she also worked as an instructor at a ski resort on the weekends, eventually realizing that she wanted to focus her attention on skiing. She moved to a ski resort in Nagano prefecture and worked there for two years. She continued to do self-search, trying to find what she really wanted to do. She concluded that she wanted to live in a place where she could truly feel that she was "living on the earth," not in a human society (*chikyū ni sunderu to iu jikkan ga waku tokoro, ningen shakai ja naku*). She said, "I wanted to feel the joy of living on the place called the earth, where there are beautiful landscapes, where I can eat flavorful food, where I can enjoy clean air, where there are mountains and the sky." Then the landscape of Lake Louise came to mind. When she was a university student, she had traveled from Vancouver to Banff with a friend. She had walked up the steep 4.5-kilometer road from the bus depot in Lake Louise Village to the lake without knowing that people usually used cars to travel from the valley bottom to the popular scenic lake in the middle of the mountain. When she reached the lake, she was mesmerized by its milky blue-green color and the glacier-capped mountain beyond. It was hard for her to shake off the strong impression made by this unimaginably beautiful and magnificent landscape. When she learned about the RMT at a job fair, Yoshiko decided to move to Banff. It was an ideal location for her, conveniently located near world-class ski hills, where she could feel that she was living on the earth.

FALLING "IN BETWEEN"

Shinohara Rei's story elucidates the challenge faced by a young woman who wanted to balance her work and private life. She explained her situation as *chūtohanpa*, or being "awkwardly in between." She had done well at the most competitive public high school in her school district in Osaka. Most of her classmates went to universities, but she went to a junior college that had been established by an American female missionary and had a respectable English department. To get a good job, she thought it would be better for a woman to go to a junior college that was known for its practical training.

As a college student, Rei was disillusioned by her classmates. Many of them still considered working as an OL a good life course for women, along with finding a good husband in a stable company and becoming a housewife. She secretly distanced herself from these other students and became further interested in feminism. She found that books on psychological topics helped her to deal with the gender obstacles that did not seem to bother her classmates. After graduating from the junior college, Rei transferred to a highly ranked liberal arts college in the southern United States and majored in psychology.

After returning to Japan in 1998, Rei applied for several jobs where she thought she could utilize the experience she had gained by studying abroad. She was selected as a final candidate for an administrative assistant position in a private English-language school and for a position as a ground agent for an airline company, but in the end, she did not receive any offers. Reflecting on her unsuccessful job search, she concluded that she was overeducated for assistant work but not educated enough for an elite position. She sensed that employers might have thought her career choice was half-baked and that she was not fully committed to the hard work required for full-time career track workers, but she was not satisfied with women's assistant work, which also was becoming scarce as it was replaced by temporary staff work. She wanted to have a good balance between work and her future family life, but it was difficult to find the stable, full-time work that would allow her to spend time with her family and pursue personal fulfillment.

Perplexed, Rei wanted to spend some time reflecting on what to do with her life. She also did not want to be dependent on her parents after graduation. She found a temporary job as a helper at a ski resort in Nagano prefecture. While working there, she thought of applying for a working holiday visa and going abroad. Meanwhile, her boyfriend, who was interested in working in the tourism industry, found a job at the RMT, and the two of them moved to Banff.

STANDS ON HER OWN FEET

Maeda Hanako experienced the mismatch of work that led many young people to leave their jobs even though full-time work was scarce. Hanako thought she was extremely lucky to have a well-paid, full-time job right after graduation in 1997. When she was a psychology student at a private university in Tokyo, she worked part-time as a computer instructor and taught the basics of Word and Excel in classes offered by a telecommunication company. The company, a subsidiary of a large telephone company, was expanding its IT section, and her boss asked her to continue working for the company after graduation. She was hired to take care of a presentation room that was equipped with the latest videophone technology for international video conferences and presentations. She was responsible for taking bookings for the room, offering technical assistance for its users, and explaining its features to its external clients. Before she received this offer, she vaguely thought that she wanted to work in the tourism industry because she liked traveling, but she accepted the job because the salary and benefits were too good for her to reject, especially when the job market was tight. As soon as she started, though, she found that it was not the job for her. She had no formal training in computer technology, and with the equipment and the programs in the presentation room continuously being updated, she found herself frequently asking for help from the company's system engineers. The engineers were kind and generously helped her. They also gave her advice and books to improve her knowledge and skills.

While she was thankful to her colleagues, Hanako felt that she had been given responsibility for tasks that were beyond her ability. She was burned out and regretted not seriously investigating what she wanted to do with her life. Every morning, Hanako set up equipment and tested it by exchanging greetings with her counterparts in overseas offices. This practice stimulated her curiosity about life abroad. She started to imagine what it would be like to live in a foreign country and became a regular viewer of the weekly television program *Umi no mukou de kurashite mireba* (If you live overseas). When she saw an episode depicting a female guide in the Canadian Rockies, she decided to go to Canada and become a guide.

Hanako told me how she was fascinated by the female guide she saw in the program. The guide drove a large tour van, showed tourists spectacular scenery, and explained the landscape through her headset microphone while driving. Hanako told me that the guide looked "so cool" (*kakkoii*) as she did everything by herself to conduct the tour. The guide seemed to embody someone who "stands on her own feet" (*jibun no ashi de tatte iru*). To Hanako, the female guide looked independent because she lived by herself in a foreign environment. The guide had "created her own connections from scratch," without depending on a familiar social network.

In contrast, Hanako felt that all aspects of her own life, including her university education and her work in a Tokyo office, had been "provided," although indirectly, by her parents; thus rather than standing on her own feet, she stood on what her parents had "set up" for her. Hanako did not dislike her work and personal life in Tokyo. She had good relationships with her boss and friends and enjoyed going out with them for meals and drinks after work. But she wanted to be part of another world in which she would feel certain that she was standing on her own feet.

While Hanako wanted to build her own life from scratch like the guide on television, she felt it would be hard to accomplish this if she stayed in Tokyo because she was already deeply enmeshed in her established social relations. Hanako found it was "so hard not to be a parasite" to her parents due to the high cost of living in Tokyo. In order to stand on her own feet, she felt she had to relocate to a completely new world. The female guide she saw on television made it clear for Hanako what she should do in her life. Hanako idolized the guide and embraced her image as a figure of independence and freedom—a person who had a solid sense of her own subjectivity and the ability to move beyond national, social, and cultural boundaries.

SEARCHING FOR THE SELF IN NATURE

Yoshiko, Rei, and Hanako, each in her own way, experienced the neoliberal economic restructuring of 1990s Japan. Their stories elucidate how drastic changes in work relations put these women "in between." They were encouraged to free themselves from conventional gender roles and pushed to enter the labor market in order to be responsible for their own livelihood, well-being, and personal fulfillment. They were not, however, in an elite position that would have enabled them to overcome gender bias and get hired for the few remaining core full-time jobs. Instead, they were urged to enter the flexible and insecure labor market, while being encouraged to be autonomous and independent subjects of this new era of economic restructuring.

Before moving to Banff, Yoshiko, Rei, and Hanako each had lived temporarily or traveled extensively in places known for their natural environment. Yoshiko and Rei had worked in mountainous ski resorts in Japan after their unsuccessful job searches. Disappointed and confused, they attempted to clarify what they wanted to do in their lives. Yoshiko tried to see if she could live as a ski instructor. Rei, who had no interest in outdoor sports, simply wanted to be away from home. Hanako loved camping and on weekends went to the beaches or the rivers around Tokyo with her friends. She also liked trekking in the mountains. At a time when she was unsure about whether she wanted to continue her office job, spending time outdoors helped her to reflect on her life trajectory and gave her a hint for a future direction. In their searches for self, these women moved away from their urban homes, and as they lived or wandered in nature in Japan, they realized they wanted to move farther away from their familiar environments.

Nature played a significant part in the guides' construction of subjectivities. Particularly, the vast image of "the earth" represented in the popular discourse of the Canadian Rockies was important for these women. The environmental protection practices in Banff National Park coincided with this notion, as the park presented its environment as a place with minimal human "intervention." The mountains were framed as evidence of the earth's long history and the current continental formation. The earth provided an image of a scale beyond national boundaries, which was, at the same time, the fundamental unit of human dwelling.

This framing of nature was significant because it stimulated the feeling of "living on the earth," as Yoshiko so eloquently articulated. Yoshiko felt that in this environment, she could escape her concerns and the predicaments she faced. At the ski resort in rural Japan, she thought the local traditional community was so strong that it was hard for an outsider to be accepted as a resident, whereas in Banff, she was a resident in a community of immigrants. Hanako also felt that she was accepted as "a dweller of the earth" surrounded by the vast natural environment. Compared with older generations of Japanese emigrants who explicitly admired the West (cf. Kelsky 2001), for many of the younger guides in the RMT, the Canadian Rockies were attractive because of their image of nature that transcends sociocultural boundaries and problems.

In the next chapter, I discuss how Canada's image as a utopian yet accessible dreamland has been constructed in popular culture and how this imaginary was constructed in relation to American "soft power" (Nye 1990) and the specific Cold War and post–Cold War geopolitics. First, I examine the work of Ōhashi Kyosen, one of the most influential post–World War II dream weavers for the emerging middle mass. Then, I introduce the life histories of three male guides whose life trajectories took their interests from American culture to Canadian nature, similar to the itinerary that Ōhashi created and popularized.

2 | Populist Cosmopolitanism

Among the many Japanese-language signs on the main street of Banff, the one on the OK Gift Shop stood out. With a large photo image of a Japanese man with thick, black-rimmed eyeglasses, it read, "This Is My Store. Feel at Home" (*Boku no mise desu. Anshinshite dōzo*). This souvenir store was owned by Ōhashi Kyosen, a popular television entertainer, former politician, and arguably the main promoter of Japanese leisure travel to Canada. Some critics argue that Ōhashi epitomizes the sensibility of the middle mass, in particular, articulating the desire for leisure and overseas travel during the 1970s and 1980s, after the restrictions for overseas travel for leisure were lifted in 1964. Through his television programs and his stores, Ōhashi popularized overseas travel as something attainable for ordinary folks, not limited to a few elites. The sign on his store represents his clever articulation of what I call "populist cosmopolitan" desire and anxiety. The goods in the store itself were not significantly different from those in the other souvenir stores, except that they offered a wider selection of items popular among Japanese tourists and some special charms that resembled Ōhashi. But the presence of the store and the sign aimed to create an atmosphere to ease nervousness for the Japanese tourists, affirming for them that it was fine to travel abroad and helping them feel at home even if they could not speak eloquently in a foreign language and were not familiar with the local customs.

Ōhashi's more recent work shifted its emphasis from leisure travel to the issue of retirement. The dream of a happy retired life overseas that Ōhashi promoted in his publications around 2000 was so influential that many tourists of various ages commented to me during the tours that "Canada is as nice as Kyosen says!" Although their understanding of actual Canadian society was initially rather vague, the image of Canada as a utopian space in nature was shared by many of the tour guides who moved to Banff. The imaginary dreamland projected on the Canadian natural landscape provided a mutual ground for interaction between tourists and the guides, and for the guides to performatively construct their subjectivity as an embodiment of the cosmopolitan dream.

Ōhashi's articulation of Canada as a destination of the populist cosmopolitan dream needs to be situated in the long-standing Japanese struggle to translate "subject" and "subjectivity." In the critical analysis of political subjectivity, populism and cosmopolitanism are often considered to be on opposite ends of a spectrum. The subject of populism is considered as the "mass" of ordinary folks. Populism traditionally expresses the sentiments of the mass, or ordinary folks, who are dissatisfied with the control of the powerful, the wealthy, and the privileged elites. Often, populism articulates this antielite sentiment with nationalism or primordial communal ties, which are imagined to exist before the expansion of external influences brought or controlled by elites.[1] Populism absorbs the sentiments of the mass of ordinary folks, whose feelings and opinions have not been expressed through established venues in representational politics. Instead of acting as individual agents and in accordance with the liberal ideal of rational and independent "citizens," the masses are considered to be elusive and responsive to the social atmosphere. The masses often seek a hero who represents their feelings through theatrical performance and mass media; in turn, the masses are mobilized and integrated into a national (and/or other) collective.

In contrast, the subjects of cosmopolitanism are often individuals— autonomous, independent, free and rational citizens of the world. Cosmopolitanism emerged from the tradition of liberal and rational citizens and further extended its reach beyond the borders of the nation-state. The cosmopolitan sphere is imagined to be based on the mutual respect of the rights, freedom, choice, and rationality of these citizens of the world. Cosmopolitanism has been developed in modern history by bour-geois intellectuals and economic elites along with the notion of a sover-eign state. It envisions the connections of citizens of the world, beyond local ties and cultural differences, as well as against the constraints of national boundaries.[2]

What populism and cosmopolitanism share is that they both place the citizen in a nation-state as a critical reference point. While the national citizen is a normalized form of subject in contemporary global politics, the assumed notion of subjectivity developed from modern Western liberal thought does not naturally fit the everyday life situations and experiences of many people whose social worlds are shaped by different intellectual histories and different understandings of subjectivity.[3]

Ōhashi's narratives absorb the populist dissatisfaction with the elite's manipulation of national (and international) politics and the people's demand for fair compensation for their hard work and contributions to the economic growth of a nation. Yet, instead of turning to national-istic or imagined primordial sentiments for a solution, Ōhashi weaves these populist demands into a cosmopolitan desire to transcend na-tional boundaries in the pursuit of freedom and the choice to live one's own life. In this formation, translating and adopting a Western-style subjectivity is crucial. In his work, Ōhashi assumes a double role as cul-tural translator between Japan and the West, and as mediator between national elites and ordinary folks (*shomin*) within Japan. Even though Ōhashi became so successful in his career that he was once listed among the top-earning entertainers in Japan, he continuously aligns himself with shomin and criticizes power elites in the Japanese social hierarchy, especially national bureaucrats. As an anonymous reviewer of Ōhashi's book *Kyosen: Jinsei no Sentaku* (Kyosen: A choice in life) writes, Ōhashi is "the most entertainer-like entertainer" who embodies the shomin's dream of postwar Japan, symbolizing economic success and a new vision of the world opened up by affluence (*Shincho 45* 2000, 268). The populist cosmopolitan dream exemplified by Ōhashi's work played an important role in mobilizing the Japanese mass population to identify themselves as being in the middle of the social strata and stimulating the idea that they were entitled to follow the lifestyles of the middle class in devel-oped capitalist society.[4]

Ironically, Ōhashi's mimetic performance of Western subjectivity also highlights the limits of cosmopolitanism, when its model is imag-ined to be "Western" liberal individualism. Seen via this model, ordinary folks in Japan are doomed to be marked as the other, the belated, or the abnormal; thus they cannot claim full membership in the cosmopolitan world unless they acquire the necessary form of subjectivity, the liberal notion of the individual rooted in Euro-American Enlightenment thought. To understand this cultural dynamic, Ōhashi's narrative performance needs to be situated within larger arguments of subjectivity.

As discussed in the introduction, *shutaisei*, the translation word for "subjectivity," is a native invention because it also includes the related concepts of independence, identity, and individuality (Miyoshi 1991, 97, 123). Miyoshi argues that the incommensurability between the English notion of subjectivity and the Japanese translation, shutaisei, reveals that although Japanese intellectuals in the mid-twentieth century had assumed the universal value of subjectivity, the concept itself was developed in the West during the modern period in response to specific historical contexts and is no less culturally and historically specific than such concepts as feudalism and Protestantism (123). He further suggests that addressing the politics of knowledge was discouraged in the political and philosophical climate of post–World War II Japan, in which the issue of subjectivity was intertwined with the discussion of responsibility for war (105). Critiquing the universal claim of the Western notion of subjectivity could easily have been labeled a return to the wartime opposition to Western powers and an expression of Japanese nationalism. In this context, serious critique of the universality of subjectivity was foreclosed, and postwar intellectuals' concerns were directed toward problematizing Japanese subjectivity as an anomaly and educating the mass to attain a subjectivity whose norm is located in the West. Miyoshi sarcastically implies that the Japanese obsession with consumption in the 1980s may be a symptom of this political and discursive predicament, as the only effective way that the mass population in postwar Japan found to express their subjectivity (125).[5]

Although earlier discussion of subjectivity in intellectual history and literary analysis has been focused on the critical writings of intellectuals, I argue that in order to understand the larger social impacts of the translation of subjectivity, we also need to examine how the issue is articulated in popular discourses. Ōhashi's popular writings suggest that the issue of subjectivity still haunts the everyday lives of many Japanese and continues to be the key predicament for articulating a culturally meaningful model of "citizenry" in contemporary Japan. Ōhashi's writings raise questions about what it means to be an active agent of one's life, and how to situate the self in the larger society.

Through an analysis of Ōhashi's narratives, I first illustrate how subjectivity is negotiated through people's demands for leisure and their concerns about retirement, both of which are entangled with their fascination with traveling overseas and the curiosity toward overseas lifestyles. In particular, I focus on his book *Kyosen: Jinsei no Sentaku*,[6] an exemplary and influential work of populist cosmopolitanism published in 2000, as well as on his related writings. Second, I examine Ōhashi's narratives as an expression of the paradoxical position of the Japanese citizenry conditioned by the political, economic, and military coalition between Japan and the United States. I discuss how the predicament of articulating Japanese subjectivity reflects this paradoxical position within the legacy of Cold War geopolitics in Asia because the spatial imaginary that Ōhashi constructed echoes that narrated by tour guides. Finally, I will introduce stories of three male guides who articulated how their interest in traveling overseas was shaped by American soft power, the power exercised by seducing and attracting the others to influence their perceptions and behaviors (Nye 1990), and how these guides revised their understanding of the world in Canadian nature.

Choose Your Own Life

Ōhashi's book *Kyosen: Jinsei no Sentaku* became a best seller in 2000. The book is part autobiography and part philosophical guide for early retirement, directed primarily at *sararīman*. As the title suggests, the fundamental concepts that Ōhashi promotes in his book are individual choice and freedom. The book's advertisement slip wrapped around the bottom part of the dust jacket reads, "To live is to live as you please! Don't be chained to your work or to the company you work for. A recommendation for Kyosen's way of life" (*Sukini ikite koso jinsei da! Shigoto ya kaisha ni shibarareruna. Kyosen ryū ikikata no susume*). He invites his readers to imagine that with "choice," one can transcend the constraints of workplace and even further, those of Japanese society. In particular, Ōhashi suggests that life after retirement is a great chance to live by one's choice and to be a "protagonist" of one's life. Therefore, he urges sararīman to change their perception of retirement: he maintains that in Japan, retirement has the negative connotation that an employee has become useless to society, but in North America, it is a sign of success if one builds his fortune early enough to be able to stop working before the traditional retirement age (Ōhashi 2000a, 31), and by using his own life as a successful example, he advocates for following the new conceptualization of retirement.

Ōhashi calls his semiretirement lifestyle a "sunflower life." Just like a sunflower that continuously turns its head to the sun, he moves across the Pacific, enjoying spring and fall in Japan, summer in Canada, and winter in Australia and New Zealand. He follows the sun and benefits from the most pleasant seasons of these countries, where he has seasonal homes and runs souvenir stores. Even though he claims that he is retired from regular television shows, he still works as an entrepreneur, and as the owner of these stores. Instead of focusing on his work and frequent travel, Ōhashi emphasizes the fun parts of his lifestyle, such as pampering himself in his summer home, picking berries, observing small wild animals, playing golf, and meeting friends (Ōhashi 2000a, 17–19). By presenting these examples of "living the way you like," Ōhashi depicts his sunflower life as active yet peaceful and freed from not only work but also the constraints of national boundaries.

Although the sunflower life seems to be beyond the reach of most of the Japanese population, Ōhashi tells readers that a sararīman can follow such a path if he makes rational choices and prepares early. Most important in pursuing a "happy second life" is to reflect critically on, and subsequently change, one's priorities in life from working in a company to exploring one's personal enjoyment. Ōhashi particularly emphasizes the need to make an active choice in designing one's life. He encourages his readers to abandon the "old" Japanese sense of priorities, such as attending a famous school, working in a good, stable company, and climbing up the corporate ladder (Ōhashi 2000a, 31). Instead of these external evaluation criteria, he advocates establishing personal measures of self-fulfillment and securing the fundamental conditions of one's life. These are (1) health, (2) a good partner (wife), (3) several hobbies, and (4) financial security (a home) (32–38). He argues that in order to live *shutaitekini*, or actively as a protagonist of one's own life, one should not be consumed by work, but rather should adopt a perception of work as merely a means to the pursuit of enjoyment in retirement. Ōhashi's advice to sararīman is to divide life into two halves, with the first half being the time to work hard and save money, and the second half being the time to enjoy life after retirement. Ōhashi suggests that with a pension and lump-sum retirement allowance, as well as active and early preparation, a happy retirement life overseas is not impossible for a sararīman.

While *Jinsei no Sentaku* advocates for actively establishing subjectivity in one's life, its sequel from the same year, *Kyosen Nikki* (Kyosen diary), emphasizes the importance of detaching personal fulfillment from material wealth and promotes an alternative view of "affluence." In *Kyosen Nikki*, Ōhashi depicts his life in Canada, Australia, and New Zealand as an example of "a modest but fulfilling life" (*Tsumashii keredo yutakana kurashi*) (2000b, 15). In these two books, Ōhashi effectively provides his readers with the dream vision of "living one's own life," free from the company and nation, the two most influential social contexts in shaping a sararīman's life. Furthermore, by shifting "affluence" from material wealth to personal fulfillment, he explains how this dream is within the reach of the ordinary sararīman.

THE VIEW FROM THE AIRPLANE: TRANSFERENTIAL DESIRE

The most striking feature of Ōhashi's narrative is the distinction between the West as advanced, liberal, dynamic, and active and Japan as traditional, constraining, static, and passive. By making this distinction, Ōhashi locates the West as the norm, and Japan as something to be saved from its own outmoded tradition. Appropriating the outsider's Orientalist point of view is central for Ōhashi when he assigns himself the role of mediator between Western and Japanese lifestyles. Specifically, in *Jinsei no Sentaku*, Ōhashi takes an aerial view and maps onto the Japanese landscape particular problems that were ubiquitous in the 1970s, such as pollution, increasing population density, and overindustrialization. He interprets the changes in the natural landscape of Tokyo as representative of the dystopic future toward which the whole country was moving. Reflecting on the time around 1970, he writes:

The Japanese economy was in the midst of rapid growth, and the whole nation was busy with "produce, produce" and "export, export." As a result, on the one hand, the nation grew richer and the standard of living was raised. On the other hand, it produced pollution: the air in urban areas was extremely contaminated. It became impossible to eat fish from the Bay of Tokyo. When my wife and I landed at Haneda International Airport in Tokyo from Canada or Hawai'i, we saw a thick layer of smog from the airplane window. We could not stop coughing when we exited the airport lobby. Unlike those people who remained in Japan, for those of us flying overseas several times for television programs, the threat of the pollution looked enormous. I picked up the issue of pollution in my Monday version of 11 PM [television show]. But I felt that the tide of the time was too strong [to stop pollution]. (Ōhashi 2000a, 25–26)

Ōhashi as the frequent overseas traveler clearly contrasts himself with most of the Japanese population, who remained in Japan in the 1970s and was, in his view, still preoccupied with working and seeking economic affluence. In this narrative, instead of critiquing specific environmental policies or industrial practices, Ōhashi sees the source of the pollution problem as the general Japanese tendency to overwork and be obsessed with material wealth. By distancing himself from Japan and locating his point of view from the air, Ōhashi positions himself as an enlightened person who has a greater awareness of the importance of leisure and personal fulfillment. From this vantage, Ōhashi critiques the Japanese sararīman as an economic animal domesticated by and dependent on the company rather than an independent individual who has a solid sense of shutaisei and makes his own decisions and choices in life.

By taking the role of an intermediary who transcends the constraints of Japanese national boundaries, Ōhashi effectively frames the issue of retirement as a site of performing the mimetic desire for "the West," or what Sakai (1997, 59) calls "transferential desire," the desire to see oneself from another's position. In this transferential desire, the West is constructed as a normative interlocutor in the Japanese imagination. The particularity of Japan is always thought out in reference to the generality or universality of the West, and "Japan" is imagined to be burdened with the existential constraint of lagging behind it, or being a distortion of it. Ōhashi creates the image of the West as a normative mirror to reflect problems in Japan, based on his observation of a particular group of Americans, Canadians, Australians, and New Zealanders.[7]

SUBJECTIVITY CONSTRUCTION THROUGH LEISURE
AND RETIREMENT

Ōhashi developed his idea of a sunflower life by observing the lifestyles of his wealthy Canadian and American friends. In *Jinsei no Sentaku*,

Ōhashi explains that it was a Canadian millionaire he met in Hawai'i in the early 1970s who transformed his idea of retirement. The Canadian man, who had built his fortune on a shopping center development in Vancouver, lived in his second house in Hawai'i during the winter. Ōhashi and his wife were invited to this man's main house on a small island near Victoria, British Columbia. During dinner on his luxurious cruiser, the Canadian friend proudly told Ōhashi that he could have retired ten years earlier, when he was forty years old, but he had postponed retirement to prevent senility. To Ōhashi, this remark was surprising and puzzling. Although he himself was getting close to forty years old at that time, the word "retire" sounded far too distant for him. Ōhashi had already built a successful career in the television industry and was wealthy enough to spend his winter vacations in Hawai'i. While mingling with wealthy people from Canada and the United States, he gradually realized that "the idea of retirement is completely opposite on each side of the Pacific" (Ōhashi 2000a, 31).

What Ōhashi learned from his rich North American entrepreneurial friends was the clear separation of work and personal life, or public and private, and the regimentation of time and space to reinforce that boundary. Whereas his Canadian friend taught him how to make the first half of life for work and the second half of life for himself, it was his American friend, a successful fashion designer, who inspired him to separate work time from private time and, accordingly, to distinguish the geographic location of the time spent for each purpose. Although the designer was living in "a luxurious condo for millionaires in Manhattan," he and his wife deserted the house every week from Friday afternoon to Monday morning. The rest of the week, they stayed in their "cabin," which was actually a mansion on Long Island. Surprised, Ōhashi asked his American friend why he would vacate his luxury condo for half of the week. The friend answered, "It helps me come up with new ideas" (Ōhashi 2000a, 24–25). He explained to Ōhashi that if he always stayed in the middle of New York City, he would be stuck with a small "urban mind," and he needed to be refreshed by spending private time in his cabin.[8]

The key lesson that Ōhashi learned from these friends was to create times and spaces for recovering a sense of authentic "self" from the disruption of work and other social obligations. In this model of the individual developed in modern Western discourses, while the essence of the self is imagined to exist in an individual, that self occasionally needs to be re-created and reminded of its integrity through detachment from external interruptions. Separating work time and recreation time, and spatially marking the boundary between the two, help reaffirm the existence of the true, authentic self. Ōhashi employs the rhetorical gesture of being "surprised" when exposed to this "Western-style" norm of the self as a free, autonomous individual independent from the external world of work and social obligations; such a gesture emphasizes the difference in the concepts of freedom, self, and subjectivity as they have developed in Japan and North America.[9] Ōhashi invites readers to adopt the ideal of the free, autonomous individual in order to overcome the stereotypical Japanese notion of passive personhood, of being overly embedded in the social world and work.[10]

This vision of retirement also gives a clearly gendered response to the creeping fears among middle-aged sararīman about their senior life. Feminist critic Higuchi Keiko (1990), in her critique of the Japanese work culture and family system, points out the phenomenon of retired husbands whose lives having been consumed by their companies and who find no space in which to occupy themselves after retirement and merely stay at home without a sense of purpose. Based on her observations at the height of corporation-based welfare capitalism, she concludes that unlike their wives, who have developed social networks through community activities, children's schools, and hobbies, the burned-out husbands are frequently at a loss about what to do outside their companies. Higuchi describes the wives' concerns for and frustrations with their retired husbands by using metaphors such as "wet fallen leaves hard to shake off" (*nureochiba*) and a hard-to-discard "large piece of garbage" (*sodaigomi*) (1990, 68). According to Higuchi, feminist sociologist Ueno Chizuko, in an even sharper critique, uses the term "industrial waste" (*sangyō haikibutsu*) to describe retired husbands (Higuchi 1990, 68). Ōhashi's *Jinsei no Sentaku* was published in a series called Ōgon no Nureochiba Kōza (Golden wet fallen leaves seminar), a title that reflects the editor's wish that men will shine like gold even after retirement. In contrast to the negative image of wet fallen leaves, the cover design of Ōhashi's book offers deep green leaves on a deep blue background, symbolizing tranquil but vibrant energy.[11]

The Politics of Leisure: Popularization of Shutaisei

Ōhashi's narrative performances must be situated against the haunting concerns with subjectivity in post–World War II Japan. The most influential argument on subjectivity, or shutaisei, is articulated by Maruyama Masao, the leading postwar political scientist at the University of Tokyo. Maruyama aims to interrogate the origin of Japanese political thought in order to consider the problem of identifying the responsibility for Japan's wartime aggression. In contrast to German and Italian fascism, in which the location of political responsibility seemed clear, the responsibility for Japan's ultranationalism remained obscure. Although the war was conducted under the name of the emperor, the emperor system persisted after the war. This obscures the question of responsible subjectivity: Who exactly was responsible for the wartime aggression? The war was narrated as if it happened "naturally," and ordinary Japanese people were framed as the victims of the war.[12] Maruyama ([1952] 1983) problematizes this obscurity and tries to discover the source of this problem by tracing the development of Japanese thought under the influence of the Zhu Xi (Chu Hsi) school of neo-Confucianism. In particular, he contrasts the two influential schools that have served as competing sources for envisioning social order in Japanese intellectual history. The first is that of Motoori Norinaga (1730–1801), which emphasizes *shizen*, the word used for the translation of "nature," indicating the force that reflects the order of the universe; the other is that of Ogyū Sorai (1666–1728), which values *sakui*, or "invention," the forces of human agency that intervene to create social order. Maruyama chooses to valorize human invention as it seeks to overcome the forces of nature that constrain rational political actions, suggesting that in order for Japanese to re-enter the international community, they need to establish shutaisei, or human subjectivity, to overcome nature (268–269).

Many postwar intellectuals, both leftist and liberal, including Maruyama, regret that the previous nature-nation configuration led to ultranationalism and the oppression of people. These intellectuals have striven to disarticulate the prewar equation of nation with natural order, particularly the link between a naturalized national social order and the genealogical metaphor of the emperor's family. Postwar intellectuals struggled to provide a better vocabulary with which to envision the new democratic Japan. As the leading political scientist, Maruyama searched for a model of the Japanese citizen as an independent, autonomous, and rational modern subject who could resist the totalitarian national force by using the vocabularies of modern Western thought.

Ōhashi's promotion of freedom and choice entails a strong enlightenment agenda. His goal of choosing to value one's own life echoes Maruyama's advocacy of overcoming the passivity led by "nature," in order for the Japanese to achieve a modern subjectivity following the European model of the autonomous citizen guided by a particular modern notion of rationality. As historian Julia Thomas points out, "nature" is considered "modernity's unconsciousness," to be overpowered and mastered by the modern rational consciousness (Thomas 2001, 21). Ōhashi encourages the sararīman to overcome the passive attitude of being "domesticated" to the company and of later finding himself as "industrial waste." He urges the sararīman to use his imagination to design his own life instead of being subjected to nature and being manipulated to work to increase the nation's net domestic product.

In this sense, both Ōhashi and Maruyama try to establish Japanese shutaisei, or subjectivity, with "transferential desire" (Sakai 1997). However, Ōhashi's notion of subjectivity operates quite differently from that of elites such as Maruyama. As the historical sociologist Oguma Eiji (2002) notes, however "democratic" Maruyama's vision of shutaisei may have appeared, his arguments were still not free of an elitist viewpoint or sentiments (96). For Maruyama, shutaisei was the basis for overcoming the constraints of nature and the source of rational decision-making for political participation. A vision of the nation as the site of citizens' political participation was the most urgent concern of postwar intellectuals like Maruyama, and inevitably, there was a tendency in their discourses to mold people into new national subjects following the model of liberal democracy.[13]

For Ōhashi, shutaisei is the vehicle for ordinary folks to pursue their personal fulfillment and well-being, to be a protagonist of one's own life, and the nation's role is to secure a site for individual life and happiness. Maruyama's stance was that of an elite intellectual searching for a collective vision of shutaisei to lead a nation into a Western-modeled, modern democracy; Ōhashi, however, looks for modern subjectivity from a shomin's point of view, with the haunting memory of being brainwashed by the national elites.

In 1973, Ōhashi's popular television show 11 PM aired a special episode commemorating the twentieth anniversary of Japanese television broadcasting, and Ōhashi proudly reflected on his own role as an entertainer who has been promoting the *teizoku*, or vulgar. He repeatedly and heatedly explained his intention to promote "vulgarity with subjective agency" (*shutaiteki teizokusei*) and "vulgarity that will not be controlled by the dominant social system" (*taisei ni kontorōru sarenai teizoku*). Media critic Kanetaka Masao points out that early Japanese commercial television had a stronger tendency toward antiestablishment perspectives, as opposed to the established highbrow media, such as the publicly funded Nihon Hōsō Kyōkai (NHK; Japan Broadcasting Corporation) and daily newspapers. Kanetaka suggests that the early television personalities, represented by Ōhashi, were well-educated, highly intellectual figures who used their wit to develop alternative cultural expressions and who expressed popular sensibilities that could not be articulated by other media (Kanetaka and Morohashi 2001, 36).[14] The world of pleasure Ōhashi promoted was a means of disrupting the morality with which the state, intellectuals, and social and cultural elites tried to educate the populace for national interests.[15] Ōhashi's intentional expression of the vulgar and the nonsensical and his valorizing the practices of leisure were strategies to resist the disciplining power of the elites.

Ōhashi shifted the focus from the national collectivity to the individual and identified the natural landscape as the site in which an individual could exercise his or her natural right of pursuing freedom and happiness. To achieve this, it was first necessary to erase the haunting specter of the national landscape and clean the slate for a new geographic imaginary.

Shomin's Dream Mediated through Affluent "America"

The autobiographical section of *Jinsei no Sentaku* takes the form of a success story describing how Ōhashi survived and adapted to drastic postwar Japanese economic, political, and social changes. Although the degree of his success is exceptional, Ōhashi's autobiography is not only about his own experiences: he narrates his story in such a way that it echoes the larger social context while also offering a medium for the audience to reflect upon their own struggles. As a powerful dream weaver for shomin, Ōhashi narrates his story as essentially that of a shomin's response to changing Japanese society since the time of immediate postwar poverty. The memory of severe poverty and social disorder is meshed with hope for a new democratic society following the defeat of the wartime totalitarian regime. The story then rides the wave of high economic growth attained by hard work and the post-bubble economy that is a reflection of the hyperconsumerism of the 1980s and 1990s.

Although he focuses on his wealth and success, Ōhashi also emphasizes his origins as the son of a camera merchant in *shitamachi*, the downtown Tokyo district historically associated with relatively lower-class merchants and craftsmen. Ōhashi also positions himself as opposed to state authoritarianism by highlighting his boyhood experience of conversion to democracy at the end of World War II. Born in 1934, Ōhashi was eleven years old at the end of the war. He describes himself as a former "imperial boy" (*kōkoku shōnen*) who had absorbed his wartime imperial elementary education and dreamed of becoming a soldier to fight for the nation and "for the emperor" (Ōhashi 2000a, 45). He fought physically with his father, who claimed that Ōhashi's schoolteacher's death in military battle was meaningless. After the announcement of Japan's defeat, Ōhashi gradually realized that his father had been right. Ōhashi points to this boyhood experience as the defining moment when his skepticism toward state authority began and he became "a liberal, existential individualist" (49).

This experience of conversion is rather typical among Ōhashi's generation, many of whom observed adults who suddenly reversed their values at the end of the war. The emperor, considered a god during the height of ultranationalism, turned out to be a mere human being; teachers who had taught that Americans were demon enemies suddenly started admiring them, as if the Americans might determine the destiny of the Japanese; the English tongue that had been prohibited as an enemy language became a tool of survival, used for panhandling or as a means of bringing oneself closer to the Americans (see Dower 1999; Oguma 2002). Yet, Ōhashi presents his authentic lineage of the resistant shomin when he highlights his conversion from an imperial boy to a true believer in democracy by depicting his father as the pillar of his morality. For Ōhashi, his father was the embodiment of Taishō democracy, a movement that demanded liberal democratic rights for the mass population. According to Ōhashi, his father did not waver, even though the fearful wartime special surveillance police harassed him for his "antinational" sayings (Ōhashi 2001, 20–21).

After the war, Ōhashi discovered American popular music as a means to express his antiauthoritarian stance.[16] Contrary to Japanese wartime military songs that had encouraged listeners to sacrifice their lives for the national interest, American popular music was pleasantly shocking for the teenage Ōhashi. It opened up his postwar vision with a liveliness that "made his heart lift up and his body swing cheerfully and spontaneously" (2000a, 78–80).[17] Gradually, as a young adult in the 1950s, he moved into the world of jazz music. Ōhashi entered the journalism program in Waseda University, but he dropped out to pursue his entertainment business.[18]

Under the wartime totalitarian regime, the pursuit of individual pleasure was considered to be oppositional to the national interest. Wartime slogans such as "Luxury is an enemy!" (*Zeitaku wa teki da!*) represented the ideology that all energy and resources, including personal belongings, were to be directed toward the national goal of winning the war. The personal was suppressed and subsumed by the public interest. Even a small expression of personal aesthetics was considered a sign of antinationalism; for example, a person with permed hair could be accused of being selfish and rebellious (see Tōyama et al. [1959] 1989, 164). In the immediate postwar period, how to conceptualize the relationship between individual freedom and the public interests in the new democratic nation became the important issue discussed among a wide spectrum of thinkers from the communists to the old-liberalist conservatives. Yet, after the defeat of the anti-US-Japan Security Treaty movements and Japan's full integration into Cold War politics, the topic of political debates shifted from visions of the new nation to the distribution of the benefits of economic growth. At the time of high economic growth and with the decline of the political power of the left, democracy was conflated with the emergence of the middle mass. As Oguma suggests, the pursuit of individual interests and the freedom of expressing personal desire were discussed as if they represented the essence of the postwar democracy (2002, 655). The 1960s and 1970s, a time of "miracle" economic growth, saw the blooming of Japanese consumerism, which became entwined with the politics of pleasure. In this synthesis, the pursuit of personal pleasure became a political ground for establishing shomin's subjectivity, as a reaction against the oppression from above, a departure from the sedimented remains of the highly stratified premodern feudalistic society as well as manipulation by the national elites.

In 1965, Ōhashi was invited to host a new late night television show, *11 PM*, which he continued to do until 1986. The show's significance in the history of Japanese television and Ōhashi's central role in the program have been extensively discussed in the popular media, as well as by some intellectuals. The program started as a new form of informational show, or a genre called a "variety show," a hybrid of news report, political commentary, talk show, and entertainment, with the host playing the significant role of mediator. The novelty of Ōhashi's show was that it combined the "heavy" topics of politics and economics with the "light" genres of entertainment and pleasure, including erotic segments. As Ōhashi describes it, the program covered everything "from politics to striptease," so that he could stimulate political awareness of the striptease spectators (Ōhashi 2000a, 54).

Media critic Imamura Yōichi describes the show as "a cutting-edge program that challenged the taboos of the television industry at that time" (2001, 29). Imamura explains that Ōhashi's contribution to this longtime popular program was to invite viewers to imagine that leisure activities, such as mah-jongg, gambling on horse races, and golf, are not mere pastimes but "a whole new cultural world so wonderful and unimaginably deep to explore" (29). Imamura argues that what marked Ōhashi's contribution to Japanese popular culture was his introduction of American-style entertainment into Japanese TV programs. According to Imamura, Ōhashi actively emphasized how vast and dynamic American culture was and introduced to his audience the excitement of "thinking big." Ōhashi was shown traveling overseas, golfing with American celebrities in Hawai'i, making high scores in bowling games, interpreting American football games, and fishing off the coast of the United States and Canada. These programs reflected not only Ōhashi's individual tastes but also the vast scale of enjoyment of American mass popular culture that the Japanese audience eagerly sought. Overseas leisure travel was affordable to only a very limited number of Japanese in the 1970s, but by the 1980s, many ordinary Japanese people started to travel, as if following Ōhashi's lead (30).

In addition to *11 PM*, Ōhashi hosted many popular variety and quiz shows, which introduced interesting trivia about overseas life. From 1983 to 1990, he aired *Sekai marugoto how much* (The world all around— how much), a quiz show that introduced exotic goods and services from foreign countries that were unfamiliar to the Japanese audience and asked panelists to guess their price. As the title indicates, he stimulated the desire to travel the world and to encounter and consume the local culture of other countries.

As Simon Partner (1999) explains, the role of television has been significant for mobilizing the Japanese mass population into a "middle mass," especially in the late 1950s and 1960s. As a key product in the electronic appliance industry, the television set contributed to the postwar recovery of the Japanese economy and produced consumers yearning to purchase the symbolic new "bright life" provided by electronic appliances. Once they had been widely distributed, television sets became an important medium for selling images and dreams. Marilyn Ivy argues that although an elaborate commoners' culture was developed in urban areas in the Edo period and the prewar era, the postwar Japanese mass culture has developed in a radically different way, through electronic media represented by television. She points out that "the historical accident that the United States, the original and prototypical mass culture, was the dominant occupying power determined the structures that later Japanese culture industries were to assume" (Ivy 1993, 245). The large-scale production, dissemination, and consumption of television, in conjunction with rising affluence, led most people to think of themselves as middle-class; television programs, by showing the middle-class "American way of life," taught this newly formed Japanese middle mass what they should aspire to and what they should consume.

This internalization and embrace of "America" by the Japanese mass should be considered in the context of Cold War geopolitics in East Asia. In particular, the establishment of the People's Republic of China clearly determined Japan's role within American military strategy as a "breakwater" against the expansion of communism and as a capitalist economic center (see Cumings 1993; Yoshimi 2001). Yoshimi points out that in order to achieve capitalist economic development and establish US military hegemony, political mappings in East Asia were reorganized, with the regional division of labor between mainland Japan as the center of the Asian capitalist economy and other regions such as Okinawa, Korea, Taiwan, and the Philippines given the burden of supporting actual US military operations. In this formation, most of mainland Japan was freed of the military burden and instead encouraged to focus on economic growth. By internalizing the gaze of America as the referential point, the Japanese have renewed their identity as productive workers and active consumers, while forgetting their past imperial relationship with other parts of Asia (Yoshimi 2007, 20).

As Ivy points out, while television continued to convey the dominant discourse of aspiring to American-style "affluence" in the 1960s, it also worked as a medium of social critique by showing scenes of Vietnam, the anti–US-Japan Security Treaty movements, and problems that accompanied economic development such as pollution (1993, 250–251). Ōhashi was a powerful and paradoxical figure in this dual role of television. On the one hand, he was a key player in the formation of Japanese television, an industry that produced postwar consumer subjectivity on a mass scale. On the other hand, his emphasis on the resistant shomin's subjectivity also addressed the awkward political situation in which the Japanese populace was positioned under the condition of a US-Japan coalition since the Cold War period.

Post–Cold War Politics and the Twisted Itinerary

Although Ōhashi built his career on introducing American-style leisure and entertainment to Japan, his later writings highlight Canada, Australia, and New Zealand as ideal places for retirement, rather than the United States. He claims that he is still a "true lover of American culture," but he depicts the United States as if it were the source of a dystopic Japan, a stance in sharp contrast to the hope for new democracy that American popular culture had imprinted on his younger mind. Both America and Japan are characterized by overwork, overindustrialization, high stress, and irrational political conservatism. Although Ōhashi still holds some hope in his good old America,[19] he expresses sadness when he comments on "the 'illness' of America" (2001, 179). He laments what it has become: a selfish, money-oriented society, a "society of guns" filled with violence (184).

With his recent proposal for a "modest but fulfilling life" in Canada, Australia, and New Zealand, Ōhashi challenges the US-Japan political coalition that was consolidated after 1955. In his view, this coalition led to the long-reigning Liberal Democratic Party's political regime, and it turned Japan into a fort of American capitalism in the Asia–Pacific Rim region. Ōhashi is aware that his own success as a television entertainer relied on economic prosperity and the Japanese cultural consumption of the American dream, as it had been secured by the US-Japan politico-military coalition. Yet, from the perspective of shomin, Ōhashi also strongly opposes the Japanese elites who manipulate national politics behind closed doors, rather than direct the nation in a democratic manner and for the well-being of the populace. Ōhashi criticizes the 1955 system that turned Japan into a "vassal state" of the United States and maximized the selfish interests of the conservative politicians who sought economic benefits through a connection with American businesses. He expresses his ambivalent feeling toward America and Japanese politicians as follows:

It might be a logical consequence for Japanese to lean toward the United States because it was America, which, although being an enemy during the war, generously saved our country from the ashes and rebuilt the nation, even considering that Americans saw an advantage to themselves by preventing Japan from turning "red." I myself admired America, studied English in order to go to America, and love jazz music. These experiences helped me to become who I am today. So, I am not opposing Japan for becoming an ally of the United States. However, unless we become the fifty-first state or a special governing area under the United States, I would prefer to see [Japanese politicians] stop uncritically adopting American ways. (2000b, 135–136)

In discussing a "diseased America," Ōhashi nostalgically mourns the loss of a social landscape in the immediate postwar period before the "reverse course" of occupation policy. In Ōhashi's reflection, even though Japan had just started to recover from the devastation of the war, and the nation was still suffering economically, ordinary people in the midst of their desperation had a strong desire for freedom and democracy in the newborn Japan.

As an alternative to American culture, Ōhashi projected his ideal onto the Canadian natural landscape. He explains how he caught "Canada fever" when he was first invited to come to Canada to film his program in the 1970s: "Like many Japanese, I was ignorant about Canada. Yet, I fell in love with this huge country that is twenty-six times as large as Japan while its population is only one-fifth that of Japan. . . . To put it briefly, what is good about Canada is that it is completely opposite from Japan. Clean, crisp air, tasteful water, laidback lifestyle . . . *things that Japan has lost in exchange for its postwar rapid economic growth all exist here*" (2001, 286, emphasis added). Ōhashi extols the beauty of a simple life in nature, framed by his fascination with the vast scale of the North American landscape; later, he extends his utopian frontier to Australia and New Zealand. He emphasizes not only the natural landscape but also the social welfare that these countries provide for their populations, such as the public health care system and leisure facilities that support the well-being of ordinary folks. Thus, the social world that Ōhashi projects onto

Canada, Australia, and New Zealand provides an alternative model to the excessively individualized, privatized, and commercialized America.

Ōhashi's shift of itinerary embodies a further complication of the US-Japan relationship, as it has emerged since the 1980s. Yoshimi argues that gradually since the mid-1970s, the Japanese relationship with the United States has become far more intertwined and complex than the simple binary of pro-American or anti-American. According to Yoshimi, especially since the 1980s, America became too thoroughly internalized in Japanese everyday life and started to lose its significance as "the privileged other" for reflecting on the contrasting Japanese subjectivity, diminishing the drive to see it as a norm, to catch up with America, and to obtain the American lifestyle (2007, 233–234). Ōhashi's vision of the active retired lifestyle in Canada, Australia, and New Zealand reflects Yoshimi's point that the internalized America has been losing its significance as a transcendental referent for Japanese behavior. Simultaneously, Ōhashi's narrative performance as a resisting shomin points toward an ambivalent distance from the embraced America. He critiques the US-Japan political-economic-military coalition as the source of the continuing predicament in which the Japanese mass population has to live: that is, the pursuit of one's own subjectivity and personal fulfillment relies on the dependent international relationship between the United States and Japan. His narratives also imply the challenge of translating "subjectivity." Yet, while this predicament places the Japanese citizenry in a difficult position vis-à-vis articulating their individual subjectivity, the majority of the mainstream Japanese during the Cold War period were nonetheless in a relatively privileged position at least economically, for they had been sanctioned to concentrate on economic development and to suppress the memories of their former colonial relationship with Asia and the struggles of ordinary folks in those countries.

The Predicaments of Articulating Shomin's Subjectivity

The impact of Ōhashi's pleasant postretirement life overseas extends beyond the gendered target audience of sararīman. For example, in 2001, *Caz Net*, an Internet version of *Caz*, a magazine for young working women, published a reader's survey on the question, "If you could start to live your life, the way you wanted, what kind of life would you live?" Among 2,219 responses, the most popular answer was "Quit my job and move to live overseas." Along with a comment that reads, "If everyone's dream comes true, everyone becomes like Ōhashi Kyosen," the article includes an illustration of a young woman dreaming of Ōhashi's relaxed lifestyle overseas, all beneath a headline that reads, "Re-set life! A Nation's Hundred Million Population All Turning into Ōhashi Kyosen!!" (*Jinsei o risetto! Ichioku Sō Ohashi Kyosen-ka!!*). The unexpected juxtaposition of young women and Ōhashi illustrates the popular imagination of the utopian space that is assumed to exist somewhere outside of Japan.

In fact, Ōhashi's ability to weave a dream that was attractive to both sararīman and office ladies was a talent sought by political parties. At the request of the Democratic Party of Japan, which was trying to reach the urban middle mass, Ōhashi agreed to run for the House of Councillors in the summer of 2001. He was both criticized and respected for his bravery in breaking with convention in his brief participation in the election campaign. Although a candidate is expected to mingle with his constituency to demonstrate his enthusiasm, Ōhashi returned to Canada in the middle of the campaign period after only nine days of canvassing. Masuzoe Yōichi, a rival candidate from the reigning Liberal Democratic Party who later became the minister of health, labor, and welfare, is reported to have criticized Ōhashi for "returning to Canada, a place of cool climate, while we are enduring the hellish severe summer heat in Japan" (*Shūkan Shinchō* 2001, 44). Masuzoe's idea of an election campaign was "to abandon self-interest and self-desire to ask people in the nation to back one's belief" (44). Yet the lure of Ōhashi's going his own way prevailed over notions of self-sacrifice. Ōhashi was elected—though he worked as a member of the House of Councillors for only 180 days. He resigned in January 2002 (Ōhashi 2002b, 195), disappointed with the "old-fashioned" customs of party politics, and returned to his "sunflower life." In 2003, Ōhashi published his third book about retirement overseas, *Kyosen 2: Jissen, Nihon Dasshutsu* (Kyosen 2: Escape from Japan).

Though filled with contradictions, Ōhashi's narratives have consistently expressed the sensibility of shomin, sometimes in the form of the vulgar nouveau riche, sometimes in the form of a "modest but fulfilling life." As a talented entertainer, Ōhashi has, in a hedonistic manner, presented images of an ideal society that shomin would imagine as an alternative to those provided by political and intellectual elites. He has done so by appropriating an Orientalist gaze and showing a utopia outside the nation. In other words, Ōhashi's work has been to disarticulate the naturalized configuration of nation and nature that had served as a means of controlling the population and, instead, articulating a populist, cosmopolitan admonition for shomin to establish subjectivity as active agents of their own lives, hence freeing them from national constraints.

Ōhashi powerfully weaves the cosmopolitan dream of living in an ideal space transcending national boundaries. However, he very quickly ceased offering an alternative political vision in Japan as a politician. Ōhashi's attempt to build a renewed notion of liberalism and democracy through the pursuit of individual freedom was not successfully articulated into an effective political force. Rather, in post–Cold War, postbubble Japan, the pursuit of individual subjectivity and freedom was taken over by the neoliberal camp, with the discourse of self-responsibility and independence from the welfare and protection provided by the state and corporations. The trajectory of Ōhashi's narrative performance elucidates the predicament of articulating the shomin's subjectivity in Japan: How can one be neither disciplined for the national collectivity nor absorbed into neoliberal individualism? The Japanese mass population's predicament of articulating subjectivity as "citizen," both within and beyond Japan, reflects the particular legacy of Japan's modernization process and American soft power exercised in the Asia–Pacific Rim region.

The ambivalent effects of American soft power are also evident in guides' narratives. In the following, I introduce life histories of three men who explicitly articulated how their fascination with life overseas was influenced by American culture.

"America" and Soft Power
REVISING "PEACE"

Kubo Toshiyuki had a vague yearning to live overseas. He could not identify any particular reason, but he said that perhaps the image of "America" he saw on television had influenced his admiration of life overseas. When he was a junior high school student in the 1980s, he liked to watch American television programs, such as *CHiPS* and *Charlie's Angels*, and Hollywood movies, such as *Star Wars*. For Toshiyuki, the people in these programs looked cheerful, positive, and outgoing. The sunny, bright images on the screen impressed him that there was a place outside Japan where people are joyful and forward-looking. He wanted to place himself in that environment (*nanka sō iu sekai ni jibun mo mi o oite mitakatta*).

After graduating from high school, Toshiyuki entered the National Defense Academy, a highly competitive university-level institution that trains future elites in the Self-Defense Forces (SDF). He was strongly influenced by Hollywood images of military officers, such as in *Top Gun* and *An Officer and a Gentleman*. The military officers in these films looked sophisticated and intelligent to Toshiyuki. In particular, he was fascinated by their sense of strong morality as he interpreted these officers as assuming responsibility for the sake of other people in the country and committing themselves to the hard work of maintaining peace. He thought that becoming an SDF officer was the best way to get closer to the roles played by Tom Cruise or Richard Gere, the stars of these films. He was also attracted by the job security because a graduate would be given an officer's status in the SDF immediately after completing his schooling, but the job security was secondary to his admiration of the Hollywood image of the military officers.

Soon, Toshiyuki found that everyday life in the academy and the SDF was not at all like the Hollywood images of the military officers. He described it as "a harsh and unsophisticated world, as if working in mud." After graduating from the academy, he worked as a tactical command officer of a missile battery, a position he held for two and a half years before being assigned as an English language instructor within the SDF. He reflected that it had not been the wrong decision for him to go to the academy and to work as a SDF officer. He appreciated that he had been trained to be tough both physically and mentally. He also had learned how to be responsible and considerate to others around him, both moral qualities that matter for the survival of the entire troop. He also enjoyed working with his American counterparts in the US-Japan joint drills. But he thought he had spent enough time in that world.

While Toshiyuki was working in the SDF, which was during the time that the Soviet bloc was collapsing, his approach toward peace gradually shifted its focus. After the end of the Cold War, the Japanese government passed legislation that allowed SDF officers to be sent on United Nations peacekeeping missions overseas. Toshiyuki was eager to participate, but he was not allowed to leave his instructor position. Meanwhile, he also had become interested in contributing to peace by showing people the positive sides of the world outside of Japan rather than by defending the country from the "hypothetical enemy." He was strongly attracted by the idea of enhancing mutual understanding and cultivating positive relationships with people in different countries. The change in global politics also rekindled his interest in traveling. He had fond memories of traveling to the United States during his third year in the academy and thought that travel would be a good means to enhance peace. He resigned from the SDF in 1997 and found a job as a tour conductor for a major Japanese travel agent.

While he was working as a tour conductor, Toshiyuki noticed the gradual change in the tourism industry. Although packaged tours were still popular, there was growing demand for independent travel. At the same time, he felt ambivalent about leading predesigned tours. He worried that the travel industry was too paternalistic and protective toward tourists. He felt that a packaged tour was convenient but that it might deprive tourists of freedom of movement and the "true" enjoyment of travel. He started to dream of having his own travel-related business that would allow tourists to plan their own trips and actively experience the tours by themselves. He wanted to share the joy of exploring the world and experiencing life overseas.

As a starting point, he wanted to live overseas to see how it felt. He decided to move to Banff partly because it was easier to find a job there in the tourism industry than in the United States due to visa regulations, and partly because he was impressed by the landscape of the Canadian Rockies when he visited there as a tour conductor. For Toshiyuki, the magnificent mountain landscape in Canada was an ideal location to test out his entrepreneurial dream and his pursuit of freedom and independence in a peaceful environment. While his interest in living overseas was obviously a product of American soft power, it was Canadian nature that provided him a place to revise his vision of the world and his idea of peace.

REVISING "AMERICA"

Nakata Tetsuya was six years younger than Toshiyuki. Although his interest in foreign countries was also influenced by American culture, when Tetsuya traveled to the United States in 1995, he realized that "America" was much more similar to Japan than he had expected, and it lost the allure of being a world different from Japan.

Like Toshiyuki, Tetsuya also liked Hollywood movies because of their cheerful, forward-looking, and optimistic outlooks. He yearned for a life outside his everyday routine as a high school student in a rural city and started to dream of living overseas, especially in California. He told me,

"I got the impression that the life there must be fun and pleasurable. I thought everyone lived happily every day." While attending a university, he majored in English and vaguely dreamed of working in the film industry. In his third year of university, Tetsuya traveled to California by himself. After staying there for about a week, he noticed that America and Japan were not so different after all.

Once he had satisfied his initial desire to visit Hollywood, he traveled to other places on the West Coast, going north along the Pacific. In a youth hostel in Oregon, he met a man who recommended that he go to Canada because the Canadian Rockies were spectacular and definitely worth seeing. Tetsuya had no knowledge about Canada, but he took the man's advice and made a detour to Banff. He was impressed by the beautiful mountains but did not stay there long. At that time, he was too preoccupied with revising his understanding of "America." After staying in Banff for a week, he returned to the United States and then went back to Japan.

Tetsuya's first travel abroad led to his sober realization about the similarity of everyday life in Japan and the United States. In reality, America was not a dreamland; it was not a magical space where everyone was happy and pleasant. Just as in Japan, the people in the United States also lived by their mundane, everyday routine.

But this experience stimulated his interest in travel. America became too familiar for Tetsuya to find the difference he wanted, but it had opened the door for him to venture outside Japan. Tetsuya and his friends went on backpacking trips to China and Russia, each for about a month. He found these places were more different and eye-opening than the United States, whose commonalities with Japan as a developed capitalist country became all too evident for him. Just doing basic activities, such as eating the food he wanted and traveling to his destinations, required a good amount of effort. There were always difficulties and obstacles to negotiate because things were run differently in these countries. In China, he bought the cheapest train tickets to travel to rural cities. He was astonished by how dirty and noisy the train cars were but, at the same time, strongly impressed by people's vitality (*ikiru pawā o kanjita*). He said, "In Japan, people ride the train as if they do not exist in the space, right? In China, people were so lively as if they were claiming their own space in the crowded train." He was also fascinated by people's outright expression of their curiosity. Obviously, Tetsuya and his friends stood out as the only foreigners in the train. Many people gathered around them and showered them with questions. People asked why they were wearing such dirty clothes and whether Tetsuya and his friends were really Japanese. Tetsuya was flattered by their comments, feeling satisfied that he looked different from a stereotypical image of Japanese.

Tetsuya also started to travel more in places closer to his home. He and his friends wandered in the mountains near the university. With their limited student budgets, they slept in tents and traveled on foot as much as possible. He loved these weekend adventures. He and his friends even made a raft and used it to travel down the nearby river. Tetsuya said, "We were reckless, and I enjoyed it." He also developed his interest in learning about the outdoors more systematically. He thought Canada would be an ideal place to pursue his interest. After working part-time for eight months and saving money, Tetsuya went to Cranbrook, British Columbia, and enrolled in an ESL program. He then moved onto a one-year mountain activity skills training program in a college. After graduation, he got a job as a hiking guide with the Rocky Mountain Tours.

SCIENCE OF THE FOREST

Like Tetsuya, Mori Yukio was fascinated by North American outdoor activities. He left his job in order to climb a mountain. When he had an opportunity to go on an excursion to Mount McKinley in Alaska in 1992, he decided to leave the private English-language school where he worked as an instructor.

Yukio grew up in a small city on the Kii Peninsula in Wakayama prefecture. The area was close to the Kumano forest, famous for a millennium-old pilgrimage route. On the trails in the forest, there were century-old stone carvings of deities and signs for pilgrims traveling the route. Yukio liked walking in the mountains and spent a great amount of time wandering in the forest or fishing in the rivers and the ocean. When he was a young child, his father had taken him to these places and taught him how to find edible plants and how to fish.

Yukio developed his interest in the English language when he was in elementary school, after meeting a distant relative from the United States. At the turn of the twentieth century, Wakayama prefecture had sent many agricultural immigrants to America, and Yukio's relative was a descendant of these immigrants. Yukio was fascinated by his relative, who looked like Japanese but, being an American, spoke only in English.

After high school, Yukio attended a foreign-language university in Osaka, where he majored in English. In 1984, when he was a third-year university student, Yukio spent one year as an exchange student in Montana. While there, he was introduced to American-style outdoor activities, including a visit to Yellowstone National Park with his friends. Hiking in Yellowstone was a new experience for him. The forests in his hometown were rich and beautiful, yet they obviously reflected with the long history of human presence. In Yellowstone, in contrast, nature seemed "untouched." Yukio was fascinated by the way nature was materially represented in the United States. The spatial arrangements created the effect of nature existing as something distinct and different from human intervention. Yukio became interested in experiencing this new sensation by going into nature off the road (*amari michino nai yōna tokoroni haitte iku. Shizen no naka ni haitte iku*). Soon, he was deeply into American-style outdoor leisure and sports such as backpack trekking.

After graduating from the university, Yukio taught English at a junior college and a private language school in Nagoya. While working as a teacher, he joined a mountaineering club organized by an outdoor equipment store and was able to expand his outdoor experiences and learn the techniques of rock and ice climbing as well as mountain skiing. After climbing Mount McKinley in 1992, Yukio moved to Banff in order to live near the mountains. He found a job in an outdoor equipment store, befriended Canadian outdoor enthusiasts, and enjoyed exploring the outdoors with them. Then, Atsuko-san came to the store and recruited him, offering him a guide's job at the RMT.

Along with these modern leisure outdoor activities, Yukio deepened his ability to see nature through the lens of science. Mountaineering and telemark skiing required scientific knowledge about geological formations and climate, which was essential to avoid the risk of being hit by an avalanche or falling into crevasses in glaciers. Yukio also became interested in learning more about plants, animals, birds, and insects from a biological perspective. The new scientific outlook opened his eyes to see the forest differently. The forest was not the place where spirits dwell or a place saturated by the long accumulated history of human prayers and wishes for spiritual revelation. Exploring "untouched" nature with scientific knowledge gave him the thrill of discovering the world. Yet, simultaneously, while working as a guide and studying the history of the area, he gradually learned that the "untouched" nature that fascinated him was not culturally untouched; it was a cultural construct that had been created by European settlers by erasing the presence of indigenous peoples.

The life histories of these three tour guides elucidate how their imaginaries of the world were shaped by American soft power, but their actual travel experiences redirected their interests in an unexpected direction: from American culture to Canadian nature. Although these guides were much younger than Ōhashi's targeted audience, the way they redirected their itineraries to the ideal dreamland resonates with Ōhashi's outlook. They shared a fascination with freedom from the communal routines in Japan projected onto the vast scale North American natural landscape, but also an ambivalent dissatisfaction with the "freedom" sustained by the unequal global power relations, in which US-Japanese politicomilitary cooperation was integral.

As an entertainer, Ōhashi has played the role of an intermediary who invites the audience to see the ideal world through popular media. Tour guides play a similar role by mediating between the everyday, ordinary world of Japanese tourists and "elsewhere," which is outside their normal, day-to-day life. Although each guide's audience is much smaller and his or her influence is limited compared with a popular mass media figure such as Ōhashi, sometimes guides can impress tourists even more because of their direct, person-to-person interaction. In the next chapter, I examine the process of the production of tour guides. I discuss how the young Japanese who left the company and the country performatively and paradoxically construct their new subjectivities as embodiments of Japanese cosmopolitan desire by subjecting themselves to the tourist economy.

3 | The Co-Modification of Self

A Guide as a Commodity

On the first day of guide training in early March 2000, I arrived at the Rocky Mountain Tours' office a few minutes early. All of the six other trainees—three women and three men in their twenties—were already there, quietly sitting at the round table near the back door, the employees' entrance. We exchanged a minimal greeting, saying "Hello" and giving a slight bow, but everyone seemed too nervous to engage in further conversation. We waited anxiously for about fifteen minutes in a small corner of the office, hearing the constant phone calls and busy conversations among managers and the administrative staff.

Before coming to this meeting, I was already filled with a strong image of Mr. Katori Masaki, or Katori-san, as an *oni kyōkan*,[1] a "demon" guide trainer who was extremely serious and strict. The manager, Atsuko-san, warned me, "Katori is tough. But be patient. His first impression may be a bit scary, but he is actually a very nice person at heart." Every guide I met at the RMT, and even the guides working for other companies, asked me with curiosity if I would join Katori-san's training. When I explained to them that it was a part of my research—I was interested in experiencing what kind of training a guide has to go through—everyone grinned and said, "Katori-san's training is very tough. *Ganbatte!*" ("Hang in there" or "Good luck with your training!").

Katori-san finally showed up from the other room without any explanation for keeping us waiting. A man in his mid-thirties, Katori-san was tall and regularly built and wore a blue fleece pullover over a white polo shirt, khaki pants, and light hiking boots, a standard Japanese tour guide's outfit. He began the meeting by saying, with a straight face, "Please keep in mind, in the tourist business, you yourself as a guide are a commodity." Then he asked a trainee to read out loud the first section of the company manual, which he himself had edited. It began as follows: "The service industry is an industry that deals with people. . . . Especially in the guiding business, we provide a 'service' that does not have a physical form of product. It might be rude to say, but you yourself are a commodity. You yourself as a whole are evaluated as a commodity. Do not forget this fact."

Katori-san recommended that the trainees study the tour brochures circulated in Japan and treat them as contracts with customers. The brochures include information on what the tours promise to offer tourists. Specifically, he suggested that the trainees should check the price of the tour and become aware of the amount of money a customer was paying. He emphasized that the price of the tour was not cheap, with a week-long standard package tour ranging from about 150,000 to 500,000 yen (roughly US$1,400 to $4,700 at the time of my fieldwork in 2000). He told the trainees, "The amount of money a customer has invested for a one-week tour may be as much money as you have brought to Canada for your year-long stay." He reminded them to make sure that they provided customers with high-quality work, worth the price they had paid.

I was struck by the explicit reference to a guide as a "commodity" (*shōhin*). But neither the trainer nor the trainees seemed to mind that this idea could be associated with exploitation of labor or, even worse, human trafficking or slavery. Rather, they interpreted that being a commodity was akin to being a performance artist or entertainer, whose charm and talent would satisfy the audience. In the training, the attractiveness of the guides as a commodity was assumed to come from their unique personality and sincere attitudes toward tourists. Therefore, in their discussion, achieving the status of commodity was desirable because it proved that the guide was a decent person that the tourists would want to spend time with, compared with someone whose personality was not attractive enough to present to the tourists. Katori-san encouraged the trainees to "polish" their selves (*jibun o migaku*) to become trustworthy persons by studying hard and by acting more sincerely and considerately toward the tourists and the other people around them.

Thus, among the tour guides in Banff, the idea of a guide as a commodity had a quite different connotation from that of the commodification of temporary workers (*haken rōdōsha*), which had become a burning social issue in Japan around 2000. Nakano Mami, a lawyer and the author of the influential book *Rōdō Danpingu* (Labor dumping; 2006), suggests that the foundational problem of *haken* (temporary) work is that labor is considered to be separable from the worker as a set of particular functions—such as filing documents, assembling automobiles, or fixing computers. These functions are conceptualized to be separate from the person, and thus easily imagined as thing-like objects of market transaction, freely exchanged between a seller and a buyer. In this conceptualization of labor, employers and the administrative workers in temporary staff agencies might numb their sensibilities and tend to sell haken work in the highly competitive temp staff labor market at unreasonably low prices to companies as if what they exploit are not human beings but merely their functions and services. Nakano argues the fact that, the Worker Dispatch Law has a characteristic of a law concerning commercial contracts which also contributes to the perception that what is exchanged in the temporary staff market is a specific skill or function as a commodity, detached from the worker as a person.

In contrast, in the guide training, because the commodity was considered to be a whole person, the guide's work was obviously inseparable from the guide him- or herself. As discussed earlier, many of the young Japanese came to Canada to "escape" from Japan and find out what they really wanted to do in their lives. Becoming a guide in the Canadian Rockies was the first step toward constructing their new subjectivities in a new environment. How did the guides' enactment of being a commodity relate to the construction of their subjectivity and exploration of freedom? How did nature, in particular the natural landscape of the Canadian Rockies, play a part in their engagement with becoming a commodity? And, what do their experiences elucidate about subjectivity in late capitalism?

In the pages that follow, I discuss how the tour guides and trainees interpreted, negotiated, and enacted the idea of being a commodity. The training process made it apparent that the guides' work in the mass tourism industry entailed a fundamental tension between sincerity and standardization. Sincerity was foundational to the moral value that made a guide a unique, attractive person, whereas standardization, or following the codes and regulations, was necessary to integrate the guides' service in the production of economic value within the tourist industry. Katori-san's instructions directed the trainees to conflate these incommensurable "values" as they became local tour guides in the Canadian Rockies. On the one hand, the guides were reminded that their labor would add extra value to the tour and bring profit to the company. On the other hand, Katori-san encouraged the guides to perceive tourist encounters as opportunities to improve themselves and to construct their own subjectivities with attractive personalities. In the production of tour guides, the guides' labor of producing economic value and their act of constructing a unique subjectivity were not separable. The tension was inherent in making these incommensurable values commensurable, and it was expected to be solved by the guide's constant pursuit of enhancing his or her moral virtue as a person. Thus, Katori-san urged the trainees to see "the beauty" in a person who constantly "polishes" him- or herself through work. In particular, he highly valued a person who acted with consideration and understanding toward other people.

This chapter also examines how the Canadian natural landscape plays a significant part in this conflation of different values and in the performative construction of guides' subjectivity. By juxtaposing the frustration experienced by the trainees and Katori-san's story of becoming a guide, the chapter illustrates the tension inherent in the translation of "freedom" and the coexistence of the translation word *jiyū* for the English words "freedom" or "liberation," and jiyū in *jiyū jizai*, derived from the Buddhist notion of liberation as self-detachment. Through this examination, the chapter also elucidates the complex process of the commodification of self in the service industry.

The Mass Production of Affective Workers:
Sincerity and Standardization
"DEBUT"

In the guiding community in Banff, the word "debut" refers to a milestone, indicating that a trainee has become a real guide. In the RMT, in an ideal case, a trainee would go through a few weeks of office training while settling into the community and familiarizing him- or herself with the environment. After the initial office instruction, a trainee would be assigned assistant work and would accompany experienced guides to observe how to conduct the actual tours. Then, the trainee would have an "exam" that involved leading a full-day coach tour to the Columbia Icefield, with a trainer along to evaluate the trainee's skill. Finally, the trainee would debut as a guide and go out on a tour by him- or herself. The word "debut" carried much the same weight for the guides as it would with a performing artist, yet the guides also used it with a tone of parody to highlight the absurdity of using such a dramatic term for the mass tourism industry. They were aware of tensions within the communication service industry. In the RMT, on the one hand, it was obvious that the company was pressed to standardize service products in order to fulfill the tour contracts and adhere to legal regulations. It also needed to rapidly produce a sufficient number of guides each season to serve the demands of mass tourism. On the other hand, the RMT emphasized the unique skills and personalities of each guide and promoted the authentic quality of the tourist experiences the company could offer, beyond standardized guiding services.

The RMT's training process elucidates the challenge of producing workers with the aura of performing artists for the mass tourism industry. The challenges were manifested in various forms, for example, whether to emphasize a guide's uniqueness or a standardized level of comfort and quality of service, independent of who is leading the tour; and whether to lead the tour out of the guide's personal sense of hospitality or to prioritize the tour's business liability of providing what is promised in the tour brochures and travel contracts. These questions shaped the setting in which newcomers were trained to be affective workers in the tourism industry.[2]

THE MANUAL

The tension between the sincere expression of the guides' personalities and their commodification within the tourist industry first appeared as a discrepancy between Katori-san's and the managers' encouraging each trainee to develop his or her own unique narrations, versus their insistence upon using the training manual as a tool to standardize the guides' knowledge, behavior, and appearance.

Each trainee was given a manual divided into three sections: the basics, the industry, and guiding. Among these sections, the trainees found the section on guiding, which constituted most of the sixty-page manual, to be the most intimidating. This section was organized along several popular routes in and around Banff National Park and was filled with information on the sightseeing spots that the guides would have to describe on most tours. It also included a sample guiding narration for a full-day tour from Banff to the Columbia Icefield. In the sample script, explanations of the natural landscape were interspersed with useful travel tips and spiced up with a few jokes. If one memorized the whole script and narrated it smoothly, one could pretend to be an experienced guide, able to speak continuously for four hours along the 190-kilometer (about 118-mile) trip to the Columbia Icefield.

Katori-san explained that he developed the manual to provide standards and to give a systematic overview of the complex structure of the tour. However, he did not want to standardize each guide's narration too much. He insisted that the manual was merely an aid, and that each trainee should build his or her own unique narrative. It was each guide's job to study and to find the most suitable way of explaining the scenery. Therefore, Katori-san told the trainees that they would not pass the exam if they simply recited the sample scenario.

COMMUNICATION WITH TOURISTS

Katori-san explained to the trainees that knowledge about the area was of course an integral asset, yet most important for a tour guide was being able to quickly and flexibly respond to customers' needs. He said, "Above all, what is most important is a guide's quick-wittedness and careful consideration of the customers, much more than pointing out the names of mountains" (*daiji nano wa yama no namae yori kiten*). This surprised many of the trainees because they assumed that the point of the training was to learn and remember details about the mountains and other sightseeing spots. During the training sessions, Katori-san constantly quizzed the trainees to test their wit and tact. For example, he asked, "What would you do if a customer asked to make a detour and stop at a particular scenic point off the scheduled route during a bus tour? How would you make a choice and satisfy everyone in the large group?" and "What if a customer ran out of small change and asked you to pay the tip to a bellman for him? What if other customers saw this and they started to ask you for the same thing?" Katori-san's own answers to these questions were rarely definitive. He explained the legal bottom lines established by industry regulations and the tour contracts, but as long as a guide did not break these rules, his answer was always "It depends on the situation." He told the trainees, "Use your common sense." If the guides could tune in to the nature of the tour, time, situation, group dynamic, and other factors, "the best solutions would naturally come" to them.

This naturalness is a concept that Katori-san emphasized repeatedly on various occasions. He suggested that if a guide considered what the customers already knew, what they did not know, what they needed to know, and what they would like to know, then "the narration would come naturally." For the trainees who were anxious to know what they were expected to say on a tour, Katori-san's abstract instructions were perplexing. Katori-san urged the trainees to tune themselves in to the atmosphere of the tour situation and to let things come naturally, but he stressed that they should be aware of the tour contracts so that they covered all the standard services and information the tour promised.

LANGUAGE

Throughout the training, Katori-san emphasized that a guide must speak in "correct Japanese." Correct language use was fundamental, he said, to help tourists concentrate on the information that the guide would give, to avoid confusion and misunderstanding, and to prevent customers from complaining. At first glance, Katori-san's instructions seemed to be a reflection of the managers' business interests. For a small company at the end of a subcontracting chain, a customer's complaint to a travel agency would have a serious impact on the business. Or, at least, the managers believed it would. Occasionally, the managers reminded guides of the difficulty of recovering a good reputation once it was lost. In fact, Atsuko-san remarked that one of her main jobs was "to apologize," in order to recover trust and maintain good relationships with both tourists and travel agencies when miscommunication occurred.

However, Katori-san's emphasis on correct language cannot be translated merely into a business interest. For him, it was another way of expressing moral value: to see things from the other's point of view. He constantly asked the guides to reflect on whether their behaviors and words were "honest" (*shōjiki*) and "kind" (*shinsetsu*) enough to the customers. Incorrect language use that might lead to unclear explanations went against the moral virtue that was so integral to his notion of being human, which was inherently intersubjective. Clear communication, in contrast, was part of polishing oneself and was inseparable from a guide's sincere care for the customers. To this end, Katori-san repeatedly and strongly cautioned trainees not to adopt speech habits common among service industry workers in Japan. In particular, he frowned upon the frequent use of indirect and unfinished speech, such as ending sentences with "but . . ." to indicate "I want to do this, but . . ." This expression was often used when a worker could not meet the customer's request but did not want to say so too directly. Although Katori-san understood that such expressions were used as a sign of politeness and to avoid conflict, in his opinion, this "funny habit" (*okashina kuse*) of Japanese service industry workers was a serious defect because it was unclear and confusing. He thought that confusing customers with unclear explanations was a sign of not being kind, honest, and considerate.

For similar reasons, Katori-san also listed youth slang, foreign loanwords, and trendy expressions as examples of language that the guides should avoid. The length of the list gave the trainees the impression that he was quite picky. However, at the end of his language lecture, he surprised the trainees by saying, "But dialects are okay." According to Katori-san, speaking in standard Japanese was ideal because everyone would understand it. However, as long as it would not confuse people from other regions, speaking in a local dialect was often preferable because it would give customers a warm feeling of familiarity. Katori-san interpreted local intonation as a natural and sincere expression of spontaneity.

PEDAGOGY

From the very beginning, Katori-san emphasized how hard one needed to study to become a guide. He stated that he printed the company's sixty-page manual in a small font not only to save paper but also to discourage people who might mistake guiding for fun, easy work. He emphasized the philosophy of polishing oneself through hard physical work. To the trainees, this meant that Katori-san and the managers were treating them as if they were disciples or apprentices in a premodern artisanal community or esoteric religious sect. This was especially clear when trainees wanted to obtain copies of the manual. The trainees were not permitted to photocopy it. If they wanted a copy for themselves, they had to copy it by hand. To some of the new guides this seemed like an outrageously outdated instruction.

The scheduling of training sessions caused frustration, too. Due to Katori-san's own unpredictable work schedule, the trainees never knew until the last minute when the next training session would be held. The assignment of trainees' assistant work constantly changed. Because the administrative staff were always busy handling changing tour arrangements, they were unable to explain the rationale behind these changes. This company practice further demanded that the trainees act as if they were artisanal apprentices. They had to guess what the managers and senior guides had in mind even though they did not spell out their intentions. Or they simply learned to adjust themselves to the managers' demands without questioning their reasons.

This created anxiety among the trainees. In the short term, it was hard for them to plan their schedules outside of work because they were expected to attend the training sessions unless they had scheduling conflicts with other work-related engagements, such as taking an exam for a commercial driving license. In the long term, the trainees worried about their financial situations. They had to pay rent for the company accommodations, and until they started earning a wage, their debt to the company piled up. The long period of training amplified their sense of dependency on the company, and they wondered when they could debut and start earning a decent wage. They hoped to be working full-time by Golden Week, a holiday week and the peak spring leisure season in Japan, from late April to early May. But for those who started the training in March, two months of training without a full-time wage seemed to be too long to tolerate.

VAN TRAINING

Maeda Hanako's experience during the van training highlighted the trainees' sense of bewilderment. Before testing each guide during an actual bus tour, Katori-san offered a group practice run for a full-day tour to the Columbia Icefield. The first van training was conducted in late April, right before Golden Week. There was still snow piled up on the sidewalk, and some of the sightseeing spots were closed for the winter, but soon, many tourists would arrive from Japan. Katori-san kept saying, "You should study hard so that you can debut by Golden Week."

Much more than Katori-san, Hanako and other new guides themselves were eager for the debuts so that they could start working as guides, earn a decent income, and begin paying the company back for their rent. Nine trainees—five women and four men, crammed shoulder to shoulder—participated in the training in a van. Katori-san explained that he would drive the van and the trainees would take turns giving a guiding talk for different sections of the tour. The main purpose of this session was for the trainees to match their descriptions and the scenery. Katori-san expected that the trainees would have learned the right timing and length so that they could introduce the scenery at the appropriate spot.

Hanako was assigned the third section, from Lake Louise to the Crowfoot Glacier. Compared with the other trainees, whose narrations closely followed the manual, Hanako's guiding showed her own character, incorporating her enthusiasm for outdoor activities, including an explanation of skating, snowshoeing, and camping as popular activities among Canadian youth. However, instead of evaluating her effort to add a personal flavor, Katori-san focused on correcting Hanako's language usage. He was particularly annoyed by her overuse of English loanwords, and, in a severe tone, he instructed her to use "correct" Japanese.

After the long day of training, Katori-san told the trainees that they all needed to practice talking more in order to debut. It was hard for them to judge the level of Katori-san's dissatisfaction. They were all exhausted and relieved just that the long day was over.

The day after the van training, I saw Hanako in the office. She dropped her shoulders, looking down, and her eyes were red. Hanako, Sara (a Canadian woman who had lived in Japan and spoke good Japanese), and I left the office to go home to the three-bedroom apartment that the company provided. As soon as we stepped out of the office building, Hanako told us, "I want to get away from the company!" Upset and sobbing, she explained what Atsuko-san had said to her in the office. Atsuko-san had heard about Katori-san's dissatisfaction with the van training; in particular, she was disappointed by Hanako because she had had high expectations for Hanako and had pushed hard for the company to hire her. Hanako, who was afraid that she would be fired, asked Atsuko-san what she should do. Atsuko-san's answer was simply "Study more," just like Katori-san's Zen-like instruction.

We walked into the apartment and sat in our living room, puzzled. Sara and I tried to put Hanako at ease, but we were not successful. Hanako said, "I don't understand what Katori-san wanted! I don't know what was wrong! I want him to tell me clearly!" After sobbing for a while, she suddenly stood up, tried to smile, and said, "Thank you both for listening. I'll go out." She hurried out the door. A few minutes later, Hanako called me. She told me that she could not stand to stay in the accommodations that the company provided. She stayed at her friend's house that night.

Geography of Difference

Located on the first floor with a door facing the street, the apartment I shared with Hanako and Sara became a gathering place for the trainees, who often stopped by to study together, practice guiding, and express their anxiety, frustration, or complaints over drinks or dinner. In these conversations, the central topic was often the company's disciplinary practices.

For trainees, Katori-san's instructions appeared contradictory. Katori-san's instruction to "study hard and transform oneself into a local" fit well with the newcomers' desires, but they felt frustrated by what they interpreted as "old-style Japanese" pedagogy, exemplified by Katori-san's and the management's insistence on proper and "natural" Japanese appearance, language use, and mannerisms, as well as by the lack of systematic lectures and transparent explanations of the company's business practices. Katori-san's insistence on black hair marked the initial shock for many of the trainees. In the first few weeks, when the trainees gathered, the discussion topic was Katori-san's definition of "natural" hair for a Japanese person. When Machida Yuki, another trainee, shared that she was asked to dye her hair back to black, the rest of the trainees were surprised because the deep brown color of her hair looked so natural that some of us did not even notice that her hair was dyed.

Later, when he heard Yuki's story, a fellow trainee, Hashimoto Fumiya, became furious about the company's strict regulation of appearance. Fumiya, a young man who had just graduated from a Canadian university, was most expressive about his criticisms of the company practices. Fumiya's complaints often grew out of his disagreement with specific instructions given by Katori-san on general issues of what he labeled as "Japanese" culture, society, or people's practices. For example, Fumiya interpreted Katori-san's instruction to consider the customer's point of view as a sign of "hierarchical society" in Japan that marked a clear positional difference between the worker and the customer. He repeatedly grumbled, "It would be better to interact with customers in a more normal manner [futsūni] because we are in Canada. That's why the Japanese looked weird to the foreigners!" Fumiya often complained about the company's practices as "irrational," "strange," and "old" and mapped them on to Japan as opposed to the "rational," "normal," and "contemporary" practices that he located in Canada or North America. Most trainees seemed to share this mental mapping and agreed that Katori-san's instructions on appearance were too strict and outdated.

At the same time, Fumiya's clichéd dichotomy between Japan and Canada also irritated many of the trainees who were slightly older than Fumiya and had other work experiences after schooling. They saw Fumiya's complaints as immature and naive regarding the "reality" of workers' lives both in Japan and in North America. This ambivalent feeling toward Fumiya's simple geographic dichotomy was expressed not only by the Japanese trainees but also by some Canadian colleagues. Sara pointed out that it was not only the Japanese who had to adjust their behaviors in the work situation: North Americans were also struggling with the expected social roles. She said she had seen an episode of the popular American sitcom *Friends* in which a character had to laugh at his boss's not-so-funny jokes so much that his face was frozen in a big grin even after he came home. Sara said she wanted to record the episode and show it to Fumiya and tell him to be more socially mature.

Most of the trainees understood the advantage of having the "appropriate" appearance because it would make a good impression on the customers and make their work easier. They recognized the importance of having a "costume" for a staged performance in front of the customers. However, they also noticed that Katori-san's instruction was not just to perform or to pretend to make a good face in front of the customer; he constantly urged the trainees to be "sincere" to themselves and to be "honest" to the customers. To the trainees, what was most puzzling was Katori-san's insistence on sincerity. They discussed how he made a distinction between "natural" and "unnatural" in a guide's personality, and how he would evaluate what was sincere expression for each guide. For example, to many young trainees, his judgments on language seemed arbitrary. How did he determine that dialects were natural, but that youth slang and English loanwords were unnatural? Hanako had a hard time correcting her overuse of English loanwords that she had acquired while living in other cities in Canada in the previous year. Hanako agreed with Fumiya, who said that if Katori-san insisted on naturalness, it was more

natural and true to himself if Fumiya spoke with English loanwords because he had been living in North America for several years, and such
words were part of his everyday vocabulary. Hanako understood that it
might not be good to overuse English words when speaking to older customers who were not accustomed to them. But she also wondered if using
some English words might work better for younger customers because it
would make her look more "authentic" as a local guide in Canada.

Beyond these presentation issues, what was most frustrating to the
trainees was the style of instruction itself. Even though the company
was run by a Japanese immigrant, and its main activity was to provide
services to tourists from Japan, the trainees expected that their work
relations would be "Canadian," which they imagined as being conducted
in a "rational," "modern," and "transparent" manner. Many trainees expected that the training sessions would consist of systematic lectures
on the natural and human history of the area. They thought that the
instructor would simply pass the necessary information on to them, and
all they would need to do was remember the information. They did not
expect the whole process of training to be like a *shugyō*, or practice of as-
ceticism. Together with the company's paternalism based on seniority,
and what appeared to be "unreasonable" instructions, they interpreted
that the company practice was too conservative, in fact, more "Japanese" than in many companies in contemporary Japan.

At this early stage, the trainees were not fully aware that the unpre-
dictability of the work schedule arose from the competition within the
tourism industry to meet customer demand, the flexibility expected in
a subcontracting company, and the whimsical nature of the tourism industry in general. The "quick-wittedness," or *kiten*, that Katori-san emphasized is an integral part of "quality" required for the workers in this
economy. Part of what the trainees considered "old-style," premodern,
and apprentice-like Japanese training practices actually coincided well
with post-Fordist flexible business practices.[3]

Sawayaka: Affective Production of Self

After running away from the company accommodations, Hanako returned to the apartment on the next day. Although Hanako was upset
by the company's pedagogy, she was still attracted by the end product
that Katori-san's training would offer her. Hanako, as we learned, was
fascinated by the image of a nature guide she saw on television and

wanted to become like her. The natural quality of guiding that Katori-san encouraged his trainees to attain seemed to match Hanako's ideal image of a guide in Canada, who "stands on the earth on her own feet."

The most important quality that Katori-san required of his tour guides was *sawayaka*, which can be translated as "refreshing," "cool," or "soothing." The term indicates the feeling associated with such natural phenomena as a refreshing morning, the lush green leaves of early summer, or an autumn breeze. Katori-san explained that sawayaka was a desirable quality for service industry workers in general but was particularly suitable for guides in the Canadian Rockies. The appearance of a tour guide needed to be clean, clear, natural, and sawayaka in order to match the refreshing landscape. For Katori-san, the emphasis on sawayaka coincided with his pointed tips on appearance and proper language use. Maintaining a clean, crisp, but not too fashionable look enhanced the image of naturalness and gave a fresh, soothing impression. Clear and smooth communication through "correct language" also created an atmosphere of sawayaka.

In principle, what Katori-san suggested was the subjection of the self to the environment, and the production of a guide's subjectivity coordinated with those desires the tourists projected upon the landscape of the Canadian Rockies. The guide's narration should match perfectly the scenery seen from the highway. A guide must internalize the timing of the points of interest, know how long it would take to reach the next points, and weave the story in response to the speed of the bus, the environment outside the vehicle, the time of day, the season, the weather, and the group's mood.

This dynamic should not be confused with the negation of individual freedom. For Katori-san, this perfect match between a person and his or her surroundings is the foundation for attaining freedom. Katori-san told the trainees that once a guide obtained the sawayaka quality and became attractive to the customer, he or she could conduct the tour freely and smoothly (*jiyū jizaini*). Customers would listen to a guide to whom they were attracted, and the tourists often helped the guide create a good atmosphere for the tour. This notion of freedom is constructed through virtuoso performance, responding to other people and the environment.

The experienced guides' comments also supported Katori-san's notion of a guide's freedom. Yamamoto Aya, a fourth-year guide, repeatedly said, "Once you are on the tour by yourself, you are free and in control," emphasizing how much fun it was to communicate with tourists. Iida Miyuki, a fifth-year guide, told the trainees, "Most customers are nice and gentle. They sometimes act oddly, but their odd actions are rather cute. Customers are here to enjoy their vacation, so they help you by creating a pleasant atmosphere for themselves." The experienced guides' remarks suggest that if a guide invested his or her own hard work to transform him- or herself into a desired product, then the guide could affect tourists, turning the tourists themselves into agents for making the tour pleasant. In contrast, if a tour guide lost his or her personal appeal, tourists would treat the guide as a mere service provider, more along the lines of a servant, translator, or driver, someone who simply offered a specific service function as an object of economic transaction. In a tour, a guide constantly needed to enchant tourists as an important part of negotiating his or her position, becoming an enchanting commodity with an aura to direct tourists' behaviors and feelings rather than falling into a position of a mere service provider who would be exploited by tourists' demands.

In order to present oneself as an attractive commodity in the tourist economy, the guide's appearance needed to be standardized in some form. Without some standardization or indication that a person was a commercial guide, the guide's attractiveness would not be available to tourists through market interaction. For this purpose, Katori-san used traditional Japanese discipline to package the guides into products recognizable to Japanese tourists. Performing Japanese with the "correct language" and a sawayaka appearance provided the guide and the tourists with a shared vocabulary, which in turn was fundamental in crafting a guide's new subjectivity as cosmopolitan. In the popular Japanese tourist imagination, the landscape of Canada represented not only Canadian nature but also nature on a global scale, or the generic model for the earth's natural history. Therefore, the guide's sawayaka quality that matched the natural environment was the key for the collaborative construction of a guide as a Japanese cosmopolitan, someone who originated in Japan but who could freely transcend the national boundaries by merging him- or herself with the natural landscape. This performance had an ambivalent effect: while it presented guides as Japanese, it simultaneously destabilized the very notion of what it meant to be Japanese because the attractiveness of the guides derived from matching their personalities to the landscape in the Canadian Rockies, distinct and different from those living in Japan. These ambivalent yet distinctive characteristics underwrote the value of a guide as someone with a unique subjectivity.

The experienced guides' conversations with the trainees also helped the trainees to understand the ritualistic aspects of the training. They told the trainees that only one guide—Kubo Toshiyuki, who used to work as a tour conductor—had passed Katori-san's exam in the previous year. Nonetheless, other guides were still assigned guiding jobs. Among the experienced guides, Katori-san had a reputation as a perfectionist, more severe than the previous trainers. Many experienced guides told the trainees that even though the training period was stressful, they were thankful to Katori-san because he hammered the "basics" into them, which helped them to conduct most of the actual tours in a pleasant manner and deal with occasional unexpected situations and unreasonable customers' demands.

Here, we see an interesting mixture of "work," often discussed as the characteristics of preindustrial artisanal production and the "enchantment" of commodities in mass society developed in industrial capitalism. Furthermore, this mixture was manifested in immaterial labor in postindustrial capitalism. On the one hand, the RMT's guide training practices can be characterized as work discipline continuous with that of preindustrial artisans. The worker's engagement with his or her work was not merely a means to earn a living but a process of "polishing" the self through bodily practices. Hannah Arendt ([1958] 1998) explains that the end product of this kind of work was inseparable from the worker. The product was an expression of a worker's personality because it represented the worker's devotion to improve his or her skills, as well as the mastery of material and bodily-mental coordination. The end product should be the authentic representation of the worker's simultaneous crafting of the object and the self; then, the worker would proudly present the end product in the market. In this context, a market was a meeting place in which the aura of the artisan's work was presented by the exhibition of the end product. But, in the case of a tour guide, the product is not a material object but the whole subjectivity expressed in a sawayaka, honest, and sincere person.

On the other hand, the RMT's formal company structure, the labor and wage system, and the company's business practices were those of industrial capitalism, which produces and circulates commodities for mass consumers. A guide as a wage laborer was supposed to alienate his or her labor from the self and to produce a commodity that the company sold in order to make profits. As a commodity in the mass tourism industry, a guide was expected to produce him- or herself as a marketable "type" or "figure"—a pleasant and reliable person who understood Japanese language, customs, and cultural tastes and simultaneously possessed the characteristics of an adventurous, nature-loving local resident in the Canadian Rockies. A guide who successfully transformed him- or herself into a commodity with this aura gained the enchanting power to allure the employers and tourists. A guide had to present him- or herself as if these characteristics were the essence of the guide independent from the social context of their production. Here, the idea of a guide as a commodity was used not in the sense of undifferentiated, quantifiable products, like a bushel of wheat, but in Benjamin's (1968) sense of a commodity that carries an aura, or an enchanting power to fascinate people. Interestingly, this resonates with Allison's (2009) point that biopolitics becomes biocapital: the idea that the construction, management, and care of the self become the source activities of self-marketing and capital accumulation.[4]

From this observation, it is easy to lament the decay of an authentic self caused by capitalist production and consumption (cf. Hochschild 1983). However, being situated in the context of the century-long history of Japanese struggle in translating "subject" and "subjectivity" in the Western intellectual traditions, the Japanese guides' experiences elucidate that this anxiety or the fear of self being threatened by the market economy itself is the product of the fetishism of subjectivity. The effect of fetishism is that it makes something appear to exist autonomously and independently from the history and social relations of its production. The commonsense understanding of self—a singular and authentic locus of subjectivity and an autonomous entity existing before social interactions (including those in the markets) that needs to be clearly demarcated from the external forces—itself has been constructed along with the development of modern "reason" and capitalism that presupposes this form of subjectivity. This historical production of subjectivity is often forgotten in the analysis of capitalism and, ironically, turns this notion of subjectivity into something "sacred." The true, sacred self, reflecting the specific historical and cultural legacy of the Enlightenment and Liberalism, is imagined to exist somewhere deep inside an individual and is found beneath the facade of the social role that one is required to play.

The immaterial work, which is centered on communication and emotional interactions with others, elucidates that the separation between workers and their labor is illusory. Workers' subjectivities are constructed by the exchange of affects and workers' intersubjective relations with others. It is here that Hardt and Negri (2000, 2004) try to find the subversive potential of immaterial laborers as a "multitude," an alternative conceptualization of actors, contradictory figures that exist within and against globalizing capitalism. The inseparability between workers and their labor reveals the limitation of the liberal conceptualization of subjectivity as well as new forms of human control. The Japanese tour guides as transnational immaterial laborers could be understood as a multitude. In the case of Japanese tour guides, however, what becomes more apparent is the politics of cultural translation regarding workers' subjectivity and freedom. The trainees' frustration revealed their previous assumptions that their true individual subjectivity should exist outside the work setting, independent from social relationships mediated by the tourist economy. This is the fetishism of subjectivity—forgetting that one's subjectivity is produced in interactions with other people, including work relations and the tourist economy, and being obsessed with the imagined "true" and "authentic" self, separate from and uncontaminated by the social relations involved in the production of the subjectivity. This fetishism of subjectivity stimulated trainees to look for a true subjectivity not disrupted by the obviously intersubjective social relationships in Japan.

Commodification as Co-Modification

Katori-san's own life history elucidates the process of subjectivity formation from a slightly different angle. Instead of insisting on finding an authentic, autonomous self liberated from the disruptive social pressures as a locus of subjectivity, his story was centered on what I will call "co-modification"—the modification and production of self through collaborative interactions with other people in a particular environment. Through my use of the term "co-modification," which does not correspond to the popular usage of the English word "commodification" as turning something into undifferentiated objects in the market, I would like to highlight the gap in translation between shōhin and commodity. Katori-san's story reveals how, through transforming himself into a tour guide whose work entailed responding to the needs and desires of others, he integrated his diverse interests in travel, geography, natural history, and English language into a unified, unique personality in a web of relationships.

Katori-san told me that he came to Banff in 1989, when he was twenty-two years old. He had become disillusioned by his job in a travel agency in Japan because he thought that "the service industry in Japan was very commercially oriented." He was urged to sell more and more tours and to expand the company's market share. He thought the work itself had "nothing to do with the enjoyment of travel." Selling tours merely as objects to increase the company's profits made him eager to return to what initially interested him about his work, which was to share with customers the enjoyment of travel.

Like several other guides I talked to, Katori-san wanted to free himself from Japanese work relations, and he developed an interest in seeing the world outside of Japan. But what was distinctive about his story was that he narrated his life trajectories with frequent use of the word *tama tama* (coincidentally) to describe the contingent, spontaneous, and improvisational nature of his experiences, as if he was enjoying the sense of detachment, freeing himself from the pretense of having a concrete goal or purpose. For example, he wanted to live in an English-speaking country and to use English, but he quickly added that he did not have any specific attachment to the language: it was merely the foreign language he happened to learn as a mandatory subject in high school. His choice of Canada was coincidental, too. Canada was the only country in the Northern Hemisphere with which Japan had a working holiday visa program at that time, and it happened to be spring there. Katori-san speculated that it might be easier to find a job before the summer tourist season. He flew to Toronto, simply because it was the largest city in Canada. In Toronto, he was encouraged to go to Banff to work in a souvenir store. He got on a Greyhound bus with no knowledge of what Banff was like. After the long bus ride across the prairies, he was captivated by the spectacular landscape of the Canadian Rockies. He worked in the souvenir store for a year, coming to realize how much he enjoyed living in Banff, surrounded by beautiful mountains and friends, yet he was not sure what to do. Just as his working holiday visa was about to expire, he happened to get recruited by Atsuko-san for a job as a guide.

Once he had landed the guiding job, Katori-san, thoroughly fascinated by the landscape, devoted himself to studying its history. He also bolstered his confidence in English by reading English guidebooks, which in turn opened up a new vision of the natural environment. He enjoyed the challenge of synchronizing his bus tour talk with the passing scenery. He learned how to time these descriptions perfectly by practicing them again and again. It was rewarding for him to know that tourists enjoyed his presence, and to receive requests from tour escorts for him to guide their tours. Soon, he gained a reputation as an excellent guide.

Katori-san explained that the reason he devoted himself to tour guiding was because he felt grateful to Atsuko-san for giving him an opportunity to work, and he felt obliged to return the favor by polishing himself into a valuable guide. He said, "It was important for me not to cause the people who trusted me to lose face. They dared to pick up a wanderer like me even though they didn't know where I came from." In Katori-san's narrative, work was not merely the abstraction of labor in market exchange. He could see, beyond the exchange of his labor and money, Atsuko-san's hard work of running the company, and tourists' efforts to save enough money to visit Canada. His wage affirmed his relationship with Atsuko-san, who provided him with further opportunities to work on improving himself as a person.

Transforming himself into an attractive guide, an enchanting commodity in tourism exchanges, broadened Katori-san's opportunities to build social relationships and to further cultivate and polish himself as a person. Katori-san's various interests in travel, geography, natural history, and the English language all were integrated into his unique subjectivity through transforming himself as a valuable tour guide. Yet his unique value was not the natural expression of his inert essence; rather, it was the product of these dynamics, the co-modification of himself as a tour guide, the product of social relations cultivated by selling his labor, and the exhibition of himself as a product in the market. His value as a commodity and his moral worth as a person were actualized through the tourist market interaction. In this sense, he excavated different notions of "market" sedimented under the capitalist labor market, something resembling the "fair" among artisans.

Katori-san's story also illustrates that his subjectivity was constructed as a nodal point of various social interactions that ran through him.[5] Because his subjectivity was constructed through his interactions with the people around him, including tourists, other guides, and managers, he was aware that his value as a commodity was also a product of relationships with people who exchange money, things, ideas, and feelings with him. Thus, the way tourists perceived value in him was not always predictable. Nevertheless, even though he could not assume what kind of value a tourist might see in him, Katori-san was confident that he could generate affect and conduct his tours quite freely.

Translation of Freedom: *Jiyū* and *Jizai*

The tour guides' frustration during training reveals the tension between two different notions of freedom: (1) jiyū, the notion of freedom in modern Western liberal thought, imported to Japan along with the European and American political system in the late nineteenth century, and (2) jizai, a concept that originates in Buddhism and Taoism, imported from China and incorporated into Japanese thought much earlier. Although both jiyū and jizai can be translated as "freedom," the ways these words pose the relationship between an individual and the world are quite different.

Many critics have explained how Japanese intellectuals struggled to find a Japanese equivalent for the English words "freedom" and "liberty" in the late nineteenth century when they translated works of political philosophy, such as John Stuart Mill's *On Liberty* and Henry Wheaton's *Elements of International Law* (e.g., Yanabu 1982; Kamei 1994). The notion of freedom based on the European Enlightenment idea of "natural rights" was entirely alien to Japanese intellectuals. Compared with the Rousseauian notion of liberty, which is attained when individual human freedom is recovered from political oppression, in pre-Meiji Japan, although there were many examples of resistance, there was no idea that connected political resistance to the innate value of the individual human being.

Yanabu (1982) explains that while nineteenth-century Japanese intellectuals avidly searched for loanwords from Chinese to adopt for the translation of the English word "freedom," they found that none of these captured the original meaning in European languages. They experimented with the word jiyū, as well as other terms, such as jizai and *jishu* (self-oriented). Leading thinkers, such as Fukuzawa Yukichi and Nakamura Masanao, while enthusiastic about Western political philosophy, expressed the predicament that they could not find suitable words to translate the concept of freedom. For example, Yanabu cites Nakamura's journal article, which explains that "in Western countries, the people's right called 'civil liberty' is an important foundational concept for peaceful governance and development of a nation" (1982, 183–184). Similarly, Yanabu also points out that in a footnote in his influential book *Seiyō Jijō*

(Things Western; 1866), Fukuzawa writes, "The letters in the text, *jishu nin'i* [self-determination] and *jiyū* [freedom] do not mean selfish dissipation and the ignorance of the governing law in the nation. It means to conduct one's own life by doing what he deserves and by intermingling with his fellow residents without hesitation when he lives in his country. This is called 'freedom' or 'liberty' in English. There is still no appropriate translation word in Japanese" (Yanabu 1982, 181). As Fukuzawa's note indicates, the term jiyū had been used as a synonym for "selfish" and had a negative connotation of being inconsiderate to others. With the increasing amount of Western literature circulated in Japan, the term jiyū had become a standard translation word for "freedom" and "liberty" while maintaining the conceptual gap between jiyū and these English words, along with the trace of their incommensurability.

According to Kawahara Hiroshi (1998), the concept of jizai originates in the Sanskrit word *vastiva* and represents the situation in which a person is liberated from the attachment to self and conducts his or her body and mind freely in accordance with the benefit of others. Kawahara explains that jizai is deeply rooted in Buddhist cosmology and represents the transcendental state in which the distinction between self and the world disappears into the ideal realm of nothingness. He points out that the two fundamental aspects of jizai are the principle of altruism and body-mind discipline. In this idea, freedom is important not as an individual right to pursue benefit for oneself. Rather, it is the state of being free from problems that arise from the egoistic attachment to oneself and one's possessions. To achieve this notion of freedom, it is important to train one's own body and mind, and let oneself detach from one's self-interest. Kawahara argues that the ultimate state of freedom in jizai is the unity of self and others mutually liberated from the narrowness of self-centered perceptions and behaviors. In this ideal state, things happen *naturally* for the benefit of both self and others. Seen from this point of view, the modern liberal notion of freedom is not free at all because it is preoccupied with the strong attachment to the individual self and the possession of "natural rights."

It is noteworthy that Katori-san often used the term jiyū jizai, combining these potentially conflicting words. This may have been simply an unintentional usage of this common expression in contemporary Japanese language. Yet, the training process clearly proved that these contradictory meanings of freedom coexist in the contemporary Japanese notion of jiyū, as the translation of freedom.

Before the trainees started to interact with tourists, it was hard for them to see that what Katori-san taught them was how to attain "freedom" as jizai, the ability to affect tourists in the direction a guide wishes and to naturally create a good atmosphere for the tour. Because the guides could acquire this ability only through interaction with tourists, they were required to subject themselves to common codes of value held by tourists, as well as by other people around them, such as senior guides or fellow service providers.[6] Katori-san's version of freedom is derived from the attentive cultivation of relationships, rather than from insisting on one's unique, inherent self that exists prior to one's interactions with other people and the environment. These contradictory notions of freedom coincide with the competing notions of individual subjectivity: the liberal humanist notion of the individual as a unique entity that exists prior to social interactions, and the explicitly inter-subjective notion of the individual realized only through subjection to others and the environment.

The tension between these contrasting principles of freedom and subjectivity became highly visible in the Japanese workplace when neo-liberal corporate restructuring and labor relations became influential in the 1990s. This trend was heightened with the discourse of "freeing oneself from the company," in other words, freeing oneself from the "Japanese-style" paternalistic company and becoming independent in order to find one's true self somewhere outside the bound of the old community-like company. Many of the young Japanese coming to Banff spoke of their anxiety over searching for their true selves somewhere outside Japan, while they simultaneously discussed the uncanny comfortableness of being part of an organic relationship with the workplace.

Like several other guides, Hanako expressed an unsettled feeling derived from the coexistence of these conflicting notions of freedom and subjectivity while working in Japan. She did not have a dramatically strong objection to the workplace and in fact liked her bosses and coworkers. What drove her to escape from Japan was that she sensed there was something wrong and "dangerous" about the lukewarm feeling of comfortableness in the workplace she experienced. She feared that she would lose her chance to seek her true subjectivity if she continued working in that environment. Her motivation for coming to Banff was to get out of this confusing situation, to escape familiar cultural and social conventions, and to clarify what she wanted to do. In this context, the training period was particularly stressful for Hanako, since she felt that she had been brought back to the similarly confusing situation she had experienced in her Japanese workplace. Moreover, after coming all the way from Tokyo, she had, ironically, to go through the "outdated Japanese" discipline that she had not even experienced in Japan. Before directly interacting with the customers as a commodity and realizing the self-cultivation process through mutual interactions with the tourists, she suffered from the confusion between different modes of subjectivity and freedom. As a result of this stress, she repeated the impulse to escape from the company accommodations.

Production of "Value" in Tourist Encounters

After working as a guide for one year and later as an administrative assistant in a travel agency, Shinohara Rei told me that being shōhin, or a commodity, was an advantage for a guide. By working as a guide, by presenting herself as shōhin to the tourists directly, she could interact with the customers and feel that her presence contributed to making the tour pleasant and helping the tourists enjoy their vacations. It helped affirm that her choice to move to Banff and work as a guide was a good one. She liked herself when she was guiding, for she felt she really was turning into a good, valuable person.

Even though Rei thought she was not a social person and was not good at entertaining people, she found the guiding work extremely enjoyable. The tourists treated her well, as if she were an idolized entertainer or an adored child of relatives. The tourists laughed at her mediocre jokes. They wanted to take photos with her. They looked with curious eyes in whichever direction she suggested and were excited by the landscape and wild animals she pointed out. Rei knew that most travelers were determined to enjoy the tour, so they were happy with whatever they saw and did. She thought that their desire to have fun helped her work. Everything they encountered must be nice, everything should be an object of admiration and worth the money they had spent. She felt that it was not she so much as the tourists who created the tour's good atmosphere.

Rei's interpretation of commodity, or more precisely shōhin, suggests a paradoxical and performative constitution of subjectivity (see Butler 1990). When she was working at the desk or in the office, it appeared that she owned her own labor power as an object of exchange and sold it by her rational judgment and free will. However, she did not feel she was an autonomous individual as defined in liberal economic theory. It was, rather, when Rei subjected herself as a commodity in the tourist economy that she felt her subjectivity emerged: she became someone who could affect the tourists as a unique person.

Ogura Yoshiko and Maeda Hanako, who specialized in outdoor activities, had even closer interactions with tourists. Compared with the bus guides, who speak mostly by themselves in front of twenty to forty tourists, hiking guides usually lead much smaller groups of two to nine, with opportunities to engage in conversation with each tourist. Yoshiko enjoyed talking with tourists, particularly those she described as "*jinsei no senpai*," or someone who is senior to her and walking ahead of her in life's path. Instead of a guide one-sidedly giving information to the tourists, she felt that she learned about life from the responses of those tourists who had more experience and more mature perceptions of the world. Hanako, as a novice guide, liked to learn from middle-aged tourists about their experiences of hiking and climbing in Japan. Hanako felt that in exchange for telling the tourists stories of mountains, rocks, animals, and flowers in the Rockies, she learned from them about how human beings had interacted with the natural environment in Japan. She thought what she did on her tours was a reciprocal exchange of knowledge and perceptions about the natural environment in Japan and Canada. She received money for the time she spent with the customers, but the money was not only the wage for her service but also a token of the exchange she experienced with the tourists.

Of course, not all the tours were enjoyable, and not all the guides had good experiences. Some did not like the work and left the RMT after only a few weeks, or stayed while seeking other jobs. Whether or not a guide could present an idol-like aura like Rei, or have pleasant reciprocal exchanges with tourists like Yoshiko and Hanako, was contingent on the situation, the nature of the tours, the chemistry among the tourists and the guide, and other uncontrollable elements such as the weather, the season, and road conditions. The managers' job was to make the best match possible between the guide and the tour group. Success seemed to depend on whether the guide's characteristics and his or her attitude toward work corresponded with the tourists' expectations of their vacation. Rei expressed how lucky she was to be assigned tours in which she had good relationships with the tourists. The younger guides were aware that the managers were assigning them relatively easy leisure tours. The difficult jobs were assigned to the senior guides. Thus, the younger guides did not have to deal with demanding customers and tour escorts in high-priced or specially arranged tours.

Moreover, the landscape of the Canadian Rockies played a significant role in the way tourists idealized their guides. I often observed tourists say to a guide, "I envy you that you are living in such a dreamlike place" (*Iidesune, konna yume mitai na tokoro ni sunde*). The guides' responses to this frequent remark were ambivalent. Many of them assumed that the tourists were merging the image of the place and the guide, in their insistence upon thoroughly enjoying their tours. Because the tourists transposed the soothing and refreshing image of the landscape onto the guides, the guides, as dwellers in such a dreamlike place, appeared more charming and attractive than they really were. Rei, on the one hand, was flattered by the remark because it suggested she deserved to live in a place the tourists envied. She felt that her work as a guide was successful when the tourists became fond of the place and appreciated her work as a mediator between them and the Rockies. On the other hand, such compliments urged Rei to reflect on her life in greater depth. With her friends, Rei often insisted that life in Banff was her "reality," not a "dream," full of unpleasant things just like any other place.

In addition, the guides were conscious that the tourists never witnessed the less-than-ideal aspects of their lives. The guides knew they were complicit in maintaining the fantasy, by not revealing their lingering feelings of anxiety and insecurity as flexible workers in a transnational setting. Many younger guides in particular had concerns about the seasonal nature of the job and the renewal of their work contracts and visas. The wage in the summer was decent, but if they wanted to live an entire year on that income, they had to carefully watch their budgets. The term of a work visa was usually no more than a year, with no guarantee of renewal. That led to the larger question of where they would live and what they would do in the near future—whether they would continue working in Canada, go back to Japan, or go elsewhere. Their uncertainty about the location of work and living was tied to their family situation. This was a serious issue especially for those who had a sick parent, or for a single person who wanted to be involved in a serious relationship. Many guides found it was a challenge to find a good partner in a small community. Many left Banff because they could not bear the anxieties and insecurities.

Yoshiko half jokingly told me that a guide was a professional white liar. The guides were good at turning negative things into positive ones.

For example, if it was cloudy, she would say that the lighting was perfect to see the fine color gradation in a glacier because the delicate colors were not disrupted by the strong sunlight. Even though she wished she could also show the tourists the mountain in the beautiful blue sky, she focused on things they could appreciate in any given circumstance. If the service in a restaurant was inefficient, she turned it into a sign of the slow, relaxed lifestyle in Canada as opposed to the stressful life in Japan, where everyone felt constant time pressure. Through the repetition of these white lies, Yoshiko convinced not only the tourists but also herself that what she said was true. Yoshiko sometimes felt tired of going to the same hiking trail, but when she saw the customers' amazement at the color of the glacial lakes, she recalled her own feeling of awe and wonder when she first encountered the landscape. This helped refresh her feeling of being healed and soothed by the landscape. While a part of her was cynical because the customers could not understand her insecurity, another part of her felt that she was really living in a dreamlike place.

For many of the guides, direct interaction with the tourists helped them to construct their new subjectivities. Commodification of the self as a guide had an aspect of co-modification of self through the interactions with the people and the natural environment around them. While the guides aspired to be independent individuals, free from the particular social situation they had left behind in Japan, the construction of their subjectivities depended on interactions with the tourists, managers, and other people around them, as well as the natural environment.

The guides' performances as "Japanese cosmopolitans" were the products of this co-modification, the intersubjective construction of subjectivity among the guides, tourists, and other people and things around them. And this subjectivity construction was central to the production "value" in the tourist industry. The moral value of constructing one's sincere subjectivity was conflated with the economic value of enactment of the Japanese cosmopolitan dream. Through this conflation of values, the guides were interpellated to become transnational flexible workers. Yet, this conflation of incommensurable values also reveals the fetishism of subjectivity in liberal and neoliberal economy and opens up the potential for imagining an alternative form of subjectivity by foregrounding the intersubjective relations.

Charisma of Female Outdoor Guides

After her second season of guiding, Maeda Hanako told me that she was surprised to know how much a guide's presence could influence tourists' experiences. For example, Hanako recounted how two female schoolteachers, after having finished a series of outdoor activity tours, were full of emotion. They hugged her, cried on her shoulder, and told her how much they enjoyed meeting her. Hanako was flattered to know that they enjoyed her tours so much, but she was perplexed by their strong emotional reaction. She wondered whether her customers might have been in the midst of a career crisis, and whether seeing her eased the stress from the pressures of their daily work. She suspected that they saw her as proof that the world would not come to an end if they deviated from the expected life course of sticking with a secure job in Japan. Looking at Hanako, living modestly but happily, enjoying the mountains in a foreign country, the teachers might have been able to broaden their perspectives of what they could do in life.

Before leading actual tours, Hanako thought that tourists came to the Canadian Rockies only for the natural landscape; she assumed that they would not be interested in the tour guides themselves. In the training session, Katori-san cautioned the trainees that guides could get the tourists' attention much more than they might have assumed. He explained that the three most frequently asked questions from the tourists were not the names of the mountains or lakes, but "How long have you been in Banff?," "Where in Japan are you from?," and "Is your wife/husband [or girlfriend/boyfriend] Canadian?" But when they were in training, the guides like Hanako were not aware of the significance of Katori-san's caution. Soon after I started to go on the actual tours as an assistant to other guides, I noticed that the guides sometimes attracted much attention from the tourists. After the tourists returned to Japan, they often sent the guides letters and gifts, such as Japanese sweets, books, magazines, and photographs of the tour. Some guides had customers who returned every year to hike with them. In fact, some of the tourists I interviewed back in Japan told me that meeting the tour guides had been the most remarkable experience of their tour. Of course, not all the tourists expressed their strong emotions to the guides; especially in large tours, many tourists seemed to be indifferent to the guides. Yet the reactions, when they occurred, were often powerful.

In November 2000, after the peak tourist season, I went to Japan and interviewed several tourists to see what they got out of their vacations in the Canadian Rockies. I was particularly looking forward to interviewing Mr. and Mrs. Yamada, a middle-aged couple from Tokyo, because they seemed to enjoy their travels intensely. For the last twenty years, they had been busy running their business and taking care of their children. Two years ago, when their oldest son entered university, they felt it was time to take a break from family obligations and traveled to Switzerland. They greatly enjoyed the Alps and decided to take their next vacation in the Canadian Rockies. While there, Mr. and Mrs. Yamada were obviously excited to be in the beautiful landscape. They had nostalgically reflected on the time when they had dated and hiked in the Japanese mountains before they had children. Mr. Yamada, who was a strong, experienced hiker, used to pause whenever we approached a clear opening and calmly looked into the distance with an expression full of strong emotions. The rest of us in the party worried that he was sometimes lost in a daydream when he stood at the site for a long time.

In a Tokyo café that November, I asked Mr. and Mrs. Yamada what had been most memorable about their trip. I was expecting that they would mention some beautiful scenery that evoked a strong sense of nostalgia, or perhaps the small animals that Mr. Yamada obsessively videotaped. To my surprise, Mr. Yamada said what struck him was Ogura Yoshiko, the guide who led their hike around Lake Louise. Although Mr. Yamada had chosen the Canadian Rockies because of the beautiful scenery, seeing a young Japanese guide like Yoshiko was also refreshing for him. He was impressed by those guides who left secure lives in Japan to travel all the way to Canada and pursue their dreams. Mrs. Yamada explained to me that she and her husband stayed up late every night and diligently wrote postcards to their children. They could not wait to explain to their children how they were fascinated by the guides who devoted themselves to their love of outdoor activities. (When they returned home, they realized that they had arrived before their postcards.) Now, every night at the dinner table, Mr. Yamada feverishly told his son to reconsider his future after he finished attending university. Inspired by Yoshiko, Mr. Yamada told his son, "Graduating from a good university and entering into a top-level company is not the only choice of your life. You should pursue your dream. For example, have you ever thought about going abroad and challenging yourself to see what you can do?" According to Mrs. Yamada, their son just rolled his eyes, not understanding what had happened to his father to produce this new attitude.

It was not only the Yamadas who were inspired by a tour guide. Yoshiko was also asked by a high school teacher if he could include a photograph of her in an English textbook that he was helping to edit. Her image was published in the textbook as an example of a Japanese working actively overseas (*sekai de katsuyaku suru nihonjin*). The teacher wanted to show students alternative future options and introduced Yoshiko as one example. She was presented as a role model—an individual who was unique and independent, pursuing what she wanted to do in her life and, in the process, transforming herself into a true cosmopolitan.

Another tourist I interviewed, a young woman who worked in a large bank, was also inspired by a female hiking guide, Uchida Chie. This woman explained to me that Chie stimulated her adventurous spirit and made her want to examine what she really wanted to do in her life. She decided to quit her job and travel to New Zealand, despite her parents' strong opposition.

As these examples suggest, the way tour guides were idolized reflects tourists' concerns about their own life and work. A guide served as a reflection of the tourists' own situations, offering a seductive image of what they could do in the future, or what they could have done in another life. In many cases, the guides embodied the cosmopolitan dream that circulated widely in Japan at the turn of the twenty-first century: the dream of escaping the set course of the stable yet constraining lives of salaried workers and having a solid sense of subjectivity while living a "modest but fulfilling life" in nature.

The unexpected centrality of guides also raises interesting questions regarding modernist assumptions about nature tourism. Tourists' fascination with the guide as mediator creates tensions with the tourist industry's rhetoric that promotes a "direct encounter with nature." This dynamic also presents a challenge to the existing literature, which presumes that tourists are on a quest to experience authentic, unmediated nature. Instead, the tourists seem to enjoy the tour guides' performance as mediators of different worlds, enchanted as much by their presentation of nature as by nature itself. Despite—or because of—the stereotypical association of outdoor activity and masculine culture, female outdoor guides played a particularly significant role.[1]

The charisma of female outdoor tour guides contradicts the traditional gendered division of labor by which the Japanese tour company operates. Rocky Mountain Tours trained guides to accommodate what they interpreted as the dominant middle-class norms in Japan. In this company, outdoor guiding was traditionally considered to be male work; in practice, however, there were almost as many female guides as male guides leading the outdoor activity tours. Many female outdoor guides presented a hint of gender ambiguity or androgyny, yet it did not mean that they were merely substitutes for male guides. In many cases, male outdoor guides seemed to gain their popularity as a result of their characteristics that comfortably fit the tourists' expectations. In contrast, the appeal of the female outdoor guides seemed to originate from the unexpected surprise brought by the ambiguity of their gender and age. They performatively constructed their subjectivities as people who could transcend the dominant gendered norms. By doing so, they produced a charismatic aura and presented themselves as mediators with the special ability to go back and forth between the everyday world and an elsewhere, imaginarily staged on Canada's vast natural landscape.

How was the aura of female outdoor guides produced? What roles did ambiguity and nature play in the construction of their subjectivity? In this chapter, I examine the performative construction of subjectivity among female outdoor guides.

Guide's Work and Gender

In the RMT, the managers assigned tours to the guides based on the best match between the type of tour and the guide's personality. The company had a high reputation for its specialized guides and had contracts with some of the largest Japanese tour agencies. The managers thought that in order to maintain the company's reputation, it was crucial to send a guide whose image would conform to what its customers expected. Gender was an important category when managers considered the match between a tour and a guide, and the gender division was clearly addressed at the beginning of the training sessions. The managers considered leading a large group bus tour to the Columbia Icefield a "basic" tour and expected every guide, whether female or male, to master it because it brought in the most revenue to the company. For their first jobs, however, female guides were trained to lead a bus tour, and male guides shuttled tourists to and from the airport.

At first glance, it seemed that female guides were rather privileged because they could start with these basic tours from the very beginning of their career. Junior male guides seemed to suffer in comparison. The work of shuttling a van between Banff and Calgary, Jasper, or sometimes even Edmonton (430 kilometers or 267 miles north of Banff) was demanding. A driver guide's day often started before dawn and ended after midnight. The managers thought it was easier to assign young men to these long early morning or late night drives because they assumed that young men were physically tougher. Also, they thought that young men, especially those coming straight out of school, tended to lack the sophisticated mannerisms required in the service industry. These men, the managers reasoned, would need more on-the-job training before they could be assigned to large bus tours and exposed to the surveillance of the tour escorts who accompanied tours from Japan. Katori-san told me that he expected male novice guides to learn how to treat customers well in small-group van tours, in which the relationship between the guide and the customers was more casual than in large bus tours. At the beginning of the season, when novice male guides returned to the office from small van tours, I often heard Atsuko-san teasing some of them by saying, "You didn't need to report to me that you were successful in using the proper polite language today," or "You didn't upset customers today, did you?" However, if they stayed with the company for several years, starting from the van tours could be advantageous for male guides in the long run because they had an opportunity to learn the skills of both driver and bus guide and would be able to lead more diverse kinds of tours.

Outdoor guiding had long been considered male work because it often required driving and being responsible for tourists' outdoor safety.[2] In the RMT, outdoor activity work could be roughly divided into two categories: one involved leading the tours, which the RMT guides themselves did, including hiking, nature walks, canoeing, picnic barbecuing, and animal watching; the other involved driving customers to the Canadian operators of horseback riding, rafting, and fishing tours and working as translators. The latter job was considered to be the entry point for outdoor activity guides. On these tours, the RMT guide served mainly as a language translator for the specialized Canadian guide, who assumed both the safety and the guiding responsibilities during the tour.

Hiking was considered to be the most skilled work among the outdoor tours. First, the hiking guides were expected to have more detailed knowledge of the natural landscape than other guides. A hiking guide's special skills included acquiring enough ecological and geological knowledge to be able to identify plants, animals, rocks, and geological formations at the sites and say something interesting and informative to tourists. Second, a hiking guide assumed sole responsibility for the tourists' safety during the tour. The guide always monitored the physical and mental condition of the tourists and set the walking pace so that everyone on the tour felt comfortable while also being taken to as many interesting spots as possible.

A typical day for a hiking guide started early in the morning at the company's parking lot. The guide would retrieve the van, make sure it was clean and had no mechanical problems, pick up lunches at the contracted restaurants, and collect tourists at their hotels. Then the guide drove the customers to the trailhead, usually about forty minutes to an hour away from Banff, and lead a full-day hike. After the hike, the guide would drive back to Banff, return customers to their hotels, go back to the office to write a report, wash the van, and finally return the van key to the office. That marked the end of the long day.

Mr. Matsuda Kenji, or Matsuda-san, the executive manager who assigned most of the guides to tours, seemed to feel ambivalent about placing women in work that involved driving customers or leading outdoor activity tours. He thought that older customers would not consider driving to be female work and was afraid they would blame him if they were involved in an accident. He also explained to me that the reason he felt more comfortable assigning male guides to the hiking tours had to do with differences in male and female physical strength. In his mind, if a customer got sick in the forest, a female guide might not be strong enough to provide help. For example, he could not imagine that a female guide could carry a customer with a sprained ankle. On hiking tours, a guide had to be independent and able to take sole responsibility for a customer's well-being. By contrast, bus tour guides worked in pairs with a Canadian bus driver (most of the Canadian drivers were male, although it was not unusual to have a female bus driver). On a bus tour, a guide was securely contained in a metaphorically "domestic" realm inside the bus and was protected by the bus driver, a figure of local authority.

According to Yoshida Mari, or Mari-san, a senior guide who had been working with the company for more than ten years, when she started in the 1980s, the managers informed her that they would not feel comfortable assigning outdoor activities to women. Even though Mari-san was an experienced mountaineer and physically very strong, she was not assigned to a hiking tour for a while. She explained that the company started to assign female guides to outdoor activity tours in the 1990s when trends in Japanese tourism changed. Until the 1990s, most of the tours the company arranged were sightseeing bus tours. Since then, the number of small-group tours had increased to cater to the diverse interests of the tourists, and more outdoor activity tours became possible with the smaller groups. The rising popularity of the outdoor tours required that the company have more driver guides, as well as those who could lead outdoor activity tours.[3] Responding to this trend, Atsuko-san, the female operations manager, actively started to look for outdoor guides.

Contrary to the company's conventional association of outdoor guiding with males, it was Chie who was hired as the first outdoor specialty guide at the RMT. She had a certificate of outdoor activity leadership from a Canadian college, which attested to her ability and reassured the managers that she was qualified to lead outdoor tours. Once the female guides started leading outdoor tours, the company received many letters and e-mails expressing how much tourists had enjoyed their experiences with the female guides. These favorable responses might have helped Matsuda-san feel more comfortable assigning women to outdoor activities. By 2000, Mari-san, Chie, Yoshiko, and some other female guides had securely established their positions as outdoor guides.[4]

Gender Play

A MASCULINE WOMAN

When I first accompanied Yoshiko's hiking tour, a female tourist looked at her dreamily and whispered to me, "She is so cool! She must have been very popular among girls if she went to a girls' high school." The tourist, who seemed to be a few years older than Yoshiko, was referring to the homosocial relationship expressed in the form of same-sex fantasy, well-observed in Japanese girls' high schools.[5] In this fantasy, students with masculine appearances are idolized by other, often junior, students. She talked as if she were a junior student chasing Yoshiko.

Yoshiko was in her late twenties, relatively tall and slender. She had stylishly cropped short hair and always wore a fleece jacket and khaki pants, even during her time off from work. Her tanned skin gave an impression that she was a very athletic and serious outdoor enthusiast. She spoke in a soft, calm voice and treated tourists in a highly courteous manner. Yoshiko's image as a "cool" masculine-looking woman, and the tourist's fascination with her should be situated in the Japanese popular subcultures of idolizing female masculinity. Nakamura and Matsuo (2003) point out that the particular forms of female masculinity have proliferated in various genres of popular culture in Japan, such as comic books, animation films and theaters, and they "create spaces where both female and male fans, regardless of their sexual orientations, can temporarily transcend their everyday gender expectations and roles" (59). In particular, the way Yoshiko attracted the tourist seems to have some commonalities with the attraction of male-impersonation actresses in Takarazuka, a popular Japanese all-female revue theater.

In her book on Takarazuka, anthropologist Jennifer Robertson (1998) argues that the actress playing a male role enacts the female fantasy of the ideal man. Takarazuka was founded in 1913 by Kobayashi Ichizō, a railroad tycoon who later became a cabinet minister. Kobayashi aspired to create a modern complement to Kabuki, traditional Japanese all-male theater, in which a male actor played an ideal woman. Robertson reports that Kobayashi wanted his male-role actresses to be "more suave, more affectionate, more courageous, more charming, more handsome and more fascinating than actual males" (17). She argues that in all-female theaters, male-role actresses have been much more popular than female-role actresses because they represent "a female body performing in a capacity that transgresses the boundaries of received femininity and masculinity" (82). As Robertson suggests, the male-role actresses transport the audience to a fantasy world beyond conventional gender distinctions and confinements. Furthermore, Nakamura and Matsuo points out that the aura of Takarazuka male impersonators derive from their fictitious ideal male image as they are "outstandingly handsome, pure, kind, emotional, charming, funny, romantic and intelligent"— that is, "the complete antithesis of the salaryman $oyaji^6$ stereotype of Japanese men" (63). They point out that the charm of male impersonators derives from the "fictional construct" (67), rather than truthfully copying the real men. The male impersonators lead the audience into a fantasy world, precisely because the masculinity is enacted by the female body that indicates the transcendence from the ordinary gender categories. Like a Takarazuka male-role actress, Yoshiko embodied the fantastical female masculinity that would invite tourists to free themselves from their ordinary mundane world.

Takarazuka was created at a time when the state-led Japanese version of modern gender discourses was permeated, as well as challenged, by the rise of the urban bourgeoisie. The Meiji government (1868–1912) attempted to reorganize the population by fixing gender categorization onto the human body and regulating family structure to fit the newly built, Western-modeled nation-state. In this process, fluid and ambiguous gender categories, as well as same-sex relations, were discouraged in order to privilege the idea of families constituted by heterosexual couples as the basis of the nation (Pflugfelder 1999). Fixing gender into rigid distinctions between male and female was also the basis on which notions of private and public were reorganized, with the family as a private and domestic realm for the heterosexual couple. In contrast to the previous idea of commoners' households functioning as both dwelling and work units that were shared not only by family members but also by apprentices and workers, the modern distinction separated "home" as a domestic realm from public workplaces, such as factories and office buildings. Thus, the creation of the modern family was also in accordance with the development of industrial capitalism (Uno 1991). A new form of family that privileged a heterosexual couple united by the ideology of romance became a site for producing modern subjectivity. The family became independent from the control and responsibility of the occupational, religious, and regional community and transformed into the basic unit of reproduction in the modern industrial nation-state (Ueno 1994).

In this transition, the debates over expected social roles and appropriate behaviors of dichotomized males and females proliferated, and these modern gender categories were translated in and enforced through the Meiji Civil Code. Accordingly, institutions such as girls' schools and the cultural products promoted in girls' magazines provided sites for people to enact the newly introduced notions of "woman" and "girl" (Kawamura 1993, 1994), and a distinct women's speech style was created (Inoue 2002, 2003). As Kawamura documents, girls' high schools (*jogakkō*) were a prime location for constructing the modern Japanese idea of womanhood and femininity by appropriating Western gender discourses (Kawamura 1993), and girls' magazines were the site for testing out and producing the newly introduced modern young women's identity through the notion of sisterhood (Kawamura 1994).

The subculture of schoolgirl's fantasy for masculine women that Yoshiko's hiking tour customer mentioned had developed in this context. In the late nineteenth to early twentieth century, girls' high schools were established for the upper class and the emerging urban, middle-class, who were privileged enough to send their daughters to high school. The girls' high schools at that time served as places to educate young women according to the state ideology of "Good Wife, Wise Mother" (*Ryōsai Kenbo*) and articulate and practice the modern idea of "woman." However, Kawamura (1993) argues that in the sanctioned space of the girls' school, the students produced a community with a certain degree of freedom and autonomy from the rest of the society, and the community provided the students with a refuge from the disillusionment of domestic life and male dominance in modern society. In this refuge, the students cultivated their own specific subcultures which emphasized the moral and aesthetic values of beauty and purity against worldly concerns, and the girls' homosocial "pure" friendships, uncontaminated by the presence of males and the dominant heterosexual productive and reproductive interests, were idealized. Often, sisterhood was expressed in the form of platonic same-sex love relationships, although the relationship between the friendship of sisterhood and lesbianism was ambiguous and hard to discern.[7] Although the state gender ideology disappeared from the postwar state discourse, in which the equality of both sexes was emphasized, the legacy of "sister" relationships in girls' high schools was still observable as the girls continued to negotiate their social position in contemporary society.

Yoshiko's performance entailed a genealogical trajectory of this long-standing negotiation of gender positioning. However, as expressed by Mr. and Mrs. Yamada, Yoshiko's charm was not merely an expression of the female fantasy of transcending gender binaries. Her performance as a Japanese woman who embodied idealized masculinity was also attractive as a sign of cosmopolitan subjectivity. As Kondo (1997; also see Ueno 1994) suggests, the modern Japanese construction of gender identity was also a story of Japanese men's struggle to stand in parity with their Western counterparts, to whom they constantly deferred as the feminized Other.

On the day of hiking with the Yamadas, while walking on the switchback trails, Yoshiko casually chatted with the couple. It was the second day of the consecutive day hikes for Mr. and Mrs. Yamada. Yoshiko knew that on the previous day they had hiked Iceline Trail in the neighboring Yoho National Park with her colleague Fred, a Japanese-speaking Canadian male guide. She thought that Mr. and Mrs. Yamada would have already heard many explanations of the flora and fauna and sensed that they would rather have time for reflection, instead of being saturated with more information. This opened the door for Mr. and Mrs. Yamada to have conversations about Yoshiko's experiences of moving to Banff. They were enchanted to see a Japanese woman who embodied the idealized subjectivity that Japanese men were blamed for not having achieved: independent, sophisticated, hardworking but not consumed by work and the company, knowing how to enjoy life through leisure, and confident while working in nature as an equal to a Canadian man.

AN ETERNAL CHILD

Enacting more-than-real, fantastical female masculinity was not the only way a tour guide served as a gender-ambiguous intermediary. Chie, the first guide in the RMT to obtain a Canadian certificate for outdoor activity leadership, acted as a mischievous child and gave the impression of being an asexual, ageless person. Chie was in her mid-thirties, but to many of her colleagues, her tireless bouncing movements on the trail, her curious eyes endlessly looking for something interesting, and her abrupt speaking style, created the impression of a preadolescent child.

Late one summer, I accompanied Chie's nature walk tour. On the way back to the hotel outside the park, Chie found wild raspberries and asked her customers to taste them. The customers were cautious at first.

Chie picked a berry and threw it into her mouth, saying, "Mmm . . . it's tasty!" The customers slowly ate the wild berries and found that they were not bad. As they walked, Chie found currants and other edible berries and asked the customers to try them all. The customers gradually became comfortable tasting the unfamiliar berries and were fascinated by the fact that the area was rich with wild food. Finally, Chie found soapberries and said, with a teasing smile on her face, "Well, you might not want to taste this one . . . but would you like to try it anyway?" The customers were already in the mood for a tasting adventure, so they picked the soapberries and put them into their mouths, then immediately made bitter faces and spit out the berries. Chie laughed and said, "See, I told you!"

This fooling act could have been problematic if the guide had not already established a trusting relationship with the customers. But the customers were delighted by this experience. Chie explained to them that bears love soapberries. Just thinking about bears and eating the same food as bears excited the customers. Through these playful experiences, Chie presented herself as a mischievous child and encouraged the customers to open up their senses to the natural environment.

Chie's gender performance could be interpreted according to Judith Halberstam's notion of "tomboyism." In her analysis of female masculinity, Halberstam explains, "Tomboyism generally describes an extended childhood period of female masculinity" (1998, 5). She suggests that Tomboyism represents adolescent girls' crisis of coming of age and their resistance to adulthood itself in a male-dominated society in which boys enjoy greater freedom and mobility than girls. According to Halberstam, tomboyism may be encouraged as a sign of independence and self-motivation if it is linked to a stable girl identity (6). While the tomboyish instincts of many girls might have been transformed into the assertiveness of a mature woman, in Chie's case, instead of remodeling her tomboyishness through maturity, she presented her gender ambiguity through the image of a prolonged childhood. With her ambiguous gender and age, Chie effectively invited the customers back to a nostalgic world, the days of childhood play.

A GIRL MEDIUM

Compared with Yoshiko and Chie, Hanako fashioned herself in a way that was rather unusual among female outdoor guides in the RMT. Although

Hanako also presented both feminine and masculine characteristics, her mixed-gender performativity was similar to that of a fighting girl in popular Japanese animated films—a cute-looking young girl fighting bravely to save the world.

Hanako was in her late twenties, although many tourists and her fellow guides thought she was much younger. She was short and small with long hair, and she appeared rather fragile, although she was as athletic as the other women outdoor guides. She loved rock climbing, snowboarding, and camping. But unlike the other female outdoor guides, she did not emphasize her athleticism through her appearance. Because she did not fit the image of an outdoor guide established by the company, at first Hanako had a hard time convincing Matsuda-san to let her work in that capacity, and she was assigned work that the company considered more suitable for a young, feminine-looking woman, such as assisting a wedding tour.

Later in the summer, however, Hanako began to be assigned entry-level jobs for outdoor guides, such as accompanying fishing, horseback-riding, and rafting tours. She enjoyed these tours herself "like a customer," no matter how many times she went. In these tours, she was excited to meet Canadian specialized guides, who opened her eyes to new ways of interacting with nature. In particular, she became friends with some of the fishing guides, whose perceptions of nature—shaped by rural backgrounds as farmers, ranchers, and sportsmen—were unique and new to Hanako, who had grown up in the urban environment of Tokyo. Her own enthusiasm for these tours enhanced the customers' excitement, and she learned the thrill of the stimulating interactions among customers, Canadian guides, and herself.

During the summer, Hanako left the company's accommodations and moved into a house with environmentalists who were working with a local environmental research group. Through her housemates and their friends, Hanako also was introduced to the Canadian environmentalists' approaches to nature, mostly from people with advanced educations and urban backgrounds. These approaches also differed from what she had learned through her friendship with rock climbers, campers, and fishing guides. She learned about the controversial environmental issues in and around Banff National Park, such as the construction of the Lake Louise Convention Center and the effect of this project and other development plans on the biodiversity conservation projects. Many environmental activists in her circle were also serious naturalists. She accompanied her friends' bird-watching and animal-tracking activities whenever possible, sometimes early in the morning before going to work, or in the evening after work. By enlarging her social network, Hanako learned different, often conflicting, approaches to nature.

In her second year, Hanako was assigned more hiking and animal-watching tours. Her animal-watching tour had an especially good reputation. In late August, when I accompanied Hanako's tour with a mother and teenage daughter, I was struck by the change in Hanako's conduct; the way she spoke was dramatically different from the previous summer. Hanako now spoke in a soft, low voice at a much slower pace. Before moving to the next site, she paused and quietly calculated where and when she would be able to see animals, as if she were communicating with them. She drove a van to Lake Minnewanka to meet a herd of bighorn sheep coming down to the road to lick the salt on the ground. Hanako referred to the sheep as "these children" (*kono ko tachi*) and said, "We are fortunate to see them so close. But actually, it is not good for these children to come down to the road." She explained to the customers how human use of the park changed the sheep's habitat, exposing them to the danger of being hit by a car or fed by uninformed visitors. She spoke as if she were a mother or an older sister of the animals, worrying about the human influence on them. Her poetic talk, the pauses in her speech, and the way she explained the landscape as if she were speaking for the animals created the impression of a girl medium or the heroine in a popular Japanese animated film by Miyazaki Hayao such as *Nausicaä of the Valley of the Wind*.[8]

In the film, Nausicaä is a princess warrior who represents both the strength of a brave warrior and the nurturing generosity of Mother Earth.[9] Nausicaä reflects Miyazaki's romanticized hope for a young girl as being innocent of and sheltered from the malice of modernization often associated with adult males. Like Nausicaä, Hanako performed the idealized characteristics of the girl's power as mediator: she was sensitive, attuned to nonhuman voices, and able to smooth over tensions and conflicts between nature and humans. Like Nausicaä, Hanako also enacted some elements formerly associated with males, such as courage, adventure, and technology, appropriating them to mix with her feminine characteristics. Hanako described the efforts of the national park and environmentalists to maintain ecological integrity, explaining to the customers how they conducted ecological research and had changed regulations based on findings from their research. Together with her own stories of adventure in various remote places in both Japan and Canada, Hanako played the role of a girl medium who mediated between the mundane and natural worlds.

The guiding practices of Yoshiko, Chie, and Hanako suggest that the charisma of some female guides came from their ambivalence and "in-betweenness." The ambiguous characteristics of female tour guides who straddled various sets of two worlds—male and female, adult and child, and human and nature—embody this otherworldly sense. With their in-between characteristics, female outdoor tour guides invited tourists to a world outside everyday life—one that the tourists wanted to experience in the natural landscape of Canada.

Neverland in Nature: A Guide's Community and Fictive Kinship

A tour guide's presentation of her identity was not merely a staged performance for entertaining tourists.[10] Yoshiko, Chie, Hanako, and others cultivated their subjectivities in their everyday interactions with friends and other people around them, and they negotiated their positions to find a space in their new environment in Banff. Central to the guides' performative construction of their subjectivities was the communal living situation in Banff. The guides created a loose, fluid, family-like community, often using fictive kinship terms.

There were several circles of these quasi-familial relations. The most visible and institutionalized site was the company itself, centered on Mr. Matsuda's family. Mr. Matsuda threw parties twice a year at his home: a summer barbecue and a New Year's Eve party. He invited employees to his large house in a quiet residential neighborhood, expecting them to arrive early and help prepare the food and do other chores, as well as clean up after the party. There was a strong sense of hierarchy based on seniority. The novice guides were expected to arrive first, stay late, and work harder. The apparent model for these events was the traditional extended family in an agricultural community. Mr. Matsuda's family functioned like the main family (*honke*) that offered food and space; in turn, the employees offered their labor as if they were the relatives who support the main family. Mrs. Matsuda served as the matriarch giving orders to the employees, who were expected to work hard under her control and strive to meet her expectations. Sometimes Mrs. Matsuda criticized employees when she found the juniors who were being idle and letting the seniors work harder. After the food was prepared, the employees intermingled and enjoyed the food and drink together with Matsuda's teenage children. At the barbecue, some would play in the backyard while others sat on the deck or in the living room and chatted. At the New Year's Eve party, they would watch the recorded *Kōhaku*, the annual year-end music show, which is traditionally viewed together at New Year's Eve family gatherings in Japan, and sing karaoke. In this ritualistic site of "company as family" (Kondo 1990), the Matsudas offered their employees the sense that they were members of this quasi-extended family.

In contrast to Mr. Matsuda's family, the less formal yet more immediate relationships were formed around Atsuko-san, the senior operations manager. One of Atsuko-san's jobs was to manage human resources for the company, but her care extended far beyond the official "management" of the employees. When she decided to hire a staff person, she would inquire whether the employee had come to Banff with his or her significant other and whether that person also needed a job. If they did, she would use her networks to find one. Atsuko-san also took care of housing arrangements and offered employees suitable rooms in the company accommodations. She always paid attention to the well-being of her staff, offered help, and did not hesitate to give stern advice and even discipline. Atsuko-san's care of her employees was not only for the benefit of the business. She often encouraged her staff to leave the company and move on if doing so was a better choice for their own pursuits in life, and she remained in touch with some of the former guides who had "graduated" from the RMT. In these ways, she consciously played the role of the guides' "mother" in Banff. She told me that she wanted to support the young people with adventurous spirits who had left their familiar environments in Japan and ventured to Canada to pursue their dreams or start a new life.

Another senior female, Mari-san, also played a significant role in setting the tone for the quasi-family relationships in Banff. Mari-san was an "auntie" for many of the guides. Even though both Mari-san and Atsuko-san were technically employees of the RMT, sometimes they had a stronger impact than Mr. Matsuda on the unofficial social relations in the company. Atsuko-san and Mari-san were close friends and were both slightly older than Mr. Matsuda, and both had worked with Mr. Matsuda since he started the company. Mari-san was respected for her knowledge, experience, and physical strength as a mountaineer and skier, not only within the company but in the Japanese guiding community in general. In fact, her reputation extended beyond the Japanese community, and she was often asked to work as a translator during official events in the national park. Backed by her professional ability and the broad trust she had gained, Mari-san was considered a moral authority for many of the guides. She also had a strong sense of righteousness and did not hesitate to criticize the policies and practices of the RMT or those of the national parks and other institutions. When the guides had a hard time making a decision, they often asked for Mari-san's opinion; they all seemed to understand that if "auntie" said something was good, then it was right.

While Mr. Matsuda, Atsuko-san, and Mari-san set the framework of quasi-familial relationships in the company's community, the younger guides created their own intimate relationships apart from the seniors. The company accommodations offered a physical site for the initial construction of their social world. Once the young guides were separated from their seniors, the company accommodations functioned like a camp or a communal residence in the age-grade system. The RMT owned four three-bedroom apartments in the town center and a large four-bedroom house next to Mr. Matsuda's home in the residential area. In these places, the same age group of people in their twenties and thirties resided communally, sharing household chores and meals. Sometimes the guides got together to study and exchange ideas for guiding. The living room often was a site for fun activities, such as celebrating somebody's birthday, gathering to watch a video, participating in a cooking contest or a haircutting party, and so on. Although each guide was given his or her own room, most of the guides spent minimal time in their rooms, and there was no clear sense of privacy. The guides also shared books and magazines, household tools, outdoor equipment, and cars. They enjoyed recreational activities together, such as hiking and skiing, and occasionally drove together to an Asian supermarket in Calgary for groceries. The communal living in Banff stood in stark contrast to the segregated nuclear family that the guides had experienced in Japan. A junior guide Shinohara Rei described the situation as "living in Neverland," a prolonged youth camp, evading the expected social norms and obligations of adults in Japan.

In this communal living situation, distinct from conventional family relations, the guides developed their own social world by playing with fictive kinship relations. For example, some of Yoshiko's male colleagues who were close to her called her *Yoshi nii*, or Brother Yoshi. Her roommate, Toda Tomoko, called Yoshiko *tōchan*, a colloquial term for a father. The rough tone of the term tōchan, as opposed to more formal and polite forms of *tōsan* or *otōsan*, connotes a close-knit, egalitarian relationship among family members and the less authoritative status of a father in a lower-class family. The term tōchan could refer to either father or husband, and Tomoko sometimes played as if she were Yoshiko's daughter or wife. For example, when Tomoko had to leave early from a gathering that Yoshiko was not attending, she used Yoshiko's jealousy as an excuse and said, "I must go home soon because tōchan would complain if I come home late" (*Hayaku kaeranaito, uchi no tōchan urusai kara*). Their friends played along with their quasi-familial relationship. Often, their friends asked Tomoko about Yoshiko by saying, "How is your tōchan doing?" (*Tōchan doshiteru?*). Although Yoshiko's social role was masculine, that is not related to her sexuality. Yoshiko occasionally talked with me and other colleagues about her fantasy of having a boyfriend.

This quasi-familial relationship and fictive kinship functioned as a social safety net for the Japanese guides who did not have "real" family nearby and had not established social networks in Canada. Yet more than merely serving a functional purpose, the playful, loose, and temporal nature of their "family" relations provided the guides with a new foundation upon which they could reconstruct their subjectivity. The guides used the conventional categories of family and kinship terms, such as "father," "mother," "aunt," and "brother," yet with their playful usage, they created a space for imagining alternative social relations and shifting away from the conventional meaning of these terms.

Gender Trouble in Nature

The guides' cultivation of personalities was their response to the dominant gender discourses in their home societies. As a consequence of this negotiation, they all insisted on how "unnatural" femininity was—not only the construction of what counted as female or male but also the binary framework of categorizing human beings according to a gender/ sex scheme. Rather, they suggested that ambiguous in-betweenness was natural. The everyday lives of these guides, especially women like Yoshiko, Chie, and Hanako, suggest a discrepancy between the contemporary Japanese dominant gender discourse and the unofficial version with which people make sense of their everyday lives. Conventional gender discourse attempts to naturalize the clear division between male and female. But the guides' actual everyday interactions suggested that such divisions do not always fit the way people understand their relationships with others.

Yoshiko told me about several occasions when male customers treated her as a male, especially when she drove a van to pick up customers at the airport. When she introduced herself, she usually clarified her gender to customers by saying, "In case you are wondering, I am a woman. Sorry if I confused you." The customers would usually take her remark as clowning around, and it would lead to ice-breaking laughter. Most customers, especially women, delightedly accepted her as a masculine woman. But some male customers, even after Yoshiko clarified her gender as a masculine woman, insisted on treating her as a man and referred to her as "he." Yoshiko was not sure whether the male customers' responses reflected their resistance to accepting her as a woman or their acceptance of her unique character.[11] In either case, the male customers' insistence suggests that choosing a gender category was not necessarily based on a biological body, but on a person's social role and position in everyday interactions.[12]

Although Yoshiko talked about her desire to have a boyfriend, she did not want to be feminine in order to attract men. She felt that it was "natural" for her to dress and behave the way she did. She said, "I'm looking for a man who accepts me as I am, the way I act naturally." Yoshiko was conscious that her gender performance did not conform to dominant Japanese gender norms, but she considered her androgynous appearance as natural; for her, presenting a feminine image would be artificial.

Like Yoshiko, Chie insisted it was natural for her not to show feminine gendered markers. When relaxing and chatting among colleagues in the company's guide room, older male guides often teased Chie about her boyish appearance and rough mannerisms. They asked repeatedly, "Hey, Chie, you are a woman, aren't you? Then why don't you act more feminine-like?" Chie responded with a mock-confrontational attitude, saying, "Feminine-like? I don't know what you mean. Leave me alone!" The joking manner of both the male guides and Chie suggested that the male guides did not intend to rewrite her as a feminine woman but rather attended, in the spirit of a willing audience, Chie's gender performance that reconfirmed her boyishness. The effect of the male guides' mock criticism was ambivalent. They reinforced the conventional binary gender norms, but they also accepted Chie's ambiguous gender.

In my interview, when I tried to understand how she had developed her unique character, Chie was obviously frustrated by my questions because the answer was so obvious to her: it was natural. Chie almost lost her temper and told me, "I don't know why I am like this! I was born this way, so nobody could help it. It is not a big deal for me, being either a man or a woman. For me, it is natural to be like this!" Chie later explained to me that femininity was something she considered *mendokusai*—a term used to describe a hesitant feeling toward something that required an effort. In fact, Chie's short temper and frank expression of her emotions were considered to be a sign of childishness by her colleagues. By acting as a mischievous and short-tempered child, Chie refused to assume the position of a sexually mature woman.

For her part, Hanako was quite conscious that her appearance as a charming young woman attracted people. Yet even Hanako told me that she sometimes felt it was mendokusai to act in a feminine manner. Since she came to Banff, she had climbed many mountains with her male friends, who helped her gain the fundamental skills in that sport. Although she was grateful to her male friends, gradually she started to develop a desire to climb with women. She explained to me that men loved to teach or help her as a woman, and she enjoyed being helped. She had come to realize that sometimes she had unintentionally acted girlish because impersonating a young, feminine Japanese woman brought her social benefits, such as friends who helped her climb mountains. Yet sometimes she was tired of impersonating femininity and wanted to rid herself of her habitual gender play. She thought that by climbing mountains with women (and without a male audience), she could remind herself of who she really was.

What Yoshiko, Chie, and Hanako highlighted was the "drag" aspect of gender construction. As Judith Butler argues, these female guides revealed that "gender is a kind of persistent impersonation that passes as the real" (1990, viii). The dominant Japanese gender discourse that attempts to inscribe femininity onto a particular anatomical body type is an institutionalized drag that makes gender inscription look natural. Butler observes that a drag queen's performance destabilizes the very distinctions between the natural and the artificial, depth and surface, and the inner and the outer through which gender discourse operates.

Drag is not the imitation of gender, but it does dramatize the signifying gestures through which normative gender itself is established. It reveals the persistent effort required to make normative gender look natural. Being female is not a "natural fact" but a cultural performance.

The RMT managers' official narrative that insisted on the gendered division of labor, the perpetual surveillance of guides' appearance, and the constant reminders to conform to the dominant Japanese gender norm reveal the unnaturalness of gender implemented by translating the gender norms developed in the process of modern capitalist nation building. Gender distinctions appeared and operated as nonfiction only when they were constantly performed in accordance with other institutionalized practices that permeated everyday life. Thus, for the guides who had been uprooted from Japan and transplanted to another environment in Banff, the assumed naturalness of gender distinction revealed a vulnerability that would easily fall apart unless a person was constantly reminded and ordered to perform.

In tour guides' gender construction, two different systems of gender categorization operated simultaneously. First, as Butler suggests, tour guides' everyday performances indicate that gender is a performative repetition that produces a reality effect—that there exists a naturally materialized entity called woman—which disguises its discursive construction.[13] Second, a gender category is also a name for a social role that positions a person in relation to others, regardless of his or her physical features or own identification. To the male customer who insisted on referring to Yoshiko as "he," although she identified herself as a woman, Yoshiko's declaration based on her anatomical body did not matter. Yoshiko did not perform in feminine drag, but rather impersonated an ideal courteous masculine character. Yoshiko's act of driving him from the airport to the hotel was not surprising as Yoshiko's impersonation matched with the role she played.[14] So, Yoshiko was a "he" in his categorization in this tourist encounter.

Nature and City

The guides' gender performances were a response to the modern production of subjectivity in which the gender/sex categorization system plays a central role. When explaining their gender identities, Yoshiko, Chie, and Hanako—each in her own way—narrated their stories in relation to the distinction between city and nature: the first as a place of enacting gendered modernity, and the second as a space where gender distinctions could be upheld, however temporarily. Their narratives associated femininity with the formality of urban settings. In this sense, the image of Banff as a base camp of the Canadian Rocky Mountains was significant. In their narratives, even though Banff had cosmopolitan conveniences, it was still not a city (*machi*) or urban (*tokai*). In their cognitive mapping, a city was a place where people needed to perform artificial and normalized gender roles; in nature, such gender markers were out of place. Even Hanako and other feminine-looking guides considered it out of place to wear makeup and skirts, which they did only when they wanted to indicate formality at work or socialize with men in a dance club, both of which were rather exceptional settings in their perception of what kind of place Banff should be. In everyday life in a natural place like Banff, they felt it was unnatural to deploy gender markers. To many women guides, Banff served as a space that provided distance and the opportunity to reflect critically on assumed gender roles.

Yoshiko's, Chie's, and Hanako's experiences differed from those of the women documented in Karen Kelsky's (2001) analysis of Japanese women overseas in earlier historical periods. Kelsky argues that women with career aspirations who find glass ceilings in Japan venture to the "West," mainly to the United States. Through their efforts to achieve upward mobility, these "internationalist women" sometimes eroticize white men and seek out romantic relationships with them to gain entry to the Western world. Alternatively, Kelsky's historical materials suggest that in their search for coalitions with Western women, Japanese internationalist women often submit to the Western women's patronizing desire to help them. Through these activities, Japanese internationalist women ironically help construct the Orientalist discourse of the liberal West versus the oppressive East.

Like Kelsky's internationalist women, Yoshiko, Chie, and Hanako told me about their dream of living outside Japan. But in their narratives, the East/West dichotomy was submerged under the nature/city dichotomy, at least in their own expressions. When I asked them in individual interviews whether they had any fascination with the West, each guide paused as if she had never consciously thought about her motivation within this framework. It seemed not to be an issue for them. Yoshiko explained that the criteria she used when she searched for a destination were, first, a place where she could concentrate on skiing; second, a safe place to live; and, third, a place where it would be easier to obtain a visa to work legally in order to pursue her adventure of living and working outdoors. She said that the reason she loved living in Banff was "because I feel that I am living on the earth, surrounded by the mountains, forests, lakes, and fresh air." What was at issue was whether the place gave her a sense of living on the earth, not in a man-made environment.

There is, of course, a long legacy of Japan's relations with "the West" that shapes Yoshiko's sense of safety and proximity living in an English-speaking North American country, as promoted through the formal education system and popular media, such as Ōhashi's television programs. Also, the working holiday visa system that encouraged many young Japanese to come to Canada can be interpreted as a product of Japanese elites' longtime efforts, since the late nineteenth century, to make Japan a modern nation-state according to Western standards and in parity with its Western counterparts. The legacy of the influence of "the West" is still predominant in shaping the lives of Japanese, including the tour guides in Banff. However, it seems to me that in their struggles to negotiate gender identities, the distinction between nature and city was more foregrounded. Their narratives and performances show us an alternative to the gendered mappings of the East versus the West shared by earlier generations of women.

Hanako, who studied feminist sociology and psychology in university, maintained that it was Westernization that promoted strict gender distinctions in Japan. If modern industrialization was the drive for a gendered division of labor in the household, and the household as a domestic realm was detached from public realms such as factories, corporations, and bureaucratic offices in this process, then Western-modeled modern nation-state building through industrialization was the origin of the confinement of women in the domestic realm. Yet, although she was critical of the Western influence on Japanese constructions of a gendered division of labor, Hanako did not care whether her own search for identity and place was in the West or the East. What mattered to her was whether she could find a place to support herself. She said, "Wherever it was, I was looking for a place where I could feel that I am standing on the earth on my own feet."

Another difference between Kelsky's internationalist women and the Japanese outdoor guides in the RMT was that, like many outdoor enthusiasts in the Rockies, these women were indifferent to upward mobility. In contrast to internationalist women who sought to climb a social ladder according to the middle-class value of upward mobility, these women guides were instead reacting against or escaping from the middle-class norms of accumulating personal property and pursuing individual material or financial success. These women had decided to leave relatively secure office work in Japan and live in Banff to play in the outdoors, even though doing so exposed them to financial insecurity. In a sense, they were already embodying modest but self-fulfilling "affluent" lives—what Ōhashi promoted as a dream for middle-class, middle-aged salaried workers—without associating the source of "affluence" in the geographic imaginary of the West. Instead of escaping from the oppressive Orient, Chie, Yoshiko, and Hanako seemed to be reacting against and escaping from the modern Western civilization as an imaginary source of industrialization and gender/sex taxonomy whose reach of power had extended to Japan.

In this sense, Banff's Japanese community provided a comfortable space for women like Yoshiko, Chie, and Hanako. Banff did more than give them a sense of being close to the mountains, where they could pursue their love of the outdoors. This cosmopolitan, transient mountain town where people come and go from many parts of the world also provided a sense of living on the earth. In addition, they found that Banff's Japanese community was an in-between place, a sort of a temporary refuge from normalized gender discourses in both Japan and Canada—away from Japan yet not integrated into mainstream Canadian society. Standing in this ambivalent in-between place, they were triggered to performatively construct their subjectivities alternatively to the modern Japanese and North American constructions of gender. Yoshiko embodied the modern masculine subjectivity, only performed by a female body as an idealized form, yearned for but not attainable in a Japanese male body. Chie invited nostalgia for an asexual body by evoking the imagination of a time before the reach of the modern trouble of fixing the binary gender categories. Hanako, like Nausicaä, enacted an alternative subjectivity to masculine modernity when the disillusionment of modernity brought by environmental destruction led people to idealize the girl's power of mediating between different worlds.

The trouble of nature at the beginning of the twenty-first century is not so much how to rationalize it by fixing the categorization, but how to correct the consequences of rationalized management. In the nineteenth and twentieth centuries, the question of nature was centered on how to govern reproductive practices through the transformation of the human body into an object of the medical gaze and how to transform natural surroundings into resources. Today, the trouble of nature has to do with remedying the consequences of modernity—the materialization and exploitation of nature. The problems are manifested in the forms of overindustrialization, global environmental decay, and the isolation of human beings from nature. These problems are also tied to the rigid categorization of human bodies as the basis of managing their productive and reproductive abilities. The gender performance of the female outdoor guides reflected the ambivalent reflexivity to modernity, operating in the in-between space of male-female and human-nature. The guides' performances simultaneously invoked a sense of nostalgic longing for a world before the problems of modernity prevailed and hinted at alternative futures, worldviews, and possibilities.

5 | The Interpretation of Nature

On the fresh snow covering the frozen Bow River, footprints of elk and humans crisscrossed, the elk's appearing first, followed some time later by the humans'. A few days later, more footprints, both elk and human, appeared. The trajectories of steps merged and diverged. The repetition of similar prints created a recognizable trail. Sometimes a set of footprints went off and created a new trail, weaving and irregular, but the path created by the overlapping footprints was mostly linear, a direct route from one side of the river to the other. Even on the main trail, however, no two sets of prints were exactly the same. Some steps looked as if they traced the previous ones, but there were always slight gaps. The aims of these steps seemed to be shared—to cross the river. Yet, things seen and experienced by the carriers of these steps might be incommensurable. Like the footprints in the snow, the ways people interpreted nature in Banff converged and diverged. Like the crisscrossing footprints, the convergence of various practices of nature interpretation simultaneously highlighted the incommensurability between them.

In this chapter, I examine the way in which Japanese tour guides engaged in the national park's new guide accreditation program administered by the Mountain Parks Heritage Interpretation Association (MPHIA—pronounced as "em-fia"). The program reflected the neoliberal reforms in park management that resulted in the work in the national park being outsourced to the commercial sector. It was commonly understood among those in the guiding business that MPHIA had been formed in response to the national park's budget cuts of the 1990s. Instead of continuing to hire their own nature interpreters, the park was increasingly outsourcing this work, and the park administrators wanted to standardize the training these commercial guides received. It was MPHIA's job to provide such training. With this new policy, the commercial guides were expected to tell the stories of nature as if they were national park interpreters.[1]

The accreditation program emphasized the importance of nature interpretation as a part of environmental stewardship. As a critical response to environmental destruction, the concept of "environmental stewardship" had been developed in conservation circles in English-speaking countries in the 1970s and had gradually gained currency since then. As the term "stewardship" indicates, the concept has its roots in the Judeo-Christian theology of human responsibility toward God's creation and has been developed by combining the theological tradition with the modern notion of citizens' responsibility and scientific rationality (see, e.g., Passmore 1974). At the turn of the twenty-first century, environmental stewardship had been employed in various conservation projects as a key strategy to educate citizens and to emphasize their responsibility in protecting the natural environment.

The version of environmental stewardship promoted by MPHIA reflected this trend in conservation movements, yet it entailed another layer of reshaping people's subjectivities: it aimed to teach the responsibility of "locals" and to transform people from transient transnational or translocal workers into "local" residents of a national park. The foundation of MPHIA's program was the deployment of the "sense of place," attained by translating nature's language based on ecological scientific knowledge. The program was designed with the idea that ecological science was the basis of understanding nature's language; as environmental stewards, guides should be able to translate nature's language into human language by learning ecological science. In this process, the transparency and universal applicability of ecological knowledge were assumed.

For Japanese tour guides at Rocky Mountain Tours, the MPHIA program posed another challenge, another rite of passage that required them to reshape their subjectivities yet again. After leaving Japan, the guides were urged to strip off their worker subjectivities as members of Japanese workplace communities and become transnational flexible laborers. This time, the guides were asked to transform their subjectivities into something like para-agents of Canada's national park, who interpret nature to tourists and pass the park's message of environmental stewardship on to the tourists. The neoliberal reform shifted the responsibility for communicating and educating national park visitors from the state to the commercial sector. This shift required the workers to internalize the norms and values of the state agency. Meanwhile, international tourism relied on immigrants and transnational workers to effectively communicate with the foreign tourists.

The Japanese guides' experiences raised a serious question about the assumption of the universal applicability of the park's notion of ecology and environmental stewardship. What is striking about the Japanese engagement is that this question emerged in the very process of their serious commitments in participating in this initiative, not in challenging the park's authority or in resisting the accreditation program. Rather, in the midst of Japanese guides' efforts to learn the national park's ecological language, a strong sense of difference emerged. After the initial tension, the Japanese guides and managers, who were eager to learn the national park's notion of ecology, enthusiastically engaged in the program. However, even after obtaining a good amount of "accurate" information and learning details about the ecosystem, many Japanese guides struggled to perform MPHIA's style of nature interpretation. In particular, they faced obstacles in passing the oral exam even though they were tested in the Japanese language. This posed a puzzle not only for the examinees but also for the examiners and instructors. The Japanese guides' participation in the accreditation program revealed discrepancies of worldviews that locate humans in relation to nature. What became apparent through the collaborative effort between MPHIA instructors, examiners, and Japanese tour guides studying to pass the exam was that knowledge about nature was in fact socially and culturally embedded much deeper than they had assumed. Specifically, what highlighted this difference was the notion of nature interpretation itself.

This chapter examines how the Japanese tour guides participated in the park's accreditation program against the background of neoliberal reform of national park management, and how they translated the idea of the "translation of nature's language." Through this examination, I will explore the complex dynamics of knowledge translation and how the guides' participation in this program shaped the way they construct their subjectivities.

Doing Business in a National Park

Winter was a quiet season for the guide business in Banff. At the RMT, there were only a handful of ski or snowboard guide requests each day. There were occasional odd tours to assist—winter school excursions or trips for businesspeople, magazine reporters, or television crews— but regular leisure tours were scarce. For some Japanese guides, winter was the time to rest after a busy summer; many went skiing or snowboarding or traveled to other parts of Canada and the rest of the world. Some ski enthusiasts worked as instructors at one of the three ski resorts in the area. Others migrated elsewhere to find seasonal jobs. Some went to Yellowknife in the Northwest Territories to fill the growing demand for Japanese-speaking guides on tours to view the aurora borealis. Others went back to Japan for temporary work, mostly unrelated to guiding, such as jobs as store clerks.

It was my weekly custom on winter afternoons to visit the RMT office before it got too dark and cold. During the summer, after delivering customers to their hotels or to the airport, the guides had to stop by the office every evening to pick up their file for the next day's tour; in winter, a weekly visit was sufficient. One afternoon in January 2001, I walked to the office from my apartment on the other side of the frozen Bow River. I opened the door, expecting to find the office as quiet as the street outside, but as soon as I stepped in, Atsuko-san, a manager, greeted me in an unusually loud and excited voice: "Ah, Satsuka-san! Have you heard about the meeting last night? It was quite a scene!"

Atsuko-san went on to tell me about the MPHIA members' meeting that had been held in town the night before. Established in 1997, MPHIA was a nonprofit organization for tour guides and guide companies, and it provided a lecture series to help commercial guides working in the park to improve their skills and knowledge. The association's activities had been developed as part of the Banff Bow Valley Heritage Tourism Strategy, a collaborative initiative undertaken by the national park, the town of Banff, and the business sector. The Heritage Tourism Strategy was designed in response to concerns about the environmental degradation of the area and to promote a sustainable tourism that aimed to balance human usage and environmental preservation. To this end, the strategy aimed to educate transient tourist industry workers and turn them into responsible "stewards" of the heritage of Banff National Park, in part by enhancing their "local knowledge" of nature. The strategy also recommended introducing a guide accreditation system in order to raise the quality of the guiding business in the national park. The national park placed a moratorium on the mandatory guide accreditation system until MPHIA could develop a relevant accreditation program. Therefore, although MPHIA courses were voluntary at that point, people in the guiding business knew that the park and MPHIA were working toward imposing tighter controls on the guides' knowledge at some time in the near future. (Although the standard pronunciation of the association's acronym was "em-fia," some people pronounced it "mafia," alluding to the organization's strong influence on the park's regulations and its implicit control over the guiding business.)

At the MPHIA members' meeting, attended by independent guides and guide company managers, representatives of the association announced their plan to lift the moratorium and to implement the guide accreditation system: starting in April 2002, in order to renew their business licenses for hiking, skiing, and snowshoeing activities within the national park, tour businesses would be required to have two-thirds of their guides accredited by MPHIA. To get the required Professional Level interpreter accreditation, a guide would need to pass a written and oral exam, and the MPHIA recommended that guides take its intensive courses to prepare for the exam.

According to Atsuko-san, those who attended the meeting had reacted furiously to the proposed requirement. "It was really like the mafia coming to town!" she joked, referring to citizens' movements in Japan to stop the yakuza (the Japanese mafia) from opening offices in their communities. The attendants complained that they had not been given enough notice, and they were angry at not being consulted. Atsuko-san mimicked a long-term resident who had yelled at the MPHIA representative, a young woman who had moved to Banff only recently: "How long have you been here? I have been here for thirty years doing my business. Why all of a sudden do I have to be told to take an exam to show how much I know about this place?" Atsuko-san told me that one of the mountain guides was particularly frustrated. He had earned a certification from the Association of Canadian Mountain Guides (ACMG),[2] an organization that was established in 1963, with the encouragement of the national park, to ensure visitors' safety during their mountaineering experiences. According to Atsuko-san, the mountain guide was angry that the national park had now created another guide association and was asking him to spend more time and money on top of the large sum he had already spent.

A guide-company manager herself, Atsuko-san was sympathetic to these Canadian guides' complaints. She shared their annoyance at the park's changing regulations. Yet she also said she felt sympathy for the young woman who had been sent to the meeting as a representative and had to explain the decisions of higher-ranked park officials and MPHIA executives. Atsuko-san was sorry to see her being yelled at by long-term residents while trying to explain MPHIA's plan as a beneficial one for the park's future.

Atsuko-san's sympathy for the MPHIA representative might have reflected her own experience in the meetings among Japanese tour operators. Foreseeing the upcoming lift of the moratorium on guide licensing based on the MPHIA accreditation requirements, about twenty Japanese tour operators in Banff had held several meetings since 2000 to discuss a possible collective response to the new requirements. Atsuko-san, who had been in contact with MPHIA executives, volunteered to take the role of communicator between MPHIA and the Japanese tour operators. In the Japanese meetings, Atsuko-san found herself a target of accusations, grilled as if she were a representative of MPHIA.

The main concerns raised by the Japanese tour operators centered on fairness, expressed as issues of language and cost. The MPHIA course, a condensed version of the national park's interpreter's training, consisted of five sections: (1) interpretation skills, (2) history, (3) geology, (4) ecology, and (5) national park management. The professional interpreter's exam included a three-hour written test and a five-minute verbal presentation. To obtain MPHIA Professional Level accreditation, a guide had to have three years of work experience in Banff and to score higher than 70 percent on the exam. The Japanese managers worried that the information contained in the MPHIA course would be too technical and sophisticated for the commercial guides. They were concerned that their guides lacked the academic background of the national park interpreters, who had university or even graduate degrees in environmental sciences or communication. Some commercial guides had higher educational backgrounds, but the hiring criteria of most commercial guide companies were based more on hands-on experience and knowledge of the techniques of outdoor activities, and on the interpersonal skills necessary to conduct tours smoothly. In particular, the Japanese managers worried that it would be an extra burden for their employees to have to learn and be tested on this technical information in English. The cost for the proposed new MPHIA course and exam, about Can $225 (approximately US$150 in 2001), was also a serious issue for the Japanese guiding community, especially because of the guides' unstable visa statuses in Canada. This was not a sum of money that individual guides had readily available, nor was it necessarily an investment that the guide companies were willing to make, since many guides were on six- to twelve-month work visas with no guarantee of renewal. The fact that many Japanese guides had to leave Banff during the winter to find jobs elsewhere also put them at a disadvantage, as many MPHIA courses and exams were scheduled for the winter off-season.

Some old-timers in the Japanese tourism community even speculated that the whole idea of guide accreditation was discriminatory. They argued that among the foreign-language tours, only Japanese guide companies would be affected by this new policy because of their unique practice of relying on locally based Japanese-speaking guides. Other major foreign-language tours, such as those from Germany, Taiwan, and Korea, often hired "through guides" who did not live in Banff and therefore were not subject to being tested for their local knowledge. A few Japanese operators even saw the specter of racism in the new requirement. In the 1980s, fueled by the fear that Japanese businesses would take over North America, anti-Japanese cartoons and letters had been published in local and regional newspapers. Some operators claimed that hate slogans had been painted on Japanese tour vans. The heightened hysteria still haunted some Japanese in Banff.

Although the Japanese managers' responses seemed reactionary on the surface, their strong concerns about "unfairness" reflected the issue of how the transnational workers were treated in this neoliberal shift of national park management and in the new configuration of the state-market complex. By outsourcing the national park's guiding service to commercial businesses, the park was requiring the commercial guides to play the role formerly conducted by the national park employees. It was an ironic situation for some of the guides who had unstable resident status to act as if they were the agents of the Canadian state. Many of them had been admitted to live in Canada with work visas that required annual renewal. Quite a few of the guides had been struggling to obtain their landed immigrant status, as their application processes did not necessarily go smoothly and some had to reapply after their applications were declined. The process not only required time, labor, and money but also had psychological effects that imposed prolonged anxiety on the applicants. The initial uneasiness expressed by some of the Japanese managers and guides reflected this situation in which transnational workers were required to transform themselves as national subjects without the guarantee of the rights and status associated with the role they were expected to play.

Before formulating any formal collective response to the new requirement, the Japanese tour company managers decided to take the MPHIA course themselves, partly to see what it was like before asking their employees to take it and partly because, given that the MPHIA would launch the program anyway, they needed to increase the percentage of MPHIA-accredited guides in their companies by counting themselves in that number. After this January meeting, MPHIA offered its first five-week evening course. Many managers who attended the course had favorable responses despite their initial concerns. At the subsequent tour operators' meeting, they recommended that the others take it. They said that even though they found the content challenging and not directly applicable to their guiding style, it was a good learning experience with high-quality course content and enthusiastic instructors.

Once the Japanese managers were satisfied about the MPHIA course content, they concentrated their strategy of addressing the unfairness on the issue of the "language barrier." They requested that Japanese guides be allowed to take the exam in Japanese, arguing that the effectiveness of their skills needed to be evaluated in the language they actually used in their work. The association agreed: the courses would be offered in English, but the Japanese guides were allowed to choose whether to take the exam in Japanese or English. This move on MPHIA's part softened the Japanese managers' attitudes and relieved their anxiety over unfair treatment, even though the issues of cost and timing, as well as how to fairly regulate the activities of nonlocal guides who were traveling from other areas, still had not been resolved. At the RMT, the management was reluctant to cover the cost but recommended that the guides take the course at their own expense. Most of the guides who had worked at the RMT more than three years took the course in 2001.

One significant factor in the managers' conversion was a sense of "inclusion" in Banff's local guide community. Given that Japanese alienation from the rest of the local population had been a recurrent concern in town, it was significant for Japanese managers to have a shared site for learning and to be able to participate in it as equal members of the community. Fundamental to this sense of inclusion was the new idea of "localness" that Banff's Heritage Tourism Strategy emphasized.

What counts as local knowledge in Banff was under contestation in this tourist town whose population consisted of a large proportion of transient service industry workers. The notion of local knowledge promoted by MPHIA was unconventional because it emphasized traveling and ecological knowledge based on park scientists' research, rather than the conventional anthropological understanding of local knowledge that is often associated with the indigenous knowledge or vernacular knowledge embedded in a community, in contrast to the expert scientific knowledge. The assumed universal applicability of scientific knowledge invited the Japanese to participate on an equal footing in this creation of local knowledge. Ecology gave them a vocabulary for community participation.

Cosmopolitan Local Knowledge
TRAVELING LOCALS

The sense of "local" as it was defined by MPHIA is the unique creation of Bob Sandford, a coordinator of the Heritage Tourism Strategy and MPHIA's history instructor. Sandford was a former park naturalist, as were many other MPHIA instructors, and is currently a historian of Banff and the Rocky Mountains. By the year 2000, he had published more than a dozen books on the Rockies, including one on Maki Yūkō's first ascent of Mount Alberta, and his books were widely read among tour guides.

In the MPHIA course, Sandford used history as a tool to understand the central predicament in Banff National Park since its beginning: the park was preserved for people to appreciate its natural landscape, yet human use of the park presents a threat to its ecological integrity. In addition to giving his version of Banff history, Sandford spent quite a long time explaining his idea of "local" and local responsibility. The unique features of Sandford's understanding of "local" were (1) that everyone in Banff comes from somewhere else, (2) that one can become a local by being transformed by the landscape, and (3) that accurate scientific information is the key to defining Banff's heritage. In an MPHIA handout Sandford stated: "Until very recently, there were not many people who were actually born in Banff. In the absence of a large local population, most of the people who lived in the park came from somewhere else."

This idea of "local," then, is not determined by birth. Indeed, Sandford's history of the region was a history of travelers—one that began with indigenous hunters and went on to include European fur traders, British expedition scientists, railway builders, horse handlers, and contemporary tourists. Through a genealogy of traveling, he narrated Banff's history in a way that allowed contemporary, transient tourist workers to trace their symbolic roots back to the indigenous peoples who came to hunt and find shelter in the area.

Sandford's rhetorical move was significant because although it was well known that indigenous peoples traveled to the area, there had been a rupture in conventional narratives between indigenous prehistory and the history of Banff that began with the European settlers. The standard narrative of the "discovery of Banff," as it had been told in many tours, books, and other presentations, was that three railway construction workers from the East Coast discovered the hot springs on their day off from work. Thinking that the hot springs could prove profitable, they claimed ownership of them. Their claim was challenged by the Canadian Pacific Railway, causing the federal government to intervene and settle the dispute by creating Canada's first national park, preserving the springs for the use of future generations of Canadians.

In his lecture, Sandford vehemently challenged this conventional narrative. He said, "One of the problems we have here is the notion of European exploration having more importance than the history of the predecessors. . . . I hear that three railway workers discovered hot springs in Banff. They did NOT!" He continued, "How can you tell, say, that the three railway workers discovered the springs, when Native people were here since before the Pyramids were built? Native people traveled here for five hundred generations. We've got this bias."

In *The Book of Banff*, Sandford states, "Though it would be difficult to tell from the current demography of Banff, the most prominent locals in the Bow Valley [in which Banff is located] were Native" (Sandford 1994, 14). He claims that these people were likely the descendants of migrants who made their way over a land bridge that crossed the Bering Strait. Mentioning archaeological studies, he points out that human beings have occupied the present-day Banff area for at least ten thousand years. The evidence of ancient campfires indicates the presence of "these seasonal visitors to the Rockies" (15). By thus narrating history to include indigenous people as the symbolic ancestors of traveling locals, Sandford provoked a new conception of the local that included those who had traveled to the area, like the Japanese guides to whom he was speaking.

COWBOY BOOTS ON A GLACIER

Sandford's expansive definition of the local did not mean that everyone who traveled to or lived in Banff could be considered a "true" local, however. The key to becoming local was the personal experience of rebirth. In his lecture, Sandford repeatedly emphasized that people in Banff became "local by choice" as they were transformed by the landscape. In the lecture handout, he states: "In Banff, landscape has always been seen as a powerful transformational force in human life. For generations visitors and locals in the Rockies have observed that in realizing the country they could realize themselves." He explains, "Overwhelmed by the grandeur of the landscape and captured by the ideal of wilderness and the unique wildlife symbolic of this wilderness, seasonal employees often stayed on just as they do today." At another point, he adds, "By coming to love where they live, these invading interlopers marvelously become locals by choice."

As an example of this local-making process, Sandford offered his own experience of personal transformation. He described the time he had walked on the glacier near the Columbia Icefield in a pair of cowboy boots, slipped, and fallen into a millwell, a hole in the glacier created by melted water on the surface. Falling into a millwell is dangerous because once one is drawn into the current under the glacier, it is hard to get out again, and staying in the icy water can cause hypothermia very quickly. As seen on the many cautionary signs that Parks Canada has placed on the toe of the glaciers, tragedies have happened to tourists who have fallen into the glacier's cracks. Sandford recounted that he fell under the ice and then was luckily pushed out of the snout of the glacier by the force of the water. He was literally washed away by the landscape.

Sandford told his audience that by immersing himself in the landscape and making some foolish and potentially dangerous mistakes like this one, he had realized the significant power of the place where he was living. Through this miraculous experience, Sandford amended his previous misconception, commonly held by Canadian urban youth, that Banff is a party town and began to realize the richness and power of the natural landscape. He elaborates on this point: "It is often a painful process, filled with setbacks and disappointments. You come. You make a few uncomfortable and even dangerous mistakes. You suffer. You fail. Something inside of you dies and something else is born. The landscape gets hold of you and somehow you grow slowly into its immensity. You begin to take the beauty personally. And gradually, any order less than the grand totality of the land seems small minded to you. The country has captured you and you call it home" (Sandford 1994, 11–12).

According to Sandford, the heritage that locals needed to protect was the landscape that had provided them with this kind of personally transforming experience. In other words, the heritage of the place was the accumulation and merging of the personal experiences of people who had traveled to the area. Such an amalgamation of personal experiences and the land necessarily made heritage elusive. In a lecture handout, Sandford wrote: "The Heritage Tourism Strategy does not presume to want to make everyone think the same way about our mountain heritage. It does, however, propose that we all may want to start with the same information as a basis for reassessing what is important about our heritage and that that information be, as much as is possible, accurate and relevant." Specifically, "accurate" information from scientific research on the park was integral. Sandford placed a particular emphasis on scientific knowledge, especially ecology and geology, which mediates diverse personal experiences and binds them into an elusive, yet collective, sense of heritage.

Within this framework of personal growth, Sandford also narrated the national park's changing policy. Just as he had become aware of the landscape by making the mistake of walking on a glacier in his cowboy boots, the administrators of the national park had become aware of the complexity of the park's ecological system through critical reflection on the past "mistakes" that the park had made, such as killing carnivores and extinguishing forest fires.

In sum, Sandford cleverly constructed Banff's cosmopolitan local knowledge around ideas of a long history of traveling locals, the elusiveness of "heritage," and the importance of scientific data to bind diverse landscape-human interactions. His story seductively invited transient workers to identify themselves as "local" and to take responsibility for becoming ecologically sensitive tour guides and environmental stewards. His invitation was highly attractive for many of the Japanese tour guides.

Ecology as Language

Among the MPHIA course offerings, Japanese participants were particularly fascinated by the lecture and field trip on ecology and geology. These were taught by James Walker, a former park scientist who managed his own environmental assessment company in Banff. Many of the Japanese tour guides I interviewed told me that they were captivated by James's ability to take the audience into a different world and to show them the dynamic relations between various inhabitants on the earth. The Japanese guides were used to explaining the ecological and geological formations of spectacular mountains and beautiful glacier lakes in their tours before taking James's course, but their tours tended to focus on the major landmarks. James opened their eyes beyond these spectacular landmarks and invited them to see how not-so-spectacular patches of land are related to the formation of those landmarks, and how the ordinary landscape is also full of interesting stories. Although the Japanese guides were daunted by the amount and depth of information James presented and felt it would be a challenge to digest and remember all that material for the exam, they were also enchanted by his interpretation of the natural landscape.

As a part of the course, James led an MPHIA field trip for about thirty Japanese guides. The focus of his interpretation was the interconnectedness of different elements in the natural world. He took the group to several familiar places, such as Bow Falls, Rundle Rock, and certain roadside spots off the old Highway 1. At these locations, James first directed the participants' attention to each piece that composed the landscape. He asked them to actually see and touch the segments of quartz, fossils, grass, or berries. Then he explained how these small pieces were connected to other pieces in the landscape of the Rockies. His story connected the millions of years of the earth's dynamism, from the sedimentation of the geological layers to the building of the mountains from plate collision and erosion by the glaciers in the ice ages, finally demonstrating how the plants brought life and experienced the forest's succession. With this ecological interpretation, these familiar places suddenly became a legible textbook of the earth's history.

At the end of the field trip, James took the group a few steps from the old highway into some aspen woods, where the ground was still covered by thick, grayish-brown grass. He asked the participants to identify what they found on the ground. The Japanese guides pointed out several short juniper shrubs. James asked if they could distinguish different kinds of junipers, and this led them to look more closely at various plants. The participants' eyes were soon glued to the ground, trying to look for diverse kinds of plants that shared this place. They noticed the differences not only among the junipers but also among the ordinary-looking weedy brown grasses, and they asked James to identify them. They were also excited to find the plants they knew well, such as wintergreen, emerging under the brown grass. At one point, somebody found a small purple orchid, about the size of a fingernail, blooming under the grass. James commented delightedly, "This is the first orchid I've seen this season," and everyone gathered around the flower. They stayed there for a while and discussed what kind of orchid it might be, describing the detailed features of the flower in order to locate the distinctive characteristics that would help identify the species. James's strategy of opening the participants' eyes to the diversity of species in the seemingly simple landscape of aspen woods was highly successful. Some participants were still looking at the orchid as James began to explain the landscape formation.

James's purpose in taking the group to the aspen woods was to explain how forest fires help preserve biodiversity. He explained how the fires had cleared the older forest of conifers, turning it into an open grass field that was succeeded by sun-loving aspens, and consequently the aspen woods provided a habitat for elk. As proof of the existence of the old conifer woods before the forest fire, James pointed out a large Douglas fir standing behind him. He hugged the tree, saying, "This is special. . . . This tree may be four hundred years old, and it has seen what has happened in this landscape." After explaining the significance of the tree, he added, "So, this tree is special enough to hug. And probably that's why developers call somebody like me a 'tree hugger.'" Nobody laughed at this joke. The participants nodded and looked at him as seriously as they had throughout the field trip. Given that his joke was not met with laughter, James kept talking in his serious instructor mode. He pointed out the scar on the trunk, told how this tree had survived the forest fire, and described how the fire had given life to the flowers they were fascinated to see on the ground. As soon as he finished his story and stepped back from the tree, the course participants walked up to the Douglas fir. A man put his hand on the trunk and looked up to the top of the tree. A woman patted it as if she were departing from a friend. A few men and women quietly hugged the tree as they left the spot.

Right after this field trip, I asked James to share his reflections, in particular, whether he had noticed any difference between the Japanese and other course participants he had taught. His first response was that he was frustrated by the "language barrier." He was not sure whether he had communicated his ideas clearly to the Japanese audience because the participants did not ask questions at the times he expected they would. He noted that it was challenging to explain complex issues in such a short course to an audience that did not necessarily have an academic background in environmental studies, and that often he needed to leave out some of the explanations he wanted to include. When he did this with English-speaking participants, they would usually ask questions about the missing pieces; the Japanese audience, however, had simply listened to him without actively responding. This lack of questions appeared to him as a lack of interaction, and without that interaction, he could not tell whether his lecture had made sense to the Japanese participants.

At the same time, however, James observed that the Japanese participants were "more tuned in to the fine details," saying that he was impressed by their fascination with the small orchid. He found that the Japanese participants especially liked plants and rocks, asking him to identify ones that were new to them, whereas English-speaking audiences were usually drawn primarily to animals. These differences in interest and response made him realize that the ways people connect with the landscape were much more fundamental than he previously thought. Because his graduate training included critical environmental studies, James already was aware of the diverse ways people perceive nature. However, observing the Japanese participants firsthand, he began to wonder about the specificity of the approach advocated by MPHIA.

For James, what particularly highlighted "cultural difference" was the Japanese participants' mimicking the action of hugging the Douglas fir. Unlike his English-speaking audiences, the Japanese did not laugh at James's self-mocking identification of himself as a "tree hugger." At first, James thought their lack of reaction was the result of the language barrier, but by the end of the day, it seemed as if the Japanese participants might have a deeper spiritual connection to the tree than could be described by the English term "tree hugger." He wondered if perhaps Japanese culture still maintained an aesthetic and spiritual connection between human and nonhuman that most of his English-speaking audiences did not have.

Although James was cautious about making any comments on "culture" because he knew he was not a cultural specialist, this realization of difference led him to reflect on his own North American "cultural baggage." James explained to me the contradictory North American attitudes toward the "wilderness," that is while North American civilization had largely removed the wilderness, in so doing it had simultaneously created a longing for it, for a power of nature that was beyond human control.[3] According to James, the North American approach to nature, which was more "scientific," reflected the history of moving the wilderness back from civilization so that people would not to have to compete with the power of nature. He speculated that the Japanese, in contrast, might have a much longer history of spiritual connection with nature, one that might be more easily recoverable from everyday life in their industrial society.

Reflecting on the cultural baggage that informed nature interpretation, James addressed the challenge in teaching nature interpretation to the Japanese participants. He told me, "Maybe a part of what might be a problem of interpretation is that we are imposing the cultural baggage on the interpretation rather than bringing something important from a different country and allowing them to facilitate their hike or whatever." James was conscious that a part of the interpreter's job was to be sensitive to the cultural baggage of both the audience and the interpreter, and to think about how the interpreter could provide the connection between the audience and the landscape. For example, he was aware that indigenous people would not express their appreciation in the same manner as he would; thus, insisting on his style of interpretation would be a problem. He said, "For me to impose my Western culture on them might ruin the experience for them. It might be better if I let them talk to me about the landscape, so they can use their own way of thinking." Similarly, he felt that if Japanese tourists did relate to the land by learning the names of things, and by gaining detailed knowledge of individual plants, this might be a good communication style to use with them, even though it was not recommended by the MPHIA course, which stressed the ecosystem approach and focused on the connection of various species, linked by cause and effect on a larger geographic scale.

Ironically, at the same time that James was becoming aware of the predicaments and challenges of communicating in the face of cultural difference, the Japanese participants were excited to be learning about ecology as a common language to communicate with their Canadian colleagues.[4] Together with Sandford's notion of "local knowledge," James's lessons in ecology and geology inspired the Japanese guides to recognize and embrace their roles as interpreters of nature in Banff, Canada's iconic national park. Moreover, for many of the Japanese guides, working as nature interpreters in Banff held a further significance beyond the park's importance within Canada. Banff is a central component of the Canadian Rocky Mountain Parks World Heritage Site, and Japan signed the Convention Concerning the Protection of the World Cultural and Natural Heritage in 1992. Since about 2000, "World Heritage Site" had become a buzzword in Japanese tourism that was actively used to boost the prestige of the Canadian Rockies as a tour destination. Kiyoko Sakata, a midcareer guide at RMT, told me that the MPHIA course had enhanced her sense of "pride and awareness" that she was "not just a guide" but a guide living and working in Canada's representative national park and a World Heritage Site. Learning how to speak the language of ecology was a reminder of the importance of her work as a nature interpreter in this special place of global significance.

Translating Nature's Words

In contrast to the sessions dedicated to geology and ecology, which fascinated the Japanese tour guides with their appeal of sharing a common language, the class on interpretation skills acutely highlighted the gap between Japanese guides and the MPHIA approach to nature. Both Canadian instructors and the Japanese participants noticed the discrepancy, and many of the Japanese participants claimed that the techniques learned in the interpretation skills class were not applicable to Japanese tours. The class instructors, Amanda Baker and Richard Smith, were former park interpreters, and at the time they designed the MPHIA course, they were working independently as nature guides. As experienced nature interpreters, like James, they were very sensitive to their audiences' reactions, and the Japanese response posed a challenge for them.

Among the key MPHIA terms, "nature interpretation" was one of the most difficult to translate into Japanese. Amanda and Richard explained to me that the use of this term was also relatively new in English; before settling on "interpreter," the park had used the terms "naturalist" and "heritage communicator" to designate the person charged with explaining the natural world to visitors. The newer term could be confusing even for English speakers, who were used to thinking of an "interpreter" as a translator between different human languages.

Amanda, Richard, and James each explained that interpretation was actually similar to language translation. Instead of translating human languages, however, nature interpretation involved translation from nature's language to that of humans. A book by Sam Ham titled *Environmental Interpretation*, widely circulated among the park interpreters and heavily used by Amanda in designing the MPHIA interpretation course, explains that "environmental interpretation involves translating the technical language of a natural science into terms and ideas that people who aren't scientists can readily understand" (1992, 3). Here, Ham equates "nature's language" with the "technical language of a natural science." He also explains that in the park setting, interpretation needs to have a message or a moral and should not merely be a transmission of facts and figures. The interpreter needs to get across "the points and meanings that he or she is trying [. . .] to communicate" (3) because the goal of interpretation is "to communicate [. . .] a message that answers the question 'so what?'" (4).

This notion of interpretation clearly includes a strong element of education. In discussing the foundations of his book, Ham cites Freeman Tilden's idea that interpretation is "an educational activity which aims to reveal meanings and relationships through the use of original objects, by firsthand experience, and by illustrative media, rather than simply to communicate factual information" (Tilden 1957, quoted in Ham 1992, 3). Ham compares a high school classroom lecture and a park's interpretation setting, explaining that, unlike the high school students, the tourists participate in a park tour voluntarily and with no external pressure, such as grades and exams, to force them to pay attention. Therefore, the interpretation must be fun and entertaining to capture and hold the interest of a voluntary audience.

Ham's book, whose subtitle is *A Practical Guide for People with Big Ideas and Small Budgets*, aimed to spread the technique of environmental education beyond North American parks, specifically to Central America. Amanda, who was struggling to design the interpretation course for commercial guides, found the book's simple message useful. The dilemma strongly felt by MPHIA instructors was that they had to translate the knowledge cultivated in the park's public sector setting to commercial guides in the private sector. As they explained to me, they needed to condense the equivalent of months of park training into a one-day lecture. They also had to design a course that would be meaningful for someone who might not have much relevant academic training and yet had already built his or her own style of communication based on hands-on experience in leading tours.

Within these constraints, in the MPHIA lecture, interpretation was boiled down to what Amanda and Richard considered to be the "basics." Borrowing from Ham, the lecture handout provided a simple definition of interpretation as "any communication process which aims to reveal meanings and relationships through firsthand experience with an object, artifact, landscape or site."[5] The handout then listed four key points: First, interpretation provokes the audience's interest. Second, interpretation has a theme; it conveys a message or a moral. Third, interpretation is pleasurable; it should stimulate the audience's curiosity and make the listeners want to stay and participate. Fourth, interpretation needs to be organized around the structure of an introduction, body, and conclusion. After this brief introduction to the concept of interpretation, the rest of the course focused on different techniques for keeping the attention of the audience, including eye contact, posture, and the use of visual aids and tools.

Lacking a Theme

In the oral exam that was held in March, the examiners (two non-Japanese-speaking MPHIA executives, one of the first two Japanese guides accredited by MPHIA, and one of the pioneer Japanese tour guides who had retired from the guide business) faced the acute difference in interpretation styles between what was encouraged in the MPHIA course and the actual presentations conducted by the Japanese tour guides and managers. Especially challenging for these examiners was how to evaluate the veteran guides who had already established a successful style for Japanese bus tours: the stories they told were interesting, and the information was accurate, but they did not impose a strong message or moral on their talks.

The following is the narrative that a veteran Japanese guide, Takagi Mamoru, or Takagi-san, presented for his oral exam (he spoke in Japanese; the translation is mine):[6]

What stands out to you in this view of the Canadian Rockies? Please take a look around. There are towering mountains with sharp cliffs, and a beautiful lake unfolding at their feet. You may have seen such landscapes or imagined what Lake Louise would be like. It is a treasure chest full of glaciers. This scenery is an emblem of the landscapes of the Rockies. It is said that such vistas were created by the erosion of glacial ice.

In Japanese, a glacier is a *hyōga*, a river of ice. When you look at Lake Louise, do you see the rivers? At Lake Louise, you can see the ice of its most prominent glacier, called the Victoria Glacier. The ice of the glacier forms from snow. As you can see, this huge mass of ice, even massive chunks that may be tens or hundreds of meters thick, all came from snow. As the snow accumulates, it gradually turns into ice.

If you step down on the snow, like this, the snow underneath changes into ice in the shape of your footstep. Let's imagine squeezing some into a ball in your hands. The snow will harden. For the ice of the glacier to form, the weight of the snow is needed. Only when the snow is tens of meters deep will the snow near the base begin to turn to ice. Even today, when we are no longer in an ice age, snow remains year round in this area on mountains higher than 3,000 meters. This is the snow line, or *sessen*. A perpetual snow forms as minuscule crystals, only a few millimeters large, repeatedly melt and then freeze. As layer forms upon layer, new glacial ice is born.

Now, this ice forms as many tens of meters of snow are compressed. Even more snow falls and sits on top. The snow grows thicker, as does the glacial ice. When the ice grows to a thickness of about 30 meters, it is said that there is a force of about 30 tons on each square meter at the base. When the ice is under this much force, the particles become uniform and assume a very unstable and fluid state. The force of gravity on the 30 or more meters of ice transforms into energy, and the ice begins to move.

If you want to define "glacier," it would be a large mass of ice that moves along the ground. In contrast, what remains beyond the glacier is called the *hyōgen*, the ice field, and is of a greater scale. It sits at higher altitudes and moves not just in one direction but in many.

A glacier will not move unless it is this large. It cannot flow. You may imagine hyōga as a river or stream that has frozen over, but a glacier is a frozen river of a completely different scale. Glaciers are immense.

Please look at the scenery to either side. The average width of this glacier, the Athabasca Glacier, is about one kilometer. It has a length of about 5 kilometers. You have been or will soon be on the ice of this massive glacier, which is 300 meters thick. Such a mass of ice carves the mountains as it moves along. It leaves behind giant valleys, U-shaped valleys. The melting water collects at the base in the valley and creates beautiful lakes. The Rocky Mountain range was pushed up by powerful tectonic forces. After the mountains were created, the glacier's role was to add decoration, carving the mountains and adding finishing touches like the lakes. The ice of the Athabasca Glacier is still moving today. Glacial ice is ice that flows.

You have landed at the thickest part of the Athabasca Glacier, which is as thick as 300 meters, and sits at 2,210 meters above sea level. Here, it is said that the ice moves forward about 25 meters each year. This glacier continues to move today. Even now, the glacier is still carving this valley.

The Japanese examiners were at a loss over how to evaluate Takagi-san's narrative as a presentation for the MPHIA oral examination. Takagi-san had a high reputation within the Japanese guiding community. His narrative was filled with facts highlighting the immense scale of the glacier, and he framed the glacier as a lively actor that had carved the landscape into the shape we know today. Takagi-san's narrative offered the "biography" of the glacier from its birth through its growth in the ice age to its current state by emphasizing the glacier's active movement. Such a narrative would effectively invite Japanese tourists to feel connected to the ice and snow in Canada as their fellow actors in the same environment on this globe. However, the examiners thought that this narrative was too subtle in conveying the message of environmental stewardship. Contrary to the MPHIA course's strong emphasis on the idea of a theme, for the examiners, Takagi-san's story did not provide a clear answer to the question "So what?" It did not convey a sense of why that information mattered for communicating the value of ecological integrity or any indication of his position as an environmental steward.

The examiners eventually passed Takagi-san because they thought the information was accurate, and they knew that this narrative would work well in Japanese tours. Nevertheless, one examiner expressed his concern that this was basically a standard tour narrative that explains the Athabasca Glacier on a Japanese tour of the Columbia Icefield, and it was not clear to him what Takagi-san had learned from the MPHIA course, especially on the topic of incorporating an explicit theme of environmental stewardship. Faced with this very different communication style, the examiners were unsure of what criteria they should use to evaluate the effectiveness of narratives like this one.

Compare Takagi-san's narrative with that of Kimura Kimie, or Kimie-san, a veteran independent guide who passed the MPHIA exam in English:

> Wildlife corridors. What are they? Why should we care? Probably most of you think that wildlife corridors are something that wild animals have chosen to use and have been using from generation to generation. But actually, they are man-made because they are something left over by humans.
>
> The whole area here in the Bow Valley used to be a paradise for wildlife, and they could move all over freely. And then, humans started to develop a town, a railroad, and beautiful highway and recreational areas. The wildlife's space shrunk. Smaller, smaller, and smaller. And eventually, it became little patches here, here, and here. And the wildlife corridors are what connect those little patches. Those patches are the space for those animals. They are the space for food, the space for shelter from rain, or hail, or snow. Or safety from predators. And it is getting even harder for them to move from one space to another.
>
> Imagine you've just checked into a hotel, which you probably did yesterday or the day before yesterday. And checking into a hotel, after a long trip, you cannot wait to take a shower. You take off your pants, take off your shoes. There's a knock on the door. Your bag is delivered. Right on time. Without bothering to put your pants back on, you just go to the door, open it slightly, and try to drag in the bag. But it gets stuck. There's no one around. What the heck? Just go outside and lift the bag. All of a sudden, you hear the door go "click."
>
> What are you going to do? The only thing you can do is to go to the front desk and get another key. By the way, the hotel you checked into is the Jasper Park Lodge. And you were fortunate enough to get a nice quiet cottage at the far corner of the property. And the front desk is over there.
>
> You just hide [yourself behind things so that others will not see you running to the front desk in your underpants]. Yes, there's no one coming. There is no smell of humans. So you rush into one bush

where hundreds of mosquitoes are swirling. Uhhhh. There's a tree. Dash. And you wonder why all these trees in the Rockies are so skinny. And then a big Brewster bus is passing by, full of Japanese tourists with their cameras in their hands. Now, a final dash to the front desk. And you hope that there's no one in the lobby. And if there are some people, you pray to God, *Please make them nice enough to pretend that they don't see me.* That's a horrible thing. You never want to have that happen in your life. But the worst thing it would mean for you is embarrassment. For wildlife, it's an issue of life and death.

So, where are they? I've brought a little town site map. At the town site, we've got a little corridor, around Cascade [Mountain], Sulphur [Mountain], Mount Rundle, and the compound. And the especially sensitive areas are closed to the public. Now, you might say, "Wait a minute. What do you mean, closed? We came all the way here to see these animals. It's not fair." Right. But if we don't protect them now, we are not going to see them anymore. It's not too late, yet.

"Coexistence." That is a word we use quite often. From a human's point of view, it means to get to know each other, get along, hopefully make bonds. But from the wildlife's point of view, it probably means "leave me alone." Maybe it's time for us to shift ourselves to a wildlife point of view in order to coexist with them.

The examiners had no problem passing Kimie-san. Although her narrative might not have flowed completely smoothly in English, she clearly understood the main point of the MPHIA interpretation course. The message of her story was clear: wildlife habitats have been severely compromised by the pressure of human use, and wildlife corridors are the only remaining routes for the animals to move across their fragmented habitats. Thus, people should respect the animals' need for wildlife corridors and keep them intact by not intruding into that space. She also used the techniques taught in the MPHIA course to connect her theme and the audience. She stimulated audience involvement by asking her listeners to imagine themselves being locked out of the comfortable habitat of a hotel room and being exposed to the hostile environment.[7] The importance of ecological integrity and humans' responsibility as environmental stewards was evident in her narrative.

The role of the guide was clearly different in Takagi-san's narrative of the glacier. Takagi-san narrated the biography of the glacier and introduced the glacier to the audience, but he left the message of the glacier open. It was up to the audience to decide what to make of the story of the birth, growth, movement, and current stage of the glacier.[8] Takagi-san believed that a guide's primary role was to enhance the tourists' satisfaction: through his narrative, the guide would remind the tourists that they had made the right choice in coming to the Canadian Rockies and that they were lucky to be in this beautiful place. Of course, the guide should inform the tourists of the park's regulations, history, and philosophy, and he should introduce the landscape with accuracy, but the meaning of the encounter with nature should not be imposed by the guide. The guide in Takagi-san's model was not a decoder of nature's message but more like a matchmaker between the tourists and the landscape.

The contrast between MPHIA's and Takagi-san's approaches could be explained as the difference between the interpretation styles of the national park and those of the commercial leisure industry. However, this explanation is only partial. Like Kiyoko, Takagi-san was proud of being a guide "in a national park" and was eager to learn the park's approach. He was confident that his guiding reflected well the uniqueness of Banff's particular environment, and that he had been successful in stimulating his customers' environmental awareness. Therefore, he considered that his presentation matched what he had learned from the MPHIA course. His style of interpretation cannot be explained simply by reference to his commercial-guide status. Nor can this kind of reduction explain the particular challenge for the Japanese commercial guides compared with their English-speaking counterparts, who rather quickly developed the knack of conveying in their narratives an explicit message of environmental stewardship.

An MPHIA executive, Ted Carter, told me that "the interpreter is the medium" by which the audience can come to understand the meaning of nature. In this model, the guide was supposed to be a medium who creates for the audience a sense of "immediacy." In other words, the guide's interpretation should enable visitors to "discover" nature's meaning for themselves. Although the audience's engagement with nature's language was conducted through the layer of translation and mediation, the tourists were led to understand that they were apprehending nature's message directly. The guide's job was thus, somewhat paradoxically, to mediate in such a way that visitors are given the sense of a direct, unmediated relationship with nature, whose meaning was already inscribed on the landscape. Both Ted and Takagi-san placed a guide as an intermediary, someone who connects and mediates between tourists and the natural world. What distinguished Ted's and Takagi-san's approaches was the configuration between "nature" and human and the location of the meaning of nature. In Ted's model, the true meaning of nature was already inscribed on the physical landscape, and the guide's job was to let the tourists "discover" it. Science was the language for deciphering the already inscribed meaning of the natural environment. In comparison, in Takagi-san's model, the meaning was not predetermined but emerged from the improvisational interaction between each person and what he or she encounters. Scientific descriptions were not necessarily the sole "accurate" understanding of nature but were among the many tools that stimulate tourists to connect with and make sense of their encounter with various living and nonliving beings on the earth.

Environmental Stewardship

By juxtaposing the MPHIA course's emphasis on theme with the "lack" of theme that marked most Japanese presentations, we can see two related underlying assumptions in the MPHIA model of interpretation. First, the idea that the interpreter has an explicit message in mind before beginning his or her talk means that the message exists independent of any interaction with the audience. Although an interpreter is encouraged to pay attention to the audience, the purpose of doing so is to effectively get the message across. In other words, in this model, interpretation presupposes an interpreter as a speaking subject whose interiority produces the meaning of the message (see Derrida [1967] 1997). Second, an interpreter is also a "translator" of nature's words; therefore, the interpreter must understand what nature wants to say. The theme of interpretation lies in the natural world itself. This idea that the interpreter translates nature's language presupposes that the meaning needs to be located in nature itself. In this sense, interpretation also assumes nature as a source of objective meaning that can be directly apprehended by anyone who understands nature's "language." Thus, this model of interpretation, with its two potentially contradictory assumptions, raises questions about where the meaning of nature originates: Does it originate in nature itself? Or is it produced in the interpreter's interiority, from which he or she extends the cognitive ability to capture the meaning of nature? In the MPHIA's model, the tension is expected to be solved by the interpreter as an environmental steward. As we can observe in Sam

Ham's book, the interpretation of nature becomes conflated with the translation of scientific knowledge. Here, "science" is rendered as a language that deciphers the meaning prescribed in nature and translates it into human language. Scientists provide the initial level of translation, and guides as nature interpreters translate the scientists' knowledge for the lay audience. This translation is assumed to be transparent in the sense that what the guides are providing the visitors is a "direct" experience of nature. By engaging in this chain of translation, people are expected to realize their role as environmental stewards.

The notion of "environmental stewardship" has been developed as a "Western" response to environmental destruction, especially as a reaction to the thesis presented by Lynn White Jr., a historian of science and technology, that the cause of environmental problems lies in the religious roots of Western science and technology. In his influential essay "The Historical Roots of Our Ecologic Crisis" (1967), White suggests that the ecological crisis derived from the modern Western techno-science, whose roots lie in Christian attitudes that place humans above nature. By providing a brief historical overview of the development of Western scientific knowledge, White argues that modern science is "an extrapolation of natural theology" and that modern technology is a "realization of Christian dogma of man's transcendence of, and rightful mastery over, nature"; therefore, "Christianity bears a huge burden of guilt" in environmental destruction (1967, 1206). White's essay triggered heated debates about the role of Christianity in science and stimulated a wide range of responses. In his response to White, the philosopher John Passmore argues that the Western tradition of "stewardship" had a good potential for environmental protection, and he advocates building "a new ethics based on the 'perfectly familiar ethics' of Western Christian tradition" (1974, 187). While pointing out the biblical origin of the notion of stewardship, Passmore also argues that environmental stewardship is "a peculiarly Western and modern concept" backed by Kantian rationality and scientific knowledge. He emphasizes that a human "has responsibilities to those who come after him, responsibilities arising out of his attempt to preserve and develop what he loves" (185). It should be noted that Passmore's notion of stewardship was developed as a defense of "liberal democratic society and science" reflecting the political climate in the 1960s and 1970s. Passmore is concerned about the influence of White's critical examination of Christianity and Western science on what he calls "mysticism" or the popular trends at that time led by the "beatniks," who sought solutions in Hinduism, Buddhism, and other spiritual traditions to address the problems caused by Western technological and industrial advancements. Passmore's writing also reflects Cold War sensibilities as he contends that the "authoritarian" or "Hegelian-Marxist doctrine" of the Soviet Union and China would not be able to solve environmental problems (185).

As a defender of "liberal democratic society," by combining modern science, rationality, and the responsibility of citizens with "familiar" Judeo-Christian ethics, the notion of environmental stewardship became a powerful tool for educating people. The concept has proliferated and been widely used in conservation agencies and environmental management. Yet, as Worrell and Appleby (2000) point out, in many actual cases in management, the term has been used quite loosely, and its religious and philosophical bases were downplayed. Worrell and Appleby argue that the underdevelopment of conceptual inquiry leaves underlying problems unexamined and might pose a challenge for practical implementation. They point out that a fundamental element of the idea of stewardship is that the world belongs to God, and a steward "is appointed by and answerable to a higher authority, and undertakes management in a way that reflects the wishes of the authority" (2000, 265–266). The idea of stewardship could foster paternalism toward other species being managed, based on the human's assigned position as manager and other beings as something to be managed. This hierarchical division between human and nature might contradict another theme in the Banff National Park's ecosystem approach that tried to overcome the assumed anthropocentrism. Moreover, although the concept has strong roots in Judeo-Christian tradition, and thus presupposes a specific cosmology and the configuration between humans and nonhumans, the way the term is used in conservation practices conceals knowledge politics, which grants this worldview primacy over others. The notion of stewardship has been uncritically expanded to a broader context to indicate responsibility in relation not only to God but to society or to ancestors, as if this concept can be easily translated into other religious and knowledge traditions, without recognizing the incommensurability of worldviews.

Although the notion of environmental stewardship was fundamental to the MPHIA project, or perhaps *because* it was such a fundamental concept, the idea of environmental stewardship itself was not highlighted as a concrete topic that should be explicated. Many Japanese guides realized the difficulty of translating the concept into Japanese, yet they did not pay much attention to the word "stewardship"; they simply interpreted it as meaning responsibility in a very broad sense. Their focus was on what they were expected to *do* as environmental stewards, and what skills they would be tested on in their presentation of nature interpretation. How did the Japanese guides translate the MPHIA's notion of nature interpretation?

Translating Interpretation

In response to the predicament felt by the MPHIA course instructors and examiners, the association decided to offer an interpretation course specifically for Japanese speakers and asked Kimie-san to teach it. Kimie-san agreed, although giving a lecture in Japanese was against her own philosophy. She had voluntarily chosen to take the exam in English, believing that because she was living and working in a Canadian national park, it was important to pass the exam in the official language of Canada. Even though she conducted her tours in Japanese, she felt that the value of her accreditation would be lessened if she were to take the exam in Japanese.

Reflecting her own philosophy, in translating the course materials from English, Kimie-san wanted to respect the authenticity of the original language as much as possible. She tried to keep the original phrasing in English and prepared an almost word-for-word translation. Her loyalty to the original presented a difficult challenge when she tried to translate the term "interpretation," which had only begun to appear in Japan in the 1990s in the context of nature interpretation, and there was still no fixed Japanese translation for it. Much of the Japanese literature on park management or nature tourism used the English loanword *intāpuritēshon* (e.g., Kawashima 1998; Yoshinaka 1996); however, Kimie-san was not satisfied with that word, which she thought would produce an ambiguous effect, allowing people to use the term without understanding what it really meant.

In her search for the Japanese equivalent, Kimie-san asked Amanda and Richard what the English word "interpretation" actually meant. Amanda explained that, in her understanding, the term was almost equivalent to the word used in English classes in high school and meant, roughly, "translate your feelings about a piece of writing." From this discussion, Kimie-san applied the term *kaisetsu*, a word commonly used in school to refer to an explanation of what an author means in a piece of writing. Kimie-san was not completely satisfied with her translation because of the awkward combination in the Japanese language between kaisetsu (interpretation) and shizen (nature). As Yanabu Akira (1982, 133) explains, the term shizen is mostly used to describe a situation that happens naturally, without human intention, the state of artlessness. This notion of shizen does not connect well with kaisetsu, in the sense of interpretation of literature, because it contradicts the sense of art and human intention with which literature is associated. Yet Kimie-san still thought that using kaisetsu was better than adopting the phonetic copy of the English word.

Lydia Liu, a comparative literature scholar, has suggested that translation entails the simultaneous impossibility and necessity of communication across languages because different language communities operate with different epistemologies. Through her examination of Chinese translation practices in the early twentieth century, Liu argues that insisting on finding equivalent words in the "host language" forces that language to transform to accommodate the desired communication with the "guest language." Thus, translation entails an imbalance of power over determining normative concepts. Liu states, "The business of translating a culture into another language has little, if anything, to do with individual free choice or linguistic competence" (1995, 3). Following Talal Asad's (1986) discussion on power/knowledge relations in cultural translation, she argues that Western languages in the past few centuries, as guest languages, have produced a desired knowledge in non-Western host languages based on a set of political-economic relations that allowed the Western languages to have more manipulative and forcible effects on the others. In this sense, the translation of MPHIA's notion of "interpretation" forced Japanese speakers to create a new linkage between shizen as nature and kaisetsu as interpretation, a mismatched combination in the epistemological framework prior to this particular act of translation.

Liu also suggests, however, that in the process of cultural interpretation, more complex power dynamics take place: although translation is often a consequence of asymmetrical power relations between different language systems, it also provides a site for negotiation and mutual appropriation. Liu illustrates this negotiation with the example of Heidegger's pursuit of an equivalent word for "language" in Japanese and his Japanese interlocutors' conclusion that there was no such equivalent. She points out that this dialogue was an example of the European inquirer insisting on the existence of an equivalent word although the notion of language has been developed in a specific sociocultural and historical context and entails the particular configuration of a person and the words enunciated. This kind of translation inquiry creates the effect of "lack" in non-European languages not only of the concept of language itself but also of the essential categories in European languages such as "self," "person," and "individual" as an enunciator, which make the assumed existence of "language" possible (Liu 1995, 3–10). Liu goes beyond merely indicating the asymmetrical power relations in this translation process by pointing out the possibility of a non-European host language that will "violate, displace, and usurp the authority of the guest language in the process of translation as well as be transformed by it or be in complicity with it" (27).[9] Just as his Japanese interlocutors' complicit gesture of "lacking" the equivalent Japanese word for "language" led to Heidegger's appropriation of the non-European perception of language and helped him to formulate his famous self-reflective inquiry into "Being," non-Western subjection to Western knowledge could open up a possibility for critical interrogation about the assumptions underlying the hegemonic knowledge.[10]

Indeed, as in the case of Heidegger's dialogue, Amanda, Richard, and James, faced with the predicament of exchanging incommensurable ideas with their interlocutors, were moved to critically reflect on the constitution of their own knowledge. James reflected on his own cultural baggage, while Amanda and Richard asked Kimie-san to present a lecture catered to the Japanese audience as an experiment to see if she could find any solutions for the problem of cultural difference. The realization of incommensurability turned their gaze back to the dominant framework of nature interpretation. The discrepancy between MPHIA's notion of interpretation and the Japanese appropriation of the concept revealed not only a difference in communication styles but also a difference in the perception of nature itself and humans' position in relation to other living and nonliving beings.

Theme as Punch Line, Steward as Shaman

As Yanabu (1982, 36–37) points out, a translation word has an aura of something new and important even though the contents are unknown. The special effect of a translation word, with its ambiguous aura, signals the tension within the word and the difficulty of comparison between the imported word and the similar concepts in one's indigenous language. The notion of nature interpretation promoted by the MPHIA attracted the Japanese guides like a mysterious jewelry box with an aura of something new and exciting, just as their experience of Sandford's lecture on local history and James's teaching of ecology and geology had done. Yet at the same time, many of the Japanese guides I talked to had ambivalent feelings about the notion of nature interpretation: learning the MPHIA model caused a sense similar to what Homi Bhabha has described as "almost the same, but not quite" (1994, 89). The difficulty of translating the concept, the predicament of the examiners, and the examinees' own anxiety about what they were being asked to do all attest to this ambivalence.

Despite the Japanese managers' and examiners' concerns about the discrepancy between MPHIA interpretation skills and Japanese guide practices, many of the younger guides appreciated the skills they learned from the course. While they shared the feeling that the interpretation skills they were being taught did not easily fit their own communication style, they respected the interpretation skills class as a part of the larger project of learning ecology as a common language.

Among those I interviewed, Nakata Tetsuya, a third-year guide in the RMT, most explicitly elaborated his appreciation for the interpretation skills he was learning. He said, "I am impressed by the Canadians' imagination [toward their audiences]. I think the reason why Canadians are good at explaining things is that they know that a listener could easily lose attention if the explanation was not easy to understand." Building on his observation about easily distracted tourists, Tetsuya also appreciated the MPHIA course emphasis on the importance of a theme. He understood that at the end of a talk, a theme should connect all the elements; a theme was like *ochi*, or a punch line. He equated a theme in nature interpretation with ochi in a comedy routine because both entertained the audience and produced a delightful sense of "Aha!" He said, "I don't understand those [Japanese guides] who complain that interpretation and guiding are different. Every guide's talk should have ochi. It is the same with a theme."

Yet, when I asked him what the themes of his guiding would be, he answered, "I don't have my own theme." That did not mean he did not communicate any message in his tours; rather, he said, "I don't have anything that I want to tell everyone in the same way. It varies according to the customer. But still, I feel I am doing interpretation." He elaborated that

in a successful tour, a theme should emerge naturally through the interaction with the customers. Instead of originating from inside himself
or from the landscape, a meaningful theme should take shape depending on the customers and the conditions of the day, such as the weather,
the specifics of the place, and the things encountered in the specific
tour. For Tetsuya, interpretation is not the technique of capturing the
true message of nature that already exists out there but the act of con-
necting his clients and plants, animals, and other beings by providing
information and stimulating bodily experiences in the particular physical landscape. The ochi, or theme, should emerge "naturally" in the intersubjective and embodied interactions.

Sano Naoto, also a third-year outdoor guide, said he was fascinated by
the idea of a guide being "a translator of nature's languages." Unlike Tetsuya, Naoto was indifferent to the techniques taught in the interpretation course, finding them rather superficial. Yet, Naoto appreciated the
core concept of translating the language of nature for humans. When he
reflected on the satisfactions of guiding, his description sounded very
similar to the ideas of the MPHIA interpretation class. He said: "When I
do it [guiding] well, a customer naturally goes into nature. A customer
would realize a tree by his or her heart's eyes. When I seize the right moment to let the customer open his or her eyes to nature, I feel good."

Following the course's notion of interpretation, Naoto explained that
he wanted to motivate a customer to feel the tree directly. However, his
idea of the guide as translator also reflected a discrepancy between this
approach and what was taught in the course. Like Tetsuya, he thought
the meaning of a conversation should emerge "naturally" from the interaction with individual customers and the specific things they encounter
in the tour. He cautioned that "nature guides should be humble," because a single person could not understand the whole richness of nature. He suggested that having a moral message in mind before starting
a tour was arrogant; to do so implied that a guide could understand nature by him- or herself. Thus, although he respected scientific knowledge and was keen to update himself with the latest research by the park
scientists, he did not want to privilege ecological knowledge as the only
way to understand nature. Instead, he insisted that nature was much
larger than any person's ability to grasp it. For him, an ideal hiking tour
was one in which all the participants, both the guide and the customers,
could share with each other what they knew about nature. I observed
that in his day hike, he routinely started the tour by telling his custom-

ers, "There are many approaches to feel nature. So, please share your insight."

In fact, what Naoto idealized as a source of his guiding inspiration was closer to a shaman-like spiritual medium who could be possessed by nonhumans in various forms, including animals, birds, insects, trees, grass, lichens, rocks, mountains, and rivers, or at least could hear the "voices" of these beings. He often told me that if one honed his or her senses while walking in the woods, one could hear these voiceless things. He thought people forgot about this ability in their busy everyday lives, and he wanted to help his clients to recover it. Once people relearn how to tune their senses, they can "naturally" hear these voices. For Naoto, a guide could not convey the messages of these beings; the messages would emerge naturally or contingently in the particular encounter between these beings and humans. What Naoto could do was to create a site for sharing the experiences of each participant of his tour to help each other to recover the communicative abilities with nonhuman beings.

Indeterminacy of Translation

The Japanese guides' ambivalence about imposing a message is consistent with a tension within the Japanese word for nature itself. Yanabu (1982) explains that within the contemporary Japanese word shizen (nature), there coexist at least two conflicting meanings developed out of different epistemological trajectories. One meaning is a translated concept for the English word "nature," which indicates objective existences in the material world in contrast to the human spirit. Another meaning has been developed from the Taoist concept of *ziran*, which describes the condition of artlessness or a situation happening without human intention (Yanabu 1982, 132–133). As a translation of "nature," shizen works as a noun, as a material object of human perception or action based on the binary framework of human as subject and nature as object. In contrast, shizen as a Japanese elaboration of ziran works as an adjective or adverb, and the conceptual framework it relies on does not include a distinction between the objective external world and the internal human spirit. Yanabu suggests that the contradictory coexistence of these two meanings within a single word creates a third meaning, which emerges as a hybrid indeterminacy (148). The term shizen moves constantly between the two poles of subject/object distinction and the amalgamation of the two. When the concept of nature was introduced, shizen was objectified, in contrast to "self" or "human" as subject. Yet, the self discovered in this process did not persist in its subjective position. As soon as the self was discovered, it tried to merge with nature and to return to the condition in which subject and object were amalgamated. In this sense, nature became an indeterminate movement between the discovery of the self/other distinction and the return of a merging between self and other. The imported meaning of nature did not take over the prior notion of shizen; instead, the hybrid formation of the third meaning emerged while retaining the inherent contradiction (147–148).

The notion of nature for the Japanese guides, as seen in Tetsuya's and Naoto's narratives, constantly moves between the two poles of the translated word shizen, or nature: one pole consists of nature as translation of an English word, a noun and an object, the other as translation of the Taoist notion of ziran amalgamated into animistic understanding and the Buddhist notion of *jinen*, an adjective or adverb. On the one hand, the guides were fascinated to discover the natural world through an ecological, "objective" framework. On the other hand, they also sought to return to the merged realm where the meaning takes form "naturally" through the mutual interaction between themselves, their customers, and other beings and phenomena in the environment.

The language of ecology thus formed a point of articulation that allowed different worldviews and cosmologies to merge and enabled this joint project among people with different interests and aspirations. In the Japanese participation in MPHIA nature interpretation, two different notions of nature interpretation merged: (1) an assumption that the universal message of nature is already inscribed and must be deciphered by interpreting nature's language; and (2) a decentralized interpretation that proceeds from a belief that each being, animate or inanimate, has its own whole cosmos within itself, and its meaning emerges as a result of a contingent encounter. This convergence was possible through the common acts of interpreting the natural landscape through ecological knowledge and of rendering the interspecies relations that constituted that landscape.

Yet, at the very moment of convergence, diverging trajectories and genealogies also appeared, as a sense of cultural difference, the contrast between ecological science as it has developed from the Greek and Judeo-Christian tradition and Japanese folk knowledge, which itself is the product of constant translation between new ideas and the sedimentation of the past translations of various knowledge traditions, including animism, Taoism, Confucianism, and Buddhism. A sense of cultural difference emerged in the very midst of the collaborative efforts among the MPHIA instructors and the Japanese guides who try to build the shared language and perceptions that would generate the common behaviors of environmental protection while containing the tension within the collaboration: participation in the MPHIA course led the Japanese guides to reflect on their conviction that the meaning of nature emerges through interaction—among the tour guides, visitors, and whatever they encounter along the tour. In this sense, nature interpretation is a contingent social action that involves many actors with various positions and backgrounds. The meaning of nature was not assumed to be something already inscribed as a legible text, to be discovered by an individual. Nature interpretation is not a linear process of passing nature's message from scientists to nature interpreters to visitors.

By contrast, the MPHIA's model of nature interpretation assumes the notion of nature whose meaning is attainable by people regardless of their sociocultural background. This notion of nature is imagined as something separate from society, and free from the specific social conditions from which the very notion of nature is produced. However, the Japanese tour guides' difficulty in grasping MPHIA's notion of nature interpretation and environmental stewardship reveals that this division between nature and society is itself produced out of specific social interactions. As Latour (1993) argues, the "purification" of nature from the society is constituted by a series of socially specific translation processes rather than the preexisting condition of translation. The negotiation between the MPHIA instructors and the Japanese guides also illustrates that the discourses of cultural difference, the distinction between Western and Japanese, have been produced along this imagined division between nature and society, as the universal applicability of the Western science is imagined as opposed to the cultural peculiarity of the Japanese understanding of nature. Even though both the Japanese guides' and the national park's notions of nature interpretation are the products of long histories of diverse sociocultural interactions, in MPHIA, their version of nature interpretation backed by ecological science was assumed to be neutral and to transcend specific cultural traditions. The Japanese guides' complicit production of these divisions, in turn, stimulated their aspirations to become cosmopolitan subjects who had transcended cultural difference.

In the next chapter, I discuss how the Japanese tour guides' engagement with the park's ecology complicitly constructs its authority as universally applicable knowledge despite their own experience of puzzlement and struggles. I explore how their engagements were shaped by the legacy of technologizing science in the modern Japanese history, and consider the implication of this legacy in understanding the politics of translation in the contemporary context.

6 | The Allure of Ecology

A Guide's Ecological Integrity?

Right before the Mountain Parks Heritage Interpretation Association examination scheduled for late May 2001, I paid a visit to Noda Hiroshi's apartment. Five guides who had taken the course had gathered there to prepare for the exam by exchanging notes and helping each other clarify some concepts. When I entered the apartment, they were focusing on the parks management segment and discussing what exactly "ecological integrity" meant and how it could be translated into Japanese. They were puzzled by the idea that connects ecology and "integrity." The guides generally understood that it meant that the environment was properly protected. However, they wondered why the word "integrity" had been chosen, and what the park officers who served as MPHIA course instructors wanted them to understand by using this particular word and concept. Who or what exactly was supposed to have integrity? Hiroshi suddenly interrupted the discussion. He asked in a loud and frustrated voice, "What happens to a guide's ecological integrity!?" (*gaido no ekorojikaru integuritī wa dōnarunda!?*). Everyone laughed. He continued, "[My] brain is full of fragmented patches caused by environmental disturbances! [My] ecological health is in danger due to various environmental stressors!"

Hiroshi's parodic use of "ecological integrity" was nonsensical. It was obviously wrong to use the phrase to describe a person's mental state. However, Hiroshi's expression captured the feeling of confusion, or the fragmented coexistence of incompatible elements in his conceptualization of nature. With the introduction of the park's ecological approach to nature, the idea that nature was an entity with integrity was supposed to share a site in his epistemological system. However, this notion of nature did not quite fit with his perception of the world.

Hiroshi's remark was an example of the Japanese guides' efforts to obtain a lived experience of foreign concepts by deploying them in everyday language. In this case, Hiroshi had used English words to express new and foreign concepts, such as "ecological integrity," "environmental disturbance," "ecological health," and "environmental stressor." But his comical misuse also implicitly pointed to the assumptions underlying the discourse of ecological integrity. Just as it sounded awkward to use this term to describe a person's mental state, it was strange for him and his friends to imagine concepts of integrity attributed to nature. By explicitly shifting the context from nature to the human, Hiroshi's remark also reveals how the park's notion of ecological integrity itself was actually constructed by shifting the notion of integrity from human health to nature.

In this chapter, I examine Banff National Park's discourse of environmental integrity taught in the MPHIA course. In the course, ecological integrity was presented as central to the park's ecosystem management plan and as the key term that marked the shift from human-centered to ecosystem-centered approaches in environmental protection strategy. The notion of ecological integrity was constructed in specific philosophical and aesthetic traditions, yet it was introduced into the park's management plan as a scientific term and as if it were culturally neutral. This assumed neutrality of ecology as science had a set of contradictory effects. On the one hand, the assumed universal applicability of the park's notion of an ecological approach had a strong allure for the Japanese tour guides. Many of the guides were excited to learn this approach because they thought it was a key to joining a community of people who share this scientific knowledge. On the other hand, the unstated cultural specificity and the underlying epistemological frameworks of the park's ecosystem approach posed a hidden obstacle for the Japanese guides, who found these ideas hard to grasp. In particular, they were puzzled by the tension within the park's ecology, specifically, regarding how to understand change and stability in ecosystems and the ambiguous position of the human in relation to other beings in the systems.

I argue that the challenge the Japanese tour guides faced was the result of the park's and the guides' complicit construction of ecological science as universally applicable knowledge. When certain knowledge achieved its status as "scientific" based on the premise that the knowledge could transcend the cultural framework of the knowledge holder, it became valued highly in the contemporary bureaucratic regime of knowledge and gained the strong authority necessary to inform policy and management plans. Yet, this complicit construction conceals the specific philosophical traditions that had shaped the knowledge and presented it as if it were detachable from its social and cultural context, making the issue of cultural translation void. By avoiding the issue of cultural translation, the Japanese guides placed themselves in an ironic situation. While the allure of ecology as science offered them a dream of sharing the knowledge regardless of the difference in their cultural backgrounds, epistemological systems, and intellectual traditions, it also conceals the cultural politics that has privileged certain knowledge traditions and underprivileged others, including their own. The Japanese guides' experiences indicate a challenge in simultaneously pursuing environmental protection and multiculturalism, two key areas in which Canada has assumed a self-assigned leading role in the world. Why and how were the Japanese guides getting involved in this ironic situation? In this chapter, I explore this question and contextualize the Japanese guides' engagement in the Canadian park's environmental conservation initiative in relation to the particular legacy in which Western science has been translated in Japan.

Ecological Integrity in Park Philosophy and Management

The MPHIA's 2001 spring course handout titled "Park Philosophy and Management" includes the Banff National Park Management Plan, released in 1997, which emphasizes ecological integrity as the "first priority" in the current park management plan. The plan responds to the fundamental dilemma in North American national parks about how to balance park usage with environmental protection (Campbell 2011; Fluker 2010). The national parks have been established to raise people's awareness of the natural landscape and to protect the landscape from being exploited by aggressive industrial and commercial usage. For people to understand and appreciate the significance of natural landscape, however, it was important to secure their rights for recreational usage. The people's visitation and usage would inevitably impact the natural landscape, which is a dilemma the national parks have faced since their establishment in the late 1800s, beginning in 1872 in the United States with Yellowstone National Park, and in 1885 in Canada with Banff (Bella 1987; Burns 2000; Dearden and Dempsey 2004; Grusin 2004; Hermer 2002; Lowry 1994; Marty 1984; Searle 2000; Sellers 1997). The concerns about visitors' impacts on the environment have been heightened since the 1960s, when leisure and recreation became available to the mass population. Reflecting these concerns, since the 1970s, the emphasis of park management has shifted from visitor usage to ecological conservation (Campbell 2011). The idea of "ecological integrity" was adopted by Parks Canada's management in the 1980s (Woodley 2010) and has become the park's core philosophy, undergirding management strategies since it was first mentioned in the 1988 amendments to the National Parks Act.[1]

The *Banff National Park Management Plan* (Parks Canada 1997) reflects this trend and, in particular, responds directly to the 1996 Banff Bow Valley Task Force's report that raised strong concerns regarding Banff's environmental degradation. The task force's report made a number of concrete recommendations to ensure ecological integrity in the park and neighboring areas. The management plan explains that although there still exist sizable areas of "wilderness" in the Central Rockies Ecosystem (in which Banff National Park is located), intensive human land usage has caused fragmentation of wildlife habitat. It also points out that the older park policies were not effective in maintaining ecological integrity; on the contrary, ecosystems were "radically altered" as a result of those former policies, such as fire suppression and predator control. The document emphasizes the "need to reduce stress on the park's ecosystems and to restore natural processes" because Banff National Park is "an important cornerstone of Canadian identity and an international obligation to World Heritage" (Parks Canada 1997, 9).

The core vision, quoted from the Banff-Bow Valley Study Round Table, states: "Banff National Park reveals the majesty and wildness of the Rocky Mountains. It is a symbol of Canada, a place of great beauty, where nature is able to flourish and evolve. People from around the world participate in the life of the park, finding inspiration, enjoyment, livelihoods and understanding. Through their wisdom and foresight in protecting this small part of the planet, Canadians demonstrate leadership in forging healthy relationships between people and nature. Banff National Park is, above all else, a place of wonder, where the richness of life is respected and celebrated" (9). To realize this vision, the management plan introduced a number of key initiatives to be taken in the decade following its implementation, including environmental stewardship practices for sustainable heritage tourism, restoration of natural flow in aquatic systems, the reintroduction of native fish, controlled forest burns, managing elk populations, the relocation of horse carrels, and the elimination of the National Army cadet camp.

The park's concept of ecological integrity is explained in the section "A Place for Nature" as "a condition where the structure and function of an ecosystem are unimpaired by stresses induced by human activity and are likely to persist" (Parks Canada 1997, 11).[2] A notable feature of the plan's explanation of "ecosystem-based management" is that it emphasizes "change" as a natural process and states that "humans are an integral part of the ecosystem" (12). The management plan states that "ecological integrity is not a static end-point, but rather a continuum of characteristics that a landscape or area should possess" (12).

The plan's characteristics reflect the notion of "resilience," a term in ecological science that was introduced by C. S. Holling (1973) and is generally defined as "the capacity of a system to absorb disturbances and reorganize while undergoing change so as to still retain essentially the same function, structure, identity and feedbacks" (Walker et al. 2004). While the exact meaning of resilience has been debated among experts, in the park's management plan document, it is translated as a function of "ecosystem health" and the system's "ability to continue evolving and developing" (Parks Canada 1997, 12). To explain ecological integrity to the course participants, the MPHIA instructors also included the park's information sheet for the public, titled "Fire Management," which uses the human body as a metaphor:

Ecosystem integrity is a little like human health. The state of health, or integrity, is one where the body, or ecosystem, is complete and functions properly. To have integrity, an ecosystem must have all its native species, complete food webs and naturally functioning ecological processes. Moreover, it must be able to persist over time. Just as people under stress may develop disease, ecosystems under stress can suffer damage. Human activities can stress ecosystems by making rapid changes they cannot adjust to. Symptoms such as the loss of a species or the inability to retain nutrients may signal the breakdown of ecosystem integrity. (Parks Canada, n.d.)

The management plan recognizes that the ecosystem is constantly changing as it is affected by "human and naturally induced stresses" (Parks Canada 1997, 12). The plan lists several kinds of natural disturbances, such as flooding, avalanches, and insect infestations, and explains that these contribute importantly to ecosystem dynamics. Although they may look disruptive, in the long run, these disturbances stimulate succession among various species and help "maintain a diversity of vegetation types and wildlife habitat" (13). As for human-induced stressors, the plan identifies two types: first, fires set by aboriginal people and, second, the "development" that took place throughout the twentieth century after white settlers began occupying the region in the 1880s. While the former human-induced stressor is mentioned very briefly along with natural disturbances—the document almost gives the impression it is a natural disturbance—the development-related stressor is explained more thoroughly, with details such as population growth in the town of Banff; increases in the number of park visitors; whose use of the park contributes to air pollution, sewage, waste, and water quality issues; the nationwide transportation systems that cross the park, including the Trans-Canada Highway and the Canadian Pacific Railway lines; and the park's past ecological management, which included policies such as fire suppression and predator control. The management plan lists a number of environmental concerns caused by these human disturbances, such as landscape fragmentation, loss of habitat connectivity between major wildlife protected areas, human-caused wildlife mortality, altered vegetation successional patterns, altered predator-prey relationships, wildlife-human conflicts, and the introduction of nonnative plants and fish (13).

Banff's management plan clearly states that Parks Canada's management takes a comprehensive approach that integrates "ecological considerations with economic and social factors," in which visitor usage is considered an integral part. Therefore, maintaining ecological integrity is "the foundation of the park's appeal as a tourist destination" (Parks Canada 1997, 12). In order to balance ecological integrity and visitor usage, it addresses the need for "appropriate information and plans to reduce and manage human induced stresses" (12). The document emphasizes the importance of science as a means to properly assess the situation and the need to communicate and spread this scientifically sound information to visitors. In this regard, the management plan sets its goals as follows:

- To use communication, orientation and education programs as a means for achieving ecological integrity
- To work with others, outside Parks Canada on the diversity of key ecosystem management messages
- To focus on key 'multiplier' audiences including local businesses, private interpretive operators and the media. (15)

Among the measures to be taken to achieve these goals, the plan suggests that communication include "information about the ecosystem in training programs for the staff of businesses and for private guides" (15).

The MPHIA course handout communicates the park's changing policy and the challenge of the new management practices in a very frank manner and emphasizes the park's commitment to science. It states, "We've learned a lot over the last century, but we are still dealing with the results of our past beliefs. If we are to manage Banff 'unimpaired for future generations' we must adopt a new approach to managing the park in the future. To understand where we are headed, we have to take a quick look at where we've been." The handout continues, "Our beliefs, values and perceptions affect how we manage our national parks. An explosion of new information in recent decades has caused park managers to reconsider some long-held beliefs, and in turn reassess how we will manage Banff in the new millennium." Following this explanation, the handout lists several concrete examples of changing perceptions by using the paired phrases "We thought . . ." and "What we've learned . . ." For example, it explains that the parks were considered to be "intact relics of pristine wilderness that had remained virtually unchanged for thousands of years," but now they are acknowledged to be "part of a larger, dynamic ecosystem that has continually changed through time." The information sheet also explains that these changes in beliefs reflect "a move away from a human-centered management approach" to a more "ecologically-centered" approach. Moreover, it stresses that "good science" is central to an ecosystem-based approach because it "helps us identify threats to ecological integrity and helps managers make the best possible decisions as to how to restore or maintain ecological integrity."

Change and Stability

The guides in the RMT were eager to learn about and understand the park's position and perspective. In their efforts to comprehend ecological integrity, the guides tried to connect the concept with what they already knew. They understood that ecological integrity was the philosophy that supported the "three basic rules in the national park," which they explained to tourists at the beginning of every tour: (1) do not leave garbage, (2) do not feed wild animals, and (3) do not take away rocks and plants from the park. The guides emphasized that the park was a space for nature and that Parks Canada had made tremendous efforts to protect this nature by conducting scientific research and carefully making management plans. When asking tourists to cooperate with the park, some of the guides used popular English expressions translated directly into Japanese, such as "take only pictures, leave only footprints" (*toru no wa shashin dake, nokosu no wa ashiato dake*) and "leave nature as it is" (*shizen no mono wa shizen no mamani*).

As they learned more about the park's philosophy beyond these practical tips, however, many of the guides expressed a sense of puzzlement, especially when they tried to understand the narratives in the park's documents and how the park philosophy applied to some of the concrete conservation policies and practices. For Hiroshi and many of his fellow Japanese guides, the park's idea of viewing the human as part of a changing ecosystem was reasonable; however, the location of the human in the park's vision was hard to grasp. Where exactly did the park locate the human in relation to other beings in the constantly changing ecosystem dynamics?

Many of the guides expressed their respect for the park's attempts to find a good balance between usage and protection. The guides themselves were strongly attracted by the "vast nature" of the Canadian Rockies and were invested in preserving the magnificent landscape. But they liked to use the park for their outdoor activities; moreover, they were making a living by helping tourists use the park. Some younger guides told me that they were strongly moved by the park's communication efforts. For example, Maeda Hanako, Nakata Tetsuya, and Sano Naoto said that they were impressed by the sincerity and braveness of the park officers who explained the past policies and management practices as wrong, describing how they did not work, what kind of problems they had caused, and how the park learned from these past mistakes and continues to make efforts to establish better policies and management plans. Hanako told me that it would be hard to imagine that a Japanese governmental institution would admit its past wrongdoings, actively share that information with the public, and openly acknowledge changes made to address those previous inadequacies or lack of knowledge.

Despite their respect and sympathy toward the park's efforts, however, it remained unclear to the guides to what extent the ecosystem was to be restored and protected. While the park management document explicitly states that the ecosystem is constantly changing and that ecological integrity is "not a static end-point," the practice of restoration obviously presumed a point to which the landscape was to be restored and a condition in which the "health" of the recovered ecosystem was imagined. This conceptual tension over change and stability led to ambiguity, and a number of related questions emerged. Which point in history did the park officers set as a reference point to evaluate the health of the ecosystem? How far back did they go to find a model landscape in which ecological integrity was maintained? Did they want to restore the "ecological health" to a point before the Trans-Canada Highway was opened in the mid-twentieth century? Or to before the Canadian Pacific Railway was built in the late nineteenth century? Or were they envisioning the time when the indigenous peoples used the area for hunting?[3] To these Japanese guides, the park's practices and approach were confusing and ambiguous on many of these issues. For example, although the park's management plan recognized that drastic changes had occurred as a result of railway construction, it was quite obvious that the railway and major highways would remain in the park because they form an integral part of the nationwide transportation system.

The guides were also aware of the park's ambiguous treatment of "aboriginal people." Although the park management plan acknowledges that their use of fires and other practices contributed to forming the present ecosystem, they did not seem to fit into the present plan. While the MPHIA instructors excitedly explained recent archaeological findings that documented the early presence of the indigenous people, this was framed as a story of a remotely distant past; in the contemporary park setting, fire use and hunting contradicted established management practices.[4] As these examples illustrate, the guides sensed that there was an underlying tension between "change" and "stability" in the park's management plan: on the one hand, the plan views ecosystems as constantly in change; on the other hand, the notion of "integrity" presupposes a point in history toward which the "restoration" efforts were to be made, although where the reference point should be set remained unclear.

Human Power and Responsibility

The issue of fire control was a topic around which the convergence and divergence of the park's approach and the Japanese tour guides' understanding of nature became apparent. In the MPHIA course, fire control was used as a concrete example of how the park had changed its management strategy in light of up-to-date scientific information. Until the mid-twentieth century, the park had actively extinguished forest fires because its efforts were targeted toward protecting the scenery. After the ecosystem approach was adopted, however, the park began to respect the processes of change that occurred "naturally," including fire due to lightning and sparks carried on the wind. This policy that respected natural processes easily fit the Japanese guides' understanding of nature. This was in contrast to the policy of prescribed burning, which the guides thought indicated a strong underlying belief in human power and rationality to control the successional processes of the forest. The practice seemed based on an assumption that humans could calculate and manage environmental change on behalf of all the beings in the forest, reflecting the idea that humans had the ability to determine what was right for the forest succession process and when a fire was needed. It was quite astonishing for many of the guides to observe this practice on such a large scale.

Similarly, the guides were fascinated by the park's large-scale, intensive intervention practices, especially regarding wildlife population control. I heard about the issue of elk control many times in various types of tours. While the accounts varied depending on the guide and the type of tour, the basic story line was as follows: although hunting was prohibited in the park in 1890, elk were almost eliminated by the early twentieth century due to overhunting in the surrounding areas. To increase the population, the park reintroduced elk by bringing in a large number from Yellowstone.[5] Meanwhile, the park also controlled predator populations by killing wolves and other carnivores. Due to the decrease of predators, elk flourished. However, the park's plan of increasing the elk population succeeded more than had been anticipated. Now, elk gathered in the town of Banff, where they presumably felt safer because predators were more cautious near humans. The increased numbers of elk in town caused serious friction with humans, and there were several cases of elk charging and occasionally seriously injuring tourists. The animals also affected the surrounding vegetation by severely grazing aspens, which in turn led to reduced habitats for beavers and other species that relied on the vegetation. The overpopulation of elk was causing a "headache" for the park, and park officers were making tremendous efforts to relocate them. Park employees had captured a herd and transported it to less populated areas on the other side of the mountain range. In the woods near the entrance to the town of Banff, park wardens could sometimes be seen chasing out elk with dogs or shooting their rifles into the air to scare them off.

In many of the guides' stories, the reintroduction and relocation of large mammals, such as elk, were narrated as comical stories of human hubris in attempting to control nature, with unexpected responses. But these narratives also conveyed the guides' sense of amazement at the underlying assumptions of this approach: these management practices indicated confidence in the ability and power of humans to "protect" nature. Humans were not viewed as humble beings whose ability was limited to responding to the events that were considered "natural" but were a special kind of animal with a "responsibility" to protect other species and the entire ecological system.

The guides liked to tell this kind of story as an anecdote to entertain and impress the Japanese tourists about the vastness of Canadian nature and the large-scale thinking of Canadian park managers. But the more they learned about the park's philosophy, values, and perspectives in the MPHIA courses, the more questions they had. Some of the younger guides, especially those who were strongly interested in environmental issues, occasionally shared their sense of puzzlement with me: Wouldn't these intervening efforts contradict the principle of "leave nature as is"? What was the source of the park's confidence that it was making the right management decisions? And, more fundamentally, where did this belief about humans' power to protect other creatures come from?

Sometimes the park's decisions seemed to be arbitrary to the guides. For example, in casual conversations with me, Uchida Chie often expressed her confusion about the issue of dogs traveling with hikers, especially in the backcountry. One day when I accompanied her hiking tour, we saw an American backpacker and "environmentalist," heading for some overnight camping in the backcountry with his dog. Chie was puzzled, asking, "Wouldn't his idea of 'environmentalism' contradict bringing a dog to the backcountry? What would he do if the dog encountered a wild animal and acted in an unexpected manner?" She also asked, "Wouldn't the park care about the dog's presence, since it prohibited the introduction of foreign species?" The MPHIA course described the intensive efforts to eliminate the bull trout and other nonnative fish species, so why were dogs allowed in the mountains? The dog might accompany the hiker out of the park, but what about the swarm of insects and microbes traveling with the dog? Could they be overlooked? What would the park do if people started to bring in other kinds of pets? Chie was not personally invested in whether or not dogs should be allowed in the park but was simply puzzled, especially after learning that the scope of the park's research program had shifted from prioritizing "charismatic" wildlife, such as bears, to including vegetation, aquatic species, and invertebrates, such as snails or liver flukes.

The guides sometimes also raised questions about the presence of horses in the park. Some justified the use of horses, arguing that they were better than motorized vehicles, especially for wardens who needed to move around in the backcountry. But other guides asked about the recreational horseback-riding tours. Some guides wanted the park to keep allowing these tours because they gave them more work. Generally, though, in many of these conversations, such as my ones with Chie, the RMT guides did not have strong personal preferences. They were willing to follow the park's decisions and to accept the park's rationale, but the decisions and enforcement practices sometimes seemed arbitrary and reflected culturally constructed affection toward specific kinds of mammals among mainstream Canadians without elucidating these specific perceptions and cultural traditions. Tension between the treatment of ecological science as universal knowledge and the culturally constructed affective sensibilities caused puzzlement for the Japanese guides, who were trying to learn ecology as a shared language in the park and were being led to believe that scientific knowledge is culturally neutral and universally applicable to people with diverse backgrounds.

The Aesthetics and Affects of Integrity

Although the MPHIA course presented ecological integrity as if it were a culturally neutral scientific concept, the idea was developed within specific philosophical and aesthetic traditions. Laura Westra, an environmental ethicist and a key advocate of the concept of ecological integrity, explains that its philosophical background is indebted to Aldo Leopold's notion of a "land ethic" that should respect the "intrinsic" value of life (Westra 2000, 27). She cites Leopold's famous quote, "A thing is right when it tends to preserve the integrity, stability and beauty of the biotic community. It is wrong when it tends otherwise" (Leopold [1949] 1966, 240). Westra argues that Leopold's idea led to a "radically new approach" to environmental ethics, "one that is based on a wider, actual reality, and one that recognizes the primacy of natural wholes, in line with the new science of ecology" (27). She maintains that with Leopold's principle, both moral theory and public policy must be "integrative rather than re-ductionist, holistic, rather than individualistic or aggregative; and most of all fundamentally non-anthropocentric, as they must recognize the value of all life, human and non-human" (28).

This philosophical tradition influences the park's management approach, and the preceding quote from Leopold is also included in the MPHIA handout. In his essay "Land Ethic," Leopold further explains, "The 'key-log' which must be moved to release the evolutionary process for an ethic is simply this: quit thinking about decent land-use as solely an economic problem. Examine each question in terms of what is ethically and *esthetically* right, as well as what is economically expedient" (Leopold [1949] 1966, 240, emphasis added). This ethics is obviously constructed in the specific social context of growing concerns over industrial development in North America in the early to mid-twentieth century and with the specific cultural, aesthetic, and affective sensibilities toward "wilderness" and its disappearance as a result of settler colonialism, which sees "stability" as an important component of ethics and aesthetics.

Westra (2000, 35) argues that respect for the intrinsic value of nature is compatible with a nonanthropocentric stance. For her, this is possible because the foundational ethical value underlying the idea of ecological integrity is "not to inflict harm," an ethical tradition that emerged from a canonical genealogy of Western thinkers, including notably Jeremy Bentham, John Stuart Mill, Immanuel Kant, and John Rawls and finally articulated by Leopold in the context of environmentalism (Westra 2000, 28). She further explains that a science of integrity is basic to the formulation of the ethics of integrity: "It is because through integrity as a *factual condition* we recognize the need for a holistic, integrated approach that the ethics of integrity supports a moral stance quite different from that of other traditional moral approaches" (32, emphasis added).

The ethical foundation of ecological integrity is further elaborated by philosopher Peter Miller (2000, 61), who identifies the "social contract" as the basis for the concept. Miller explains that while "people can engage in rational negotiation to protect their individual interests, . . . most people's interests are not exclusively self-centered" (61). He maintains that "love and care" can be extended to humans and nonhumans; therefore, "mutual self-interest in life-support systems" and "love of living things and the exuberant system of life" could "converge in a concern for the wellbeing, health or integrity of ecosystems and the ecosphere" (62). It is notable that Miller points out that ecological integrity is a socially constructed perspective and "not a scientifically documentable biological condition of an ecosystem in and by itself" (67). On this Miller diverges from Westra's notion of integrity as a "factual condition" backed by science. Nevertheless, these philosophers and ethicists who advocate for ecological integrity share an idea of the ecosystem as an object or a whole entity to which a humanistic ethics can be extended, drawing on a "holistic" approach from ecological science.

Of course, there is an issue of translation from the field of science to ethics or to bureaucratic administration, in which the nuanced arguments of scientific experts are simplified and reduced for ease of communication.[6] Nevertheless, there should be some underlying conceptualization of nature in the scientific debates in ecology that allows the interpretation of the ecosystem as an entity onto which humanistic ethics can be extended.

As many critics and ecologists have pointed out, there has been an ambiguity in the term "ecosystem" since it was first introduced by the British plant ecologist Arthur Tansley in 1935, and this ambiguity has opened up "the flowering of a bewildering array of theoretical views and applications" (Voigt 2011, 185). The concept of an ecosystem has been developed by incorporating various systems approaches from the thermodynamics, cybernetics, and information theory and, more recently, catastrophe and chaos theories, as well as the postnormal scientific theory of nonequilibrium thermodynamics and self-organizing holarchic open systems (e.g., Kay et al. 1999). Systems approaches have played a key role in ecologists' attempts to understand the interconnections among organisms and their biotic and abiotic environments. Peter Taylor, a science studies scholar, explains that these approaches were taken in order to establish ecology as a robust science and to construct "well-bounded systems, which have clearly defined boundaries, coherent internal dynamics, and simply mediated relations with their external context" (2011, 87). He emphasizes that the central challenge for ecologists has been how to conceptualize the "unruly complexity" of life in a scientific framework (Taylor 2005, 2011). The concept of "system" allows ecologists to capture all the complex, unruly relations they must consider within a whole and to turn the system into an object of study; thus, ecologists' work inevitably entails the tension between life's rich unruliness and their attempts to discipline the complexity in order to produce scientific knowledge.

Although the tension between scientists' desire to attend to unruliness and to discipline it in order to produce systematized knowledge exists in other disciplines, it is particularly visible in ecology. In particular, Taylor argues that ecology has been facing a number of challenges, including conceptualizing ongoing change in ecosystem structure, the dynamics among heterogeneous components, and the embedded interconnections among these components. Moreover, Taylor points out that the notion of "model" is ambiguous in the ecosystem approach. He asks, are "models idealized representations of ecological reality . . . or heuristic devices to generate further theoretical questions?" (2011, 88).

This question is important, as ecologist Wolfgang Haber points out, because there has always been "a temptation" to slide the ecosystem concept "from the metaphysical construct into tangible reality of nature" (2011, 224).[7] The slippage of "ecosystem" from an analytic concept to a description of reality can be framed as the tension between constructivist versus realist views of the ecosystem. This tension needs to be situated in relation to two other sets of tensions, which Annette Voigt (2011), a historian of science, frames as mechanicist-organicist and reductionist-holistic perspectives. She suggests that a major set of debates that shaped the development of ecosystem approaches have reflected these tensions: for example, whether to see the ecosystem's wholeness as analogous to a machine or a larger organism; as an abstracted idea based on the observation of actual objects (thus reducible into parts) or a starting point existing apart from the "sum of its parts"; as an observer's mental construct or a real entity with spatial boundaries.

Within this larger framework of debates, Voigt argues that the ecosystem can be likened to an organism insofar as the functions of the ecosystem are conceptualized "in such a way that its purpose is self-preservation, i.e. it is an end in itself" (2011, 190). She also suggests that the systems approach can lead to the perception of a community of organisms as a "higher-level individual" when individual organisms' characteristics and relations with their environment are examined with regard to their contributions to the overall function and maintenance of the community (189). These organicist and holistic perspectives of the ecosystem allow the transfer of the idea of "individuality" from an individual organism to a larger organic community.

This perception of the ecosystem—as a real entity with individuality—is compatible with technocratic perspectives and practices because it renders the ecosystem not only an object of scientific study but also one in need of management. Voigt explains that this conception of the ecosystem, in responding to the environmental movements that have emerged since the 1960s and 1970s, has been well aligned with public interests and expectations that ecosystem theory could "offer a deeper understanding of the effects of human action on 'nature,' as well as providing, on the one hand, an ultimately technocratic solution to the environmental crisis and, on the other, a new, holistic human-nature relationship" (2011, 188). This notion of ecosystem has a strong affinity with the discourse of ecological integrity. In the park management plan, the metaphor of human health allows for the slippage of the ecosystem concept into a real entity like a human body, clearly bounded and with its integrity threatened by external influences.

The Paradox of Nonanthropocentric Approach

The perception of the ecosystem, which treats this assemblage of organic and nonorganic beings in the metaphor of a human body, allows an extension of a humanistic ethics of integrity. How can we understand this extension of humanist ethics to nonhumans? It seems contradictory with the idea of a "nonanthropocentric" approach and the park's emphasis on a shift away from a human-centered to an ecosystem-centered orientation. Some Japanese environmental critics point out a paradox in the nonanthropocentric discourse. This discourse might have a powerful effect in challenging the primacy of the human in the modern Western humanist philosophical tradition, and within a conceptual framework based on a clear human-nonhuman distinction. However, it remains puzzling for those who do not share this philosophical tradition and conceptual framework. For those outside of or at the fringe of this tradition, it is contradictory to claim to be nonanthropocentric while extending a basic human ethics to other creatures and assuming the human's powerful position and responsibility for the well-being of those other creatures.

Kitō Shūichi (1996, 34), one of the leading Japanese environmental ethicists, who introduced many Western environmental ideas to Japan, points out that in the development of Western environmental ethics, a central issue has been how to "protect nature" and how to overcome anthropocentric approaches for the purpose of environmental protection. In his historical review of environmental thought, he argues that environmental "protection"—the conscious and explicit effort to protect the natural environment—is a new attitude that became prevalent in the nineteenth century. He argues that in the past, people used various practices to tame nature's power and to receive its benefits, which could be interpreted as "protection" from today's point of view. However, for Kitō, there is a fundamental difference between the conceptualization of nature in these older traditions and the more recent idea of explicit "protection." The discourses of protection were possible only after people shifted their perception of nature and stopped seeing it as something beyond human power, something to be in awe of for its capricious power to bestow blessings or cause harm. In other words, the protection discourse emerged when nature became an object of human manipulation. Even though this discourse tries to overcome the human-centered approach of industrial exploitation, both the environmental ethics of protection and industrial exploitation are the product of modern Western humanistic thought, and they share the same epistemological framework that views humans as distinct from nature because of their ability to exercise power over nature as an object, whether this human power manifests in the form of exploitation or protection.

Based on this perception, Kitō raises a question about the effectiveness of the anthropocentric versus nonanthropocentric argument. He suggests that the nonanthropocentric approach encounters a fundamental difficulty in that it is based on a clear division between the human and the nonhuman and has tried to solve this problem by extending a humanistic ethics—such as not to harm others—to nonhuman beings. Kitō points out that the problem of environmental ethics based on a human-nature binary is that it tends to ignore the difference between modern industrial activities that exploit nature and those human practices and wisdom accumulated in the long history of people's everyday activities and their close interaction with nature. The framework that maintains this binary leads to an understanding of all human activities as antagonistic to nature and pays little attention to the fact that the most fundamental part of the human relationship with nature lies in the everyday practices of making a livelihood.[8] Kitō emphasizes the fact that humans cannot live without having some impact on nature.

Kitō also points out a similar paradox in the discourses of "the intrinsic value" of nature, which have often served as the basis of nonanthropocentric approaches because the idea itself is the projection of a certain human value. It is logically difficult for humans to conceptualize the value of nature that exists independently from the act of interpreting the value from their perspective. He argues that even if nature had value beyond human utilitarian needs, this value is revealed to humans only through their very interaction with that nature. The basic assumption underlying the discourse of intrinsic value is the idea that nature is an objective entity existing independently from human beings, while its wholeness can be perceived by human beings. However, Kitō states, "It is impossible for humans to capture nature as a whole, as it is" (1996, 123–124). His critique implies that this perception is possible only when humans put themselves above nature. This critique echoes Donna Haraway's caution concerning the "god trick of seeing everything from nowhere" (1991, 189) that slipped into modern scientific perceptions of nature.

Instead of assuming the human ability to understand the intrinsic value of nature separate from humans, Kitō argues for recognizing that humans have been developing a wide variety of connections and networks with nature. Humans have been entangled in these networks with other beings through varieties of livelihood practices and lifestyle activities, including religious rituals, as well as social and economic activities. The diverse cultures that humans have developed are modes of human-nature relationalities. According to Kitō, the argument of intrinsic value ironically extracts a part from this complex web of human-nature relationalities and projects an ideal state of whole integrity onto a limited part of nature that is comprehensible to humans. Thus while Kitō appreciates the contribution of Western environmental movements, he also points out the underlying premise of a clear distinction between the human and nonhuman and suggests the limitations of the universal applicability of the "protection" framework.

Instead, he advocates the necessity of generating environmental ethics that recognize the complex entanglement of the human and nonhuman in specific contexts.

Numata Makoto, an influential ecological scientist, is also critical of the "protection" discourse if it "places the human above nature" (1994, v) and allows humans to take a paternalistic attitude toward other beings. Numata served as a president of the Ecological Society of Japan and the director of the Nature Conservation Society of Japan in the 1970s and participated in a number of international conservation initiatives, including the World Wildlife Fund and the United Nations Environment Program. He introduced the new ideas and approaches developed in the international arena to Japan. However, instead of advocating for a nonanthropocentric approach, he argues for exploring an environmental ethics from an anthropocentric perspective in a strict sense. Numata's approach is based on the recognition of humans' humble position and the awareness that it is impossible for humans to see the world from other perspectives. When humans consider the "environment," according to Numata, it is the environment seen through their specific biological functions and ontological conditions. Drawing from Jakob von Uexküll's notion of "Umwelt" ([1934] 2010), the world perceived by a specific organism based on its particular sensory structure and functions, Numata points out that the environment is relational and ontologically different for various organisms. What we discuss as environment is environment that is perceived only by humans. It should be noted that Numata's idea of anthropocentric ethics differs from the development-oriented approach. He has strongly critiqued the discourses of "sustainable development" and "harmony between development and conservation," which tend to be used to justify giving preference to economic development over the conservation of nature (39–40).

While Numata emphasizes the importance of recognizing the limitations of human cognition, he stresses that the conventional ecological discourses often minimize humans' ability to physically impact the ecosystem. He states that many textbooks place humans solely under the category of "consumer" based on the understanding of them as animals, as opposed to plants as producers, microbes as decomposers, or inorganic matter, such as air or water. However, he argues that humans, with their intellectual and technological capacities, play a significant role as producers and decomposers as well, and intervene and change the abiotic aspects of the ecosystem. This perception resonates with the influential idea in ecological science that frames the human as a "keystone" species, which is also used in the park's management plan. But Numata's approach diverges from the perception of human as keystone species in the integrity discourse that emphasizes how humans exert pressure on the ecosystem as if they are an external force on the rest of the system (i.e., in a top-down sense). Numata suggests that what is called "environmental protection" should foster practices that maintain the "human-nature" systems in which humans are deeply embedded in the web of life, instead of assuming humans' transcendental capability to make value judgments for other beings and to speak for other species. Based on his understanding of the human as a biological organism, and the human's deep entanglement with ecological systems, he strongly reminds his readers that what is "good" is inevitably a human value judgment. Therefore, he advocates for an environmental ethics that reminds humans of their partial vision and of their limited anthropocentric perception that is conditioned by their specific biological features.

Kitō's and Numata's efforts in translating environmental thoughts and ecological knowledge developed in the Western intellectual traditions reveal the ambiguity of the human's position within discourses of environmental protection. These discourses sometimes emphasize the human's embeddedness in the environment and at other times treat the human as an external force that puts pressure on the ecosystem or paternalistically protects other beings. This ambiguous treatment of the human creates tension between the stated claim of being a nonanthropocentric approach and the act of extending humanistic ethics to nonhuman beings. Kitō's and Numata's accounts also suggest the underlying assumptions that shape the ethics of ecosystem protection. These are based on a worldview that privileges relative stability—relative, yet nonetheless stable—and an epistemological framework that conceptualizes the world as consisting of individually separable physical entities. However, the historical, social, and cultural specificities of these worldviews are often omitted in environmental discourses.

It should be noted that authors like Kitō and Numata are far from being restless critics or reactionary oppositionists of Western environmentalists. Rather, they have played significant roles in introducing Western environmental thoughts to Japan. Their writings clearly show respect for these ideas and present them as something that the Japanese can learn from, yet their writings address something found in the interstitial space in translation. Their efforts at translating environmental ideas developed in North America and Europe reveal the basic assumptions submerged and forgotten in the original context of intellectual traditions, as these assumptions are not shared in the Japanese intellectual context to which those thoughts are transported.

The Allure of Ecology

Despite the puzzlement and the challenge derived from the uneasiness of different epistemological traditions, the assumed scientific transparency of the ecological approach adopted by the park was attractive for the Japanese guides. As mentioned in the introduction, before MPHIA, most guiding narratives for Japanese tours were adapted from translations of existing Canadian guidebooks and tours, such as the tours offered by Brewster's. Many of these narratives were structured around stories of European explorers and their encounters with the natural landscape. Thus, the Japanese guides' narratives were already framed by Canadian stories of European exploration. The treatment of ecology as a common scientific language presented the possibility for the Japanese guides to liberate themselves from being secondary interpreters of Canadian history. Ecology as a scientific language allowed them to feel that they were engaging with the landscape of the Canadian Rockies directly. The science of ecology, as a neutral language that claims to transcend particular sociocultural contexts, further invited them to participate in the community of people who use this language.

Moreover, the allure of ecology for the Japanese guides derived from its emphasis on constantly changing forms of life, the close relationality among humans and various nonhuman beings, the significance of inanimate beings, and the deep embeddedness of humans in the environment. These aspects of ecology sounded compatible with the lay perceptions of nature among the Japanese tour guides that have arisen as a result of the constant translation of animistic, Taoist, and Buddhist knowledges as well as modern Western science. Although the ecological integrity discourse brought the substance-oriented "realist" epistemology and the aesthetics of stability back into the park's notion of ecology, there were also some elements that could be potentially interpreted as aligning with alternative worldviews rather than one based on the clear division between the human and the nonhuman, the hierarchy between animate and inanimate beings, the preference for stability and equilibrium, and the substantive perceptions of the world.

What was exciting for some of the Japanese guides was that they felt the potential of expressing their sensibilities toward relationality "scientifically" without the fear of being labeled "not modern," "traditional," or culturally peculiar. In the RMT guide training, a strong emphasis had been given to scientific explanations of the landscape. Katori-san, the RMT trainer, repeatedly cautioned the novice guides not to rely on the native legends or local myths of the place, which were not scientific. Even though these legends often contained insights on human-nonhuman relations, they were deemed as having too much affinity with unscientific, old-style Japanese narratives from which the trainer wanted the guides to keep their distance. By contrast, the ecological language that the guides learned in their MPHIA training allowed them to speak in a scientific way about interconnected natural worlds. For example, a senior guide, Mori Yukio, told me that the MPHIA course had inspired him to learn more about geology, and he had started to take an evening geology course offered at a local school. He told me that James Walker's MPHIA ecology and geology course had made him realize that rocks were fundamental to understanding the connections in "the history of the earth." "Rocks are fascinating," he said, "because if there were no rocks, then there would be no trees, flowers, animals and us, humans." James's ecology and geology classes allowed Yukio to find a point of articulation between science and his sensibility of feeling the close connection— almost like a genealogical tie—between the human and nonhuman, including inanimate beings like rocks, which he had developed in the forest near his hometown in Wakayama.

Maeda Hanako, a novice outdoor guide, also told me passionately how James's course had opened her eyes to an ordinary-looking landscape. She said that James had shown her magically how the small roadside patches of land were exciting microcosms filled with diverse beings. Paying close attention to these diverse plants and rocks reminded her of the sense of sharing the space with these other beings. James's lecture had given her a way to talk about the interconnected microcosms scientifically. While James was puzzled by the close attention the Japanese guides paid to each individual plant in the midst of his efforts to show the larger ecosystem, guides like Yukio and Hanako took from this experience a way to integrate their previous sense of interconnectedness with the newly learned scientific language. Detailing the objectively observable shapes and colors of the plants was an act of applying the scientific gaze and creating realistic representations of the observed objects. Learning the visible features of the landscape, the measurable numbers, and the historical facts was an attempt to speak a transparent language that would liberate them from the fear of having their beliefs labeled "primitive," "mystical," or "peculiar" cultural perceptions of nature.

Technologization of Science

Like Yukio and Hanako, many of the Japanese tour guides working for the RMT were enthusiastic to learn about the park's notion of ecology. But, as seen in chapter 5, even after they attended the MPHIA course, studied hard, passed written exams, and shared the same information, many guides had difficulty narrating the story of nature as expected by the park. Despite their excitement and effort, there were some invisible obstacles beyond an apparent language barrier. These obstacles caused puzzlement not only among the guides themselves but also among the MPHIA instructors, examiners, and administrators.

It seems to me that the source of this puzzling situation is the way science was treated by the park as well as the Japanese guides. There is an underlying assumption in the park's and MPHIA's understanding of scientific knowledge that makes such knowledge universally applicable regardless of the user's epistemological traditions or philosophical and sociocultural background. But this idea itself is a product of modern Western discourse, framed by the specific worldview that expects scientific rationality to liberate humans from social constraints. The way Western technoscience has been incorporated into Japanese society is complicit in intensifying this assumption.

Watanabe Masao (1976, 7), a historian of science, has pointed out that since the encounter with Euro-American colonial powers in the mid-nineteenth century, "modernization" in Japan has taken place through the incorporation of Western science and technology. In this process, while the technological and practical benefits of Western science have been focused on, much less attention has been paid to the intellectual and cultural traditions that shape Western scientific thought. In the rapid move to incorporate modern Western knowledge in order to transform Japan into a modern nation-state, little effort has been made to connect the imported Western intellectual traditions in science and existing Japanese thought. The result has been the coexistence of different intellectual traditions without attempts to make meaningful relations among them (Watanabe 1976, 7–8). This point coincides with an observation of Murakami Yōichirō (1995) that, in contrast to the Western intellectual traditions that have made clear hierarchical distinctions between science and technology that reflect the mind/body or theory/practice dichotomy, in the modern Japanese education system, science and technology have not been clearly distinguished because learning Western modern technology has been highly valued and given priority in the university system.

Watanabe argues that a basic attitude of perceiving nature as an object and an explicit belief that humans stand above nature are foundational to the development of modern Western science; thus, humans can use nature, but they also have a responsibility as subjects to manage it. Watanabe explains that this worldview is rooted in intellectual traditions that are based on the belief that there is some kind of order in nature, which can be traced back to the idea of seeing the world as "the Book of God's Creation." This worldview has played an integral role in giving implicit and explicit religious support and endorsement to the effort to understand and discipline this order (Watanabe 1976, 170–171). Watanabe contrasts this Western worldview with the Japanese tradition and argues that in the Japanese epistemological tradition the central reference point of action has not been imagined in humans but in what we now call nature (175–176). As a result, standing in the midst of these conflicting epistemological traditions, sometimes even the top Japanese scientists in the early and mid-twentieth century were led to ask, "Can the Japanese do science?"[9]

Watanabe suggests that the technologization of science has led the Japanese to ignore the uneasiness between the existing understanding of nature and the imported Western philosophical tradition. He stresses that not enough effort was made to synthesize the imported technoscience and traditional ideas as a means to construct an alternative scientific philosophy. He argues that the lack of a scientific philosophy that is compatible with the Japanese intellectual tradition and the preoccupation with technological advancement allowed mindless industrial development and led Japan to be an "advanced country of environmental destruction" (1976, 184). Watanabe's account reflects the specific social context of the 1970s, when concerns about the unexpected degree of environmental pollution as a result of this industrial development were at their height in Japan. Yet, it still offers insight in examining the challenge of decolonizing our perception of science and exploring the cultural politics of knowledge encounters.

Although the technologization of science might have been accelerated in Japan by the particular way science has been institutionalized in universities and research institutions since the turn of the twentieth century, as Murakami (1995) points out, this is not necessarily a unique phenomenon in Japan. Reflecting the need for technological innovations in the development of mass industrialization and mass education, the hierarchy between science and technology also has been blurred since the mid-twentieth century in Europe and North America. Joan Fujimura's (1987) analysis of scientific fact making in the United States elucidates the process of the technologization of science, as she describes how scientific work was broken down into "doable" tasks and packaged into a "standardized" set of procedures throughout multiple levels, including experimental, laboratory, and social levels. I would argue that these schematized standardization practices and protocols contribute to the technologization of science and lead people to forget about the deep-rooted philosophical traditions behind modern science.

The park's and the Japanese guides' complicit construction of science as universally applicable knowledge could be situated in this century-long legacy of Japanese efforts to learn Western science. The technologization of science made the issue of cultural translation invisible, and ironically posed a hidden stumbling block to the Japanese tour guides. The challenge that the guides faced was simply framed as a matter of the quantity of knowledge they accumulate rather than the uneasy coexistence of different epistemological traditions. It generated a sense among the guides that they were simply "behind," measured by a single scale of evaluation, and thus they needed to "catch up" by studying harder. For example, Kimie-san and Mari-san, when asked by the younger guides how to make sense of the concepts learned in MPHIA courses, repeatedly commented that the newer guides should study harder (*motto benkyō shinaito*) or that they might have lacked serious efforts (*doryoku ga tarinai*) to understand the concepts. Even though the guides were constantly encountering the challenging gaps of translation, they rarely articulated the incommensurability of worldviews, epistemological systems, and intellectual traditions that created these gaps. They felt the cultural difference but attributed it mostly to the peculiarity of Japanese knowledge and practices, rather than that of MPHIA, the Canadian national parks, or the Western intellectual tradition. Therefore, although the core vision of the park proposed in the Banff Bow Valley report involved inviting "people from around the world" to bring in "their wisdom and foresight" (Parks Canada 1997, 9), this goal remained difficult to meet because the Japanese guides were busy adopting the hegemonic knowledge rather than critically addressing the specificity of the MPHIA version of knowledge and the issue of cultural translation. The experiences of the Japanese tour guides suggest the challenge of incorporating multiculturalism—another pillar of Canadian national identity along with Canada's natural landscape—into the park's vision of ecological management.

Most of the guides who gathered at Hiroshi's apartment eventually passed the guide accreditation exam. Even though their puzzlement over fundamental frameworks was unresolved, especially regarding the assumptions underlying the park's understanding of the human position in relation to nature, many of the guides treated this as a nonissue. Instead, they concentrated on studying to pass the accreditation exam and treated the process as an issue of technical procedure. In this sense, they "studied hard," as Kimie-san and Mari-san suggested. The Japanese guides' experience indicates that the effects of knowledge politics are so serious and deep that those whose knowledge has been marginalized themselves have been effectively interpellated and complicitly contribute to maintaining the asymmetrical power relations.

The politics of translation is an important issue in contemporary capitalism, especially in areas where knowledge, information, intellects, and affects are considered the prime and direct sources of value production. Under industrial capitalism, the main social concern was whether workers could produce material effects by using technology; whether the workers understood the philosophical background behind the technology was unimportant. The incommensurability of worldviews of the workers and the philosophy behind the production of technology could be neglected. Consequently, technologization could have liberatory effects: those who did not share philosophical backgrounds could actively use the technology and create innovative products by transplanting the technology to a new social context. However, when the evaluation of a worker's quality involves the extent to which the worker internalizes a technology's philosophical background into his or her own knowledge and how he or she produces affects based on that background, the politics of knowledge translation becomes an unavoidable issue.

Cosmopolitan Shaman

In closing, I present the story of Hanako, whose experience with the MPHIA course will give us a hint for understanding how the Japanese guides were complicitly subjected to this knowledge politics. Her reflections about her life illustrate the significance of learning nature interpretation for the Japanese tour guides and the ways in which learning to speak the common language of ecology was central to the guides' construction of their subjectivity as mediators of different understandings of nature.

In late October 2001, I went for a hike with Hanako. It was the last hike of the year before the heavy snow would begin to fall. We went to Ha Ling Peak, named after a Chinese cook who had worked in a nearby hotel just south of the park boundary. Hanako had just gone through the MPHIA course and had worked hard to prepare for the exam. While crushing the frostcolumns on the trail with our hiking boots, she told me enthusiastically how moved she had been by Bob Sandford's history lecture. After quitting her office job in Tokyo and wandering around the mountains and remote islands of Japan, she had moved to Canada three years ago and had spent most of her time in Banff working as a tour guide. She had hiked many trails and scaled several mountain summits. She had befriended naturalists and gone bird-watching and animal tracking. In the past three years, she had immersed herself in the mountain landscape and finally felt she knew what she wanted to do with her life—live and guide in the Rockies.

She told me that she had returned to Tokyo the previous winter to visit her sick father. One night, she went for a drink with her friends, and in the bar she saw an image of Mount Rundle, an iconic landscape in Banff, projected on the TV screen. She found herself almost in tears and realized that she had a strong attachment to the place and wanted to call Banff her home. But something made her hesitate. She had not been born in Banff or Canada; she had lived there only a few years, and the transient nature of the place did not give her a feeling of home. The people she knew there came and went all the time, and nobody seemed to be settled. Yet Sandford's lecture touched her strongly, helping her realize that everyone comes from somewhere else and becomes a local by learning how to walk in the mountains, how to minimize their impact on the environment while appreciating it, and how to cultivate a strong attachment with the landscape. She finally felt comfortable calling herself a "local"—and not just to claim the local discount in stores and restaurants during the off-season.

Hanako was not naive about the economic and political interests behind Sandford's inviting story of localness. She believed that the Heritage Tourism Strategy was the park's way of using commercial guides as tools for the purpose of reducing the national park's budget, and she suspected it was MPHIA's hope to increase revenues by offering courses. The course fee was not a small amount for her, especially because she faced financial worries about her father's medical expenses. But it did not matter to her whether she was being used or not; indeed, she welcomed being used if it gave her a sense of being a "local."

Hanako told me that she treasured her participation in the MPHIA course because it expanded her social network of nature interpreters. She particularly enjoyed the group discussion with non-Japanese participants. Although she had made friends with Canadians through her various outdoor recreations, she had not previously had an opportunity to get to know nature guides outside the Japanese guide community.

Like her colleague Sano Naoto, Hanako credited the MPHIA course with helping her realize that her job was to translate nature's language in the Canadian Rockies to Japanese tourists. While most of her fellow MPHIA participants would translate it into English, she specialized in translating it into Japanese. Each translator's specialty might be different, but they shared a common task. This new conception of her work as nature interpretation allowed her to feel that she was a member of this community of translators, and this awareness stimulated her to polish her skills further. Her aspiration of becoming a good nature interpreter intensified her understanding of Banff as a place where people were "standing on their own feet" directly on this earth, and where people can liberate themselves from the old communal social ties, obligations, and constraints.

When she told me how fascinated she was by James's ecology course, Hanako was almost ecstatic. She said dreamily, "How wonderful it would be to see the world from his eyes. I want to do guiding like him. . . . I want to marry him!" James was not the only person Hanako wanted "to marry"; at different points, I also heard her say she wanted to marry Naoto, Yukio, and Eita. Hanako did not mean she literally wanted to marry all of these men, obviously, but these nature guides had helped her to see the landscape so freshly and differently that they activated her senses as if she had been in an ecstatic trance. They took her to a completely different world, and she wanted to merge with them so that she could see the world through their eyes.

Although Hanako was fascinated by her experience in the MPHIA interpretation course, she said she felt a "danger" in the notion of interpretation. She understood that there was a hierarchical distinction between those who knew about nature and those who did not. She believed that interpretation has an element of education, but she felt that a guide should be not an educator but a person who initiates *tsūyaku gokko* (playing translation) among all parties, both guides and tour participants. In her view, a guide should be aware of her responsibilities as a guard and schedule manager for the tourists because she obviously knows more about the practical realities and particularities of the local environment. But in terms of appreciating nature, she should not assume that she knows any better than the tourists.

For Hanako, the most delightful moments in her work were those in which she learned a new Japanese perspective on nature from her customers. Perhaps in part because of her youthful appearance, when she explained about animals and plants in the Rockies, senior customers often responded by sharing their own experiences of nature in Japan. For example, when she explained that indigenous people used lodgepole pine resin to waterproof their canoes and baskets, a woman told Hanako about a childhood memory of collecting pine resin for fuel during the Pacific War.

The most striking response Hanako had heard was about bears, from a man who lived in the mountainous area in northeastern Japan. During the tour, one of the tourists had asked Hanako what they should do if they encountered a bear. She explained the standard strategy encouraged in the park, which was to keep their distance and quietly retreat without showing their back to the bear. Perhaps out of slight annoyance at what seemed like an urban perception of bears as irrationally dangerous creatures, the man told her that humans and bears could share a space if humans knew how to respect them. The man said he was from a rural area, known as a country of *matagi* (which is often understood as the traditional hunting group that specialized in bear hunting as an act of receiving a gift from the mountain deity). Hanako told me that according to the man, it was only recently that bears and humans had developed an antagonistic relationship. People these days did not understand how to interact with bears, and thus threatened them and forced them to attack. For Hanako, the excitement of guiding in the Canadian

Rockies was that it could be a site for these kinds of exchanges with customers and for a chance to learn about the diverse ways that human beings engaged with nature.

Hanako treasured this kind of moment, when she felt that she was acting as a mediator at the intersection of people with different backgrounds. She admired Naoto, who thought a guide's work was ideally similar to that of a shaman, mediating between natural worlds and human worlds and among humans with different social and cultural backgrounds. The MPHIA course—with its ideas of nature interpretation, ecology as a common language, and cosmopolitan local knowledge—allowed Japanese tour guides like Hanako and Naoto to imagine their guiding work as a mediation between different worlds, a position that also enabled them to imagine transcending national boundaries, to free themselves from the "old" constraints of Japanese society and, in turn, to reevaluate Japanese culture from an external point of view.

Epilogue Found in Translation

Maeda Hanako, who had taken Bob Sandford's notion of transformation through landscape so fully to heart, did not come back to Banff in
2002. In the wake of the attacks of September 11, 2001, many large Japanese tours to North America were canceled, and Hanako was told by
the manager, Atsuko-san, that she could not guarantee that there would
be enough work in the coming season. The news disappointed Hanako
and other former guides who were looking forward to becoming part
of Banff's local community. The situation was also difficult for Atsuko-
san, who had supported these younger guides as their surrogate mother
in Canada. The bitter experience reminded Atsuko-san, Hanako, and
others in the Japanese guiding community that the tourism business
is built upon the assumed imagination of a global peace that allows the
free movement of people.

Hanako held onto her dream of returning to Banff, but reflecting on
tourism's vulnerability to global politics, she had second thoughts about
working as a tour guide. While taking care of her sick father in Japan,
Hanako became interested in Asian traditional health care. She found a
job as a massage therapist and, at the same time, went to school to study
traditional medicine. After years of training, she obtained an acupunc-
turist's certificate and began working in a clinic in Tokyo. Over several
years, she was seriously torn about whether to stay in Japan or go to
Canada again to find a job as an alternative health care practitioner. She

continued visiting Banff and maintained her connections there. Eventually, she married a Japanese man living in Banff and moved back there in 2010. She found a position as a massage therapist in a resort hotel spa.

Shinohara Rei returned to Japan in 2002 after working with the RMT for two years and another year with a subsidiary of a Japanese travel agency in Banff. She had broken up with her boyfriend and wanted to leave town. During her first few years back in Japan, she had a difficult time finding a job. She switched between several temporary jobs. She found a part-time position as a receptionist in the college she graduated from in Osaka, and later was promoted to a full-time study abroad coordinator. She married an engineer, a full-time *sarariman* in a major electronics corporation, and had two children. After the long detour, she finally settled in a stable position that was comfortable for her. She could use the experience she had gained through studying and living abroad in giving advice to students. The college's work environment suited her, as an educational institution built for women; to a certain degree, the staff were allowed to arrange their schedules in order to have a good work-life balance and spend time with their families.

Ogura Yoshiko continued working at the RMT. After years of waiting, she finally obtained permanent resident status in Canada in 2008. Her visa status was no longer conditional on her employer, and she could find a job anywhere she wanted. In the winters, she started working as a ski instructor at Lake Louise, while continuing her guiding work during the summer. She enjoyed both guiding and ski instructor work despite the fact that they did not provide much long-term financial security. Now in her late thirties, Yoshiko was concerned with how much longer she could continue this physically demanding work, though she could not imagine herself doing something else: the performative construction of herself through direct interaction with tourists was an integral part of her sense of self. She felt that her situation at the RMT was too comfortable, like soaking in lukewarm water (*nurumayu ni tsukatteiru mitai*), and it was hard to get out of even though she knew that she had to take a step sometime in the near future before she became too old.

At first glance, Hanako, Rei, and Yoshiko, each in her own way, seemed to be interpellated into some versions of mainstream ideologies (see Althusser 1972). They looked as if they had become subjects of liberalism or neoliberalism with the dream of freedom and liberation.

Hanako's life trajectory could be seen as a story of the effective assimilation of an immigrant to Canada: she ran away from the constraining social ties and obligations in the old world, liberated herself and explored a way to "stand on her own feet," and, finally, found home as a "local" in Canada's multicultural society.

Rei's personal journey could be interpreted as the successful adjustment of an overseas returnee to the dominant Japanese society. Rei's current position seemed to be ideal for a working woman in a conventional sense, with a good balance of work and family. She did not have to be entirely consumed by work because her sararīman husband assumed the main responsibility for earning an income for the family. She had some quibbles about her husband, who stayed in his office until midnight and rarely was at home. But she was also aware that his hard work freed her from the burden of feeding the family and allowed her to explore *yaritai koto* in her own work, which gave her a good amount of challenge and satisfaction, while she had primary responsibility for the care of their two young children.

Hanako and Rei enjoyed a few years of whimsical life in the Japanese guide community in Banff—"Neverland" in the midst of "magnificent nature." In this liminal space away from mainstream Japanese and Canadian societies, they played the role of Japanese cosmopolitan. But eventually, after bumpy years of further self-searching experiments, Hanako found a job in a Canadian-operated resort hotel, and Rei ended up in a college back in Osaka. They married and settled down to raise their families. Their performances as guides, as intermediaries to alternative worlds, could be understood as exceptional work experiences in their youth. Their critical reflections on the dominant social norms, work relations, gender, and family could be seen simply as a temporal stage in life that many youth experienced as a step in the process of becoming mature adults in a given society. In a way, their time in Banff's Japanese community could be viewed as a long vacation. Like tourists who experience the liminal state in their travel but then return to normal everyday life (see Graburn 2001), they experienced the time separated from mainstream society but eventually assimilated or adjusted to normal everyday life.

Yoshiko, in contrast, chose to remain a flexible laborer in Canada. In her pursuit of liberating herself from the artificial environment and of gaining a sense of "living on the earth, not in human-made society," she did not want to prioritize job stability. Her desire for freedom pushed her out of more solid, conventional work arrangements. Yoshiko's choice in her life course could be analyzed as proof of the expanding power of neoliberalism: the discourses of freedom stimulated people like Yoshiko to dream of liberating themselves from the Japanese corporate system, as well as work, family, and gender relations that support the employment system. These imaginaries of freedom were also articulated as cosmopolitan desire.[1] If their performance was successful, they turned themselves into embodiments of this Japanese cosmopolitan desire and transformed into yearned-for commodities in tourist encounters: people who could translate various notions of nature, transcend national, social, and cultural boundaries, and take tourists to a world unlike the one they knew in their everyday lives. With this dream of freedom, the guides themselves, including Yoshiko, could be seen as those who were interpellated into the neoliberal discourses and became active agents of the neoliberal economy by participating in transnational labor relations as flexible, affective laborers.

However, by tracing the personal journeys of these Japanese guides (and former guides), and their own reflections carefully, more complex processes of translation become apparent. Consider the ambivalent effects revealed by the Japanese guides' involvement in the Canadian national park's guide accreditation program. On the one hand, their participation helped build the hegemonic formation of ecology as language; on the other hand, their seemingly obedient gesture of translating the park's ecological language also opened up a critical space that destabilized the dominant knowledge. The process by which the Japanese guides translated the park's idea of "nature" elucidated the instability of the dominant notion of nature under the guise of the stability and universality of the concept. The guides' acts of translation pointed to the indeterminacy contained in the hegemonic discourse by turning the critical gaze back to the park's environmental stewardship project and revealed its social, cultural, and historical specificity. Moreover, their translation practices constantly generated new hybrid meanings of nature in the process of moving back and forth between different epistemological traditions.

Similarly, the Japanese guides' engagement with the discourse of freedom did not mean that they believed in liberal or neoliberal notions of subjectivity. As discussed in chapter 3, *jiyū* as the translation word for "freedom" contains the unsettling tension between the liberal notion of freedom, developed in the European Enlightenment, and the Buddhist notion of *jizai*. On the one hand, jiyū, as a translation of freedom stands against the external source of oppression by being supported by the individual possession of natural rights. On the other hand, jiyū as a translation of the Buddhist concept is achieved by detaching oneself from individual interest and merging the self with others in the ideal state in which both self and other transcend their egoistic desires.

The tension contained in jiyū was alive in the narratives of these women. For example, Rei said that the natural environment of Banff made her aware that she had been too influenced by what she described as an "American-style" pursuit of personal achievement, success, and freedom. Living in Banff's guide community, she realized the importance of pursuing a "peaceful ordinary life" rather than individual "success." She found that even though her wage as a novice guide was modest, she gained "richness in heart" by living in a community where people closely supported each other and shared pleasant times in a beautiful natural environment. This experience led her to be critical about the attitudes that pushed people to climb a social ladder as if it was the only way to achieve "freedom" and to measure a person's value. She started to wonder if people in contemporary society conflated the moral value of making an effort to better themselves with the socioeconomic value of attaining upward social mobility. She envisioned an ideal society that would allow everyone to find a comfortable niche and to live peacefully even though his or her skills and characteristics were not easily translated into an ability to make a living.

When she was younger, she looked down on office ladies, imagining that anyone could do such work and that the work thus was not worthwhile. But after working as a guide, she realized it was rewarding to be appreciated for her work of helping others. Even more, by working as an assistant administrator in the travel agency, she became aware that offering someone effective assistance was itself quite challenging, required skill, and therefore was worthwhile to pursue. Her experiences of working both as a guide and as an administrative assistant allowed her to see the connection between these two. Rei realized the web of mutual help among people in various positions, and she no longer looked down on assistant work as she had before. It became clear to her that everyone contributed to society in diverse ways, so anyone who did her best in her work should be respected, regardless of the kind of work.

Yoshiko's idea of freedom also did not quite fit with the typical notion of freedom in market-centered neoliberal discourse, whose model of subjectivity was to be an entrepreneur. Although several other guides started their own independent businesses, Yoshiko did not think of becoming an entrepreneur. She liked working as an employee because she did not have to worry about the management aspect of the tour guide business. She could concentrate on guiding and interacting with tourists. For her, being an entrepreneur or a company owner did not mean being "liberated." Instead, it was "freeing" to be hired by a good employer because she could be liberated from the concerns of running a business and freely concentrate on what she wanted to pursue: to enjoy the feeling of "living on the earth" by hiking or skiing with her customers.

Even Kubo Toshiyuki, who had been pursuing his dream of having his own company, did not view making a profit as his primary aim. He still held onto his passion for contributing to "peace" through cultural exchange and mutual understanding through travel. His interest in making a company was to offer an effective nodal point in society for this purpose, and he viewed business as a means to create the site for pursuing this dream, not a tool to accumulate personal wealth. He left the RMT for three years to attend a school in Calgary and to learn website design but returned to Banff and continued working at the RMT while nurturing his dream.

Neither did Mori Yukio, who left the RMT and became a self-employed freelance guide, believe in the neoliberal entrepreneurial aspiration of pursuing his economic interest. Yukio left the RMT because the more his status as a reliable senior guide was established, the more he was frustrated because he had to compromise the quality of his guiding. This was partly due to the nature of the RMT as a subcontracting company of several major Japanese travel agencies. Gradually, Yukio was assigned a greater number of complex tours that combined customers whose tour conditions were quite different. To meet the customers' different needs and satisfy tour contracts, he was required to deal with numerous logistical issues. In addition, Yukio was given more assignments that required him to entertain important clients and to perform as a local sales representative for major Japanese travel agencies rather than as a guide. Yukio felt that he had to act as if he were an employee of a large Japanese corporation, from which he wanted to free himself. Liberating himself from these constraints, he wanted to continue to "polish" the quality of his guiding. His decision to take an economic risk and becoming a freelance guide was more like that of an itinerant artisan rather than a neoliberal entrepreneur.

These stories illustrate the Japanese guides' ambivalent engagements with neoliberal discourses of freedom. On the one hand, in their effort to liberate themselves from the previously dominant regime of governance—the "Japanese-style" work relations—they were attracted by the notion of individual freedom developed in the modern European tradition of liberalism and further mutated into recent neoliberal discourses. On the other hand, as soon as they started to talk about freedom, using the translation word jiyū, they were led to articulate conflicting notions of freedom, as the detachment from the liberal notion of subjectivity, moving toward freedom as jizai, achieved by the subjection of the individual self to connectivity with others and the environment. The life trajectories of these current and former Japanese guides and their own reflections on their life courses suggest that their acts of translation helped to form the hegemony of neoliberal discourses of freedom and subjectivity, but with traces of indeterminacy, also elucidated the potential of shifting the discourses into different directions.

In this sense, their subjectivities resonate with what Paolo Virno (2004) described as an "amphibian subject," living both within and outside capitalism. Virno draws from Gilbert Simondon's idea of "individuation" and decouples the individual and the subject, the pair that has been assumed to be isomorphic in the liberal discourse. Virno argues that the "individuation is never concluded" as the "subject consists of the permanent interweaving of pre-individual elements and individuated characteristics; moreover, the subject is this interweaving" (2004, 78). In the work of immaterial workers in contemporary capitalism, the significance of the pre-individual social and material conditions, which shape the individual's subject construction, is hard to ignore. Because their work relies on communication that produces affect in others and on the worker's ability to be affected, it is apparent that "individuation is never concluded, that the pre-individual is never fully translated into singularity" (78). Virno also cautioned that this cooperation between an individual and the others around the individual is not necessarily peaceful. Rather, "it engenders crises of various kinds" and highlights that the "subject is a battlefield" (78).

So, what is found in tracing nature in translation? The guides' journey into magnificent nature demonstrates that nature needs to be understood as a constant process of translation. Translation of nature is inseparable from the cultural politics of what it means to be human and what it is like to be a "free" and "liberated" subject living in the continuously globalizing world.

As the guides' efforts in translating nature demonstrate, nature is an elusive concept. Although it is supposed to indicate a physical environment external to human beings, its boundaries are unclear—both in terms of scale and in terms of the relationship with human beings. Yet, its very elusiveness is the source of the ambivalent aura that attracts diverse people living in various epistemological and cultural backgrounds to imagine that they share the same living environment in nature on the earth. Nature also invites people to assume that they share the same nature as human beings, the universal category of our being.

The claim of the universality of nature has been further intensified by its association with scientific knowledge. Even though framing the physical environment as "nature"—as if it exists independently of and separately from human beings—is a product of specific social and historical contexts, this epistemological framework gained its hegemony from the belief that one can understand nature with objective scientific knowledge, regardless of one's social and cultural background. The claim of universality entails the obligation of accepting everyone as a subject of knowing nature, and nature becomes a point of articulation in which diverse epistemological traditions come into contact. The allure of nature is its open invitation. This inclusive potential invites people who do not necessarily share the same epistemological traditions to participate in knowing nature. This allure presents strong effects with its liberating potential, especially on the people who have been struggling to shift their position from objects of an exoticizing Orientalist gaze to achieve the status of subjects with their own subjective gaze, in their aspiration to become equal members as subjects of knowledge. Therefore, translation of nature concerns ecology not just in terms of natural environment; translation of nature is also inseparable from social ecology (the constitution of society) and mental ecology (the construction of people's subjectivities) (Guattari 2008). The Japanese guides' experiences elucidate how these three ecologies are intertwined in their practice of translating nature and how translation of nature is deeply political. Their experiences illuminate the quotidian nature of knowledge politics.

At the turn of the twenty-first century, the concern for the well-being of the physical environment has been heightened as a consequence of industrial resource extraction on a global scale. At the same time, the stresses of industrial society also stimulate people to make actual and imaginary journeys into nature in order to heal their minds and bodies. As the problem of nature has become an urgent global concern, it is important to understand the translation process of these three ecologies, and its politics among people with diverse backgrounds. It is necessary to recognize that nature is always in the process of translation, and that this translation has significant effects on the politics over visions of society as well as the well-being of people. Because the translation of nature is fundamental in people's struggle for freedom as well as for constructions of their subjectivities, any endeavors that deal with global and environmental issues have to recognize how acts of translation shape the kinds of discourse and agency that are possible.

Notes

Prologue

1. See Orvar Löfgren (1999) for the history of the development of mass tourism as the "laboratory" of subject making in Europe and North America. Pál Nyíri (2009) also documents how tourism works as a training ground for making modern subjectivity in China.

Introduction

1. The "staged" aspect of tourist representation has been a central topic in the social studies of tourism since Dean MacCannell's ([1976] 1999) pioneering work, which draws from Erving Goffman's (1959) discussion of social interaction as performance. Although this book was inspired by these discussions, its focus is slightly different. Instead of joining discussions of how the staged tourist representation is constructed, I would argue that this analytic mode, which relies on the distinction between the "stage" and "backstage," derives from a very specific modern Western epistemological framework. The notion of "authenticity" and the preoccupation with this concept are products of this epistemological tradition (see Handler 1986). Rather than revealing the staged aspect of guides' performances, this book intends to trace how the Japanese tour guides work as mediators of incommensurable epistemological frameworks. Here, I draw on Timothy Mitchell's (1988) critique of modern Western epistemological technology, which orders things based on the separation between representation and what is represented, and the strong belief that a truthful,

realistic representation can capture the authentic truth behind the facade of representation. Roland Barthes ([1970] 1982) points out that Japanese theatrical representational techniques order things differently. Based on his observation of Bunraku, traditional puppet plays, he points out that the puppet players are not hidden backstage but are obviously visible to the audience. This theatrical technique is not based on the belief that the truth, or the authentic reality "out there," should be found behind the realistic representation. Instead of truthful representation, Barthes observed that the traditional Japanese theatrical technique artfully creates the stories or evokes the world through the play of signs and forms that often include the stylized appearance of what would be placed backstage in Western representational techniques. This echoes the recent critique of the primacy of authenticity within tourism studies (see Bruner 1994 for an early critique of authenticity). A growing number of analysts point out the incommensurability of the notion of authenticity with the non-Western conceptualization of the world, whose epistemological configuration and/ or social conditions put more value in other concepts, such as sincerity (e.g., Taylor 2001; Winter 2009).

2. Names in this book are pseudonyms, except for public figures and those informants whose publications are cited in this book. In some sections, when it did not affect my arguments, I disguised minor facts in order to protect the informants' privacy. The polite postfix "san" is used to address people who were considered to be socially senior to the regular guides in the Japanese community in Banff. The Japanese speakers use several different ways to address each other depending on seniority, social status, gender, proximity, and characteristics and personality. Among the Japanese speakers in Banff, a senior man often would be called by his family name plus "san," and a senior woman would be called by her given name plus "san." But it was not rare for a senior man to be called by a given name and a woman to be called by a family name, depending on the occasion and the relationship. To make it simple for the readers, but also to capture the sense of social relations within Banff's Japanese-speaking community, I follow the most common practice throughout the book: family name plus "san" for males with senior status, and given name plus "san" for females in senior positions. I use the given name for guides of regular status, even though I used "san" for some of them in my actual communication with them.

3. See Michael Lambek (2008) for a critique of the conflation between economic value and ethical virtue.

4. I thank Alejandro Paz, who pointed out the importance of linguistic ideology by making the following comments on an earlier draft: "Even the idea of a 'literal' translation is filled with ideology. Any time a cultural mediator is called upon to find a form from across a language boundary, s/he must make a choice among different varieties, i.e., making all kinds of links— from syntactic and semantic constructions all the way to compositional

features of personhood ('voices')—and such things become institutional-ized and thus can occur seemingly instantaneously, and without a great deal of consciousness."

5. Miyoshi (1991, 123) argues that this incommensurability reveals that, although Japanese intellectuals in the mid-twentieth century had assumed the universal value of subjectivity, subjectivity was developed in the West during the modern period in response to specific historical contexts and is no less culturally and historically specific than such concepts as feudalism and Protestantism.

6. As Sakai (1997) points out, there have been two types of reactions to this constraint: one is to praise the uniqueness of Japanese thought and as-sume a nationalistic bent; the other is to take the position of the Western-ized subject and fashion oneself as cosmopolitan, as if one is free from the cultural constraints specific to Japan.

7. The translation process of "subject" calls attention to a fundamental para-dox inherent in the English word, too: How can a subject be a subject if it is also an object seen from the referential vantage point somewhere external to the self, such as in the usage "research subject"? However, this paradox has not been explored fully in the conventional discussions in Japan.

8. Although I strongly respect Ortner's work in general, I depart from her regarding her reading of Vincanne Adams's account of Sherpas (1996). Ortner (1999) considers Adams to have overprivileged the Westerner's perspective and describes the process in which Sherpas lost "authenticity" in responding to their clients' desires. I would argue that Adams raises an important question about the notion of authenticity itself by illustrating how Sherpas and the Western climbers internalized each other's gazes and mutually constructed their subjectivities. Adams's account is helpful for understanding how "authentic" identity is performatively constructed and becomes "real" through the repetitive enactments of discourses produced by certain gazes (cf. Butler 1990).

9. According to Sandford (2000), Mount Alberta is the fifth-highest mountain peak in the Canadian Rockies. Determining the height of the mountain was a difficult task due to its remoteness and inaccessibility.

10. The periodization of "golden age" varies in different locations. The golden age of European Alpinism is considered to be from 1854 to 1865, when the highest peaks were first ascended. In Canada, the golden age is con-sidered to be from 1885, when the completion of the transcontinental railroad brought climbers to Western Canada, to 1925, when Mt. Alberta and Mt. Logan were summited (Robinson 2004, see also Scott 2000). The golden age of Alpinism in Japan is considered to be about ten years from 1905, when the Japanese Alpine Club was established (Koizumi 2001).

11. On the way to New York, Maki stopped in Los Angeles and stayed with Kojima Usui, who was the branch manager of Yokohama Shōgyō Bank in LA (Maki 1991a).

12. See William Kelly (1993) and Andrew Gordon (1993) for a historical analysis of the formation of the "middle class" in Japan. The formation of "middle-class" consciousness has been much discussed in Japanese academia and the popular media. Most of the debates have been based on the "Public Opinion Survey Concerning People's Lifestyles" conducted and published by the Cabinet Office of Japan. According to the survey, since the late 1960s nearly 90 percent of respondents indicated that their living standard was "middle." The "White Paper on the National Lifestyle," which was prepared by the Japanese government's Economic Planning Agency, cited the survey results in several volumes and presented them as a proof that the middle-class consciousness was established among the Japanese population (e.g. 1970). Reflecting these data, in the 1970s, the discourse of *Ichioku sōchūryū* (All the hundred million people all middle class) emerged in the popular media, and since then, scholars and intellectual commentators have debated whether the claim that most of the Japanese population was middle class had a substantial basis or was simply an illusion (e.g., Kishimoto 1979; Murakami 1984). Alongside this debate, there has been much discussion of whether this "class" consciousness is about class in the Marxist sense or simply indicates people's perceptions of their living standard (e.g., Kanbayashi 2010).

13. See Anagnost (2008) for a critique on the usage of "social strata" over "class" in China that tames people's awareness of social inequality and encourages the expansion of middle-class values and practices.

Chapter 1. Narratives of Freedom

1. See Ogasawara (1998) for a sociological study of OLs using the ethnographic observation method. Ogasawara points out that OLs used to be called "office flowers," as their function was considered to be decorative and to encourage men to work hard (12). She also points out that even though the word is so popularly used in everyday life in Japan, the actual meaning of the term is ambiguous. While the stereotypical image of the OL is an unmarried woman working as a clerical assistant, Ogasawara defines an OL in her study as "a woman working regularly in an office who engages in simple, repetitive, clerical work without any expert knowledge or management responsibility" (27). Although many OLs might not officially have management responsibility, as Satomi's story suggests, in actual practice, they sometimes have some expert knowledge to effectively assist the career track workers.

2. The word *furītā* is a combination of the English word "free" and the German word *arbeiter* (worker). While the German word arbeiter means a worker or a laborer in general, the loanword in Japanese, *arubaitā*, refers to "part-time worker," often students. The word furītā has been used to distinguish non-student part-time workers from student workers.

3. The connection between Hokkaido and North America that the guides felt was not accidental. Hokkaido was formerly known as Ezo, settled by the Ainu, an indigenous people of Japan. Threatened by the increasing Russian influence in the region, in the nineteenth century, the Tokugawa shogunate encouraged immigration from the mainland to Ezo. In 1869, the newly established Meiji government launched the Hokkaido Kaitakushi (Development Commission) and integrated the land into the Japanese political system (Morris-Suzuki 1998, Ōsaki 1971). The government invited American agricultural specialists, such as Horace Capron and William S. Clark, to provide guidance for adapting American-style frontier development (Ōsaki 1971).

4. A working holiday visa allows young people between the ages of eighteen and thirty (twenty-five in some countries) to work part-time or full-time to supplement their funds during their travel for up to one year. After Australia, New Zealand, and Canada, Japan expanded its program to include the Republic of Korea and France in 1999, Germany in 2000, the United Kingdom in 2001, Ireland and Denmark in 2007, Taiwan in 2009, Hong Kong in 2010, and Norway in 2013. According to the website of the Ministry of Foreign Affairs of Japan, the programs "are designed to foster young people with global perspectives and enhance friendly relationships between Japan and partner countries by providing opportunities for the young people to deepen their understandings of partner countries" (Japan Ministry of Foreign Affairs 2013). According to the Immigration Bureau's white paper, Canada has been the second most popular destination after Australia among Japanese on working holidays in the early twenty-first century. In 2000, a total of 4,183 working holiday visas to Canada were issued (Japan Ministry of Justice 2003, 120).

5. Eita's comments about his work suggest that it also provided him with a means of self-cultivation and a way to maintain his well-being. Yet, in his mind, self-cultivation through work is not only for himself but also for the clients, the company, and the larger society. The process of achieving self-cultivation and well-being through bodily coordination with one's surroundings is very similar to practices among Chinese citizens who engage in various kinds of cultural and physical exercises, as documented by Farquhar and Zhang (2005).

6. Many of the guides' frustrations echo Arendt's ([1958] 1998) concerns about the intrusion of "labor" into the realm of "work." Arendt argues that, unlike "labor" in industrial capitalism, which is assumed to be alienated from a person and to be sold merely to survive, the "work" of artisans, or *homo faber*, was an expression of the worker's personality.

7. I use Dore's typology as a heuristic device to introduce different perceptions of the corporation rather than as an observation of actual practices in the workplace. Although Dore uses the term "Anglo-Saxon" which implies ethnicity, I prefer to use "Anglo-American" to highlight the specificity of

this form of corporation in British and American institutional systems. The actual operations and practices of corporations are obviously more complex than these models. As Karen Ho (2009) suggests, the conflicting models coexist within corporations in the United States. She points out that the "shareholder-favoring" model became dominant only within the last twenty-five years.

8. Many critics have pointed out that in small and midsized companies, there has been a higher rate of labor mobility even though the "community" model has been established as an ethos, and has been made the hegemonic form of organization by large-scale corporations (e.g., Takanashi 2002, 188). Takanashi also points out that the "long-term" employment practices have been developed in order to repair the damage caused by the frequent and intense labor disputes, layoffs, and strikes of the 1950s (2002, 187).

9. See Yanagisako (2002) for a critique of ethnicized typology and a discussion of the coproduction of "culture" and capital.

10. Michel Albert (1993) points out similar variations in his explanation of the "neo-American" model, which is based on individual achievement and short-term profits, and the Rhine model that emphasizes the long-term goals of collective achievement and public consensus.

11. Iwai (2003, 173–178) points out that this development bore particular mixed legacies of a wartime totalitarian economy and postwar American occupation. Both coincidentally aimed to dissolve the classic prewar elite, family-owned corporation and redistribute capital away from the few within the privileged class.

Chapter 2. Populist Cosmopolitanism

1. As many authors have pointed out, populism is a very elusive concept. My discussion here is drawn mostly from Laclau (1977); Taggart (2000); and Otake (2003).

2. This notion of cosmopolitanism is drawn from Kant (1991), as well as recent arguments on cosmopolitanism, cultural politics, and subjectivity in Archibugi (2003); Breckenridge et al. (2002); and Cheah and Robbins (1998).

3. Reflecting the complex historical development of the English terms "subject" and "subjectivity," recent anthropological discussions on "subjectivity" seem to be separated into two parallel fields. One focuses on "subjectivity" as an individual's emotional experiences, as exemplified by Luhrmann's (2006) position that follows the psychological model of subjectivity. The other examines the constitution of this mode of subjectivity itself by raising questions about an individual as a bounded entity that takes the position of "subject" as the privileged locus of subjectivity (e.g., Mol 2008), and by situating this mode of subjectivity within Western intellectual history (e.g., Rorty 2007; see also Biehl, Good, and Kleinman

2007 for an overview on this topic). My interest in this book aligns with the latter approach. I intend to show how the notion of "subjectivity" that is imagined to be located in the particular model of human itself has been the key problem in modern Japanese intellectual history, and to illustrate how the Japanese tour guides tried to translate and negotiate with this normalized model of human, individual, and subjectivity. The predicament of the Japanese guides was not only that they were torn between different codes of emotion (as in Luhrmann's example of colonial elites or homeless women) but also that they were required to live simultaneously in a social world that assumes this notion of subjectivity and another social world in which this notion of subjectivity does not necessarily fit well.

4. See Kelly (1993) for the development of postwar leisure culture in Japan.

5. Economist Kaneko Masaru (1999) makes a similar argument in his analysis of the market as a medium of the individual and society.

6. "A Choice in Life" is close to the original Japanese title. However, I translated the title elsewhere as "Choose Your Own Life" because the contents of the book were instructions for lifestyle choices for sararīman (Satsuka 2009).

7. Ōhashi calls choosing one's own life "the new Western mentality" (*atarashii oubeigata no mentaritī*) (2000a, 11). The term *oubei* literally means "European and American," with the combination of the *kanji* characters that indicate Europe and America. However, in this book and other related writings, there is little mention of European influences on his idea of retirement or work. Because most of Ōhashi's writings are about American, Canadian, Australian, and New Zealand society and culture, here I translate *oubei* as "Western" instead of "European and American."

8. Following his American friend's idea of separating the places of work and leisure, Ōhashi built a house near a golf resort in Itō, Shizuoka prefecture, about 120 kilometers southwest of Tokyo, and moved there in 1974. He spent half of the week at his house in Itō and traveled by bullet train to Tokyo, where for the rest of the week he stayed at an upscale hotel suite while working on his TV programs (Ōhashi 2000a, 27–28). In 1990, following his Canadian friend's idea of early retirement, Ōhashi announced his "semiretirement declaration." From then on, he entered into his "latter half of life," hopping between Japan, Canada, Australia, and New Zealand to follow the best golf season in each country.

9. According to Yanabu Akira (1982, 25), notions of the "individual" developed from European Enlightenment thought were not easy concepts to translate into Japanese. When the English word "individual" was imported in the nineteenth century, there was a long controversy over how to translate it. Several attempts were made to use a similar Japanese word for its translation, such as *hitori* (one) or *hito* (human). However, applying these words would confuse the meaning of "individual" because neither was able to express the sense of an individual as an independent person who is a unique

entity while also belonging to a larger category of human. Thus a new word, *kojin*, was created by combining the Chinese characters for "each" and "human" (Yanabu 1982, 25–42).

10. See Kondo (1990) for the anthropological critique of this assumed notion of "self."

11. Responding to the feminist caricature, Ōhashi depicts the traditional Japanese notion of retirement as an image of a stagnant senior passively spending time. He asks the readers, "Are you going to pass your time merely playing with your grandchildren? Living in the shadows treated like a '*sodaigomi*' at home?" (2000a, 29). He problematizes the contemporary sarariman still caught in this mind-set. In contrast, Ōhashi highlights the positive image of what he calls the "new Western style" of retirement. He urges readers to change their perceptions of senior life, abandon the traditional Japanese way of thinking, and move forward to adopt the "Western style" (11).

12. Mitsui's (2008) analysis of the atonement of the Asian Women's Fund toward "comfort women" clearly indicates that this continues to be a serious issue in contemporary Japan.

13. However, as Oguma (2002) points out, we should be aware that Maruyama was not an uncritical admirer of Western liberalism. While he reevaluates the modern notion of individual as subjective agency, he also distanced himself from a kind of liberalism, especially the tendency in the British and American liberal thoughts that assume the nation-state is a source of obstacles to pursuing individual freedom and place high value in liberating individuals from the society. Being more influenced by continental European thought, he tried to pursue the way that individuals associate with the society and to cooperate to construct social coalitions with their subjective agencies.

14. As Kanetaka and Morohashi (2001) point out, Ōhashi can be situated among the group of television and radio entertainers who were influential in forming mass sensibilities in the 1960s. These entertainers were multitalented (in script writing, program production, and acting in and hosting their shows) and articulated popular antiestablishment sentiments through their work. They also were politically opinionated, as exemplified by Ōhashi and Aoshima Yukio, who served as a member of the House of Councillors (1968–1989 and 1992–1995) and as the governor of the Tokyo Metropolitan Government (1995–1999). Others include Maeda Takehiko, Ozawa Shōichi, and Ei Rokusuke. Although Kume Hiroshi and Tamori were less explicit about their own political stances and more specialized in their roles as television show hosts, Kanetaka and Morohashi include them among the later generation of this group of entertainers who wield witty criticism against authority to express mass sensibilities.

15. Some of the words Ōhashi coined in the 1960s that still appear in slang dictionaries further exemplify his antielite strategy. In particular, *happa*

fumi fumi is a legendary phrase in nonsense subculture; it is a line from the improvisational "pop word" haiku Ōhashi made for a television advertisement for a fountain pen in 1969. In the ad, after reciting the nonsense rhyme to express the good feeling of writing with the pen, Ōhashi wittily added, "You got it" (*wakarune*). His playful words implicitly critiqued the privileges of rational communication.

16. The "America" that Ōhashi promoted through his work does not necessarily coincide with the actual society or the life of people in the United States. It is, rather, "America" as a trope, into which Japanese people can project their social imagination. In this way, it is part of the desired "America" as the post–World War II Japanese imaginary that Yoshimi (2001) pointed out.

17. Ōhashi's list of American popular music includes Benny Goodman's "Let's Dance" and Artie Shaw's "Begin the Beguine," as well as music by the Boston Pops and Paul Whiteman, the tango, and Hawaiian music. Ōhashi encountered these genres after the war when he was a middle school student and discovered a box of records in a package that had been hidden in his house in the countryside of Chiba prefecture during the evacuation. American music was prohibited during the war as "enemy's music" (Ōhashi 2000a, 78–79).

18. As Susan Pharr (1996) points out, journalism in modern Japan has a tradition of acting both as a strong critic of the government and as an institution to disseminate the dominant social perception; thus it stands in an ambivalent position to authority.

19. Ōhashi (2000b, 165) writes nostalgically of his hero Joe DiMaggio as a representative of the lost good old days—a man of sincerity and honesty who achieved success by hard work, and not for greedy, selfish reasons but for the love of what he does and with a sense of social responsibility. He also praises the movie character Forrest Gump, "who single-mindedly and sincerely devotes himself to others before thinking of his own benefit" (Ōhashi 2001, 87).

Chapter 3. Co-Modification of Self

1. *Oni* is a Japanese folklore demon spirit. It is fearful but sometimes also has a humorous connotation. The term is commonly used to describe a severe instructor, teacher, or supervisor or someone who is very serious about his or her work.

2. Similar dilemmas have been addressed by Hochschild's (1983) work on flight attendants and Russ's (2005) work on hospice care workers.

3. See Emily Martin (1994) for a discussion of "flexible" bodily practices in post-Fordist work relations.

4. Comaroff and Comaroff (2001, 3) argue that this is a capitalism that presents new forms of enchantment with a gospel of salvation and

prosperity, articulated in the new form of fetish of nation-state as well as the expansion of the neoliberal discourse of civil society. They argue that in millennial capitalism, there emerges "a more radically individuated sense of personhood" in which social traits, including class, became objects of a person's possessive traits or lifestyle choices (15). I would add that at the very foundation of this articulation lies the fetish of personhood, the iterated figure of modern liberalism, who has an intrinsic unique inner self that is imagined as free from external influences.

5. This should not be confused with the negation of individuality; rather, it is the core of actualization of individual uniqueness, which is similar to what Deleuze and Guattari call "haecceity," a mode of individuation different from the modern liberal notion that presupposes the existence of the individual as an independent, autonomous subject. Deleuze and Guattari argue that haecceities "consist entirely of relations of movement and rest between molecules or particles, capacities to affect and be affected" (1987, 261).

6. This process of attaining freedom through discipline is similar to what Erika Evasdottir (2004) observes as "obedient autonomy" among Chinese intellectuals.

Chapter 4. Gender in Nature Neverland

1. See Manzenreiter (2011) for an example of the association of masculinity and climbing in Japan. As Manzenreiter points out, traditionally, women had been banned from entering some mountainous religious areas because of the "impurity" associated with the female body. See Suzuki (2002) for more detail about the complex history of *nyonin kinsei*, or the prohibition of women in the mountains. Although mountain climbing and related outdoor activities had often been associated with masculinity, these activities recently have been popularized among women, and the term *yama gāru* (mountain girls) was coined to indicate women who love the outdoors. It should also be noted that there are several internationally outstanding female alpine climbers in Japan, including Tabei Junko, who, in 1975, was the first woman in the world to reach the summit of Mount Everest.

2. Different companies had different policies regarding gender for hiring and assigning tours. For example, one company in Banff was known for hiring many young female guides, many of whom led hiking tours, whereas another company had mostly male guides.

3. Evaluating the expansion of women's work opportunities has been the recurring theme in feminist debates in Japan since the early twentieth century. Because work outside the home was associated with Western-modeled modern industrialization, the debates also intersected with the question of whether the modern Western notion of the individual as subject is applicable to Japanese society and whether the imported modern

notion of gender equality would "liberate" or "oppress" Japanese women. The most well known was the early "maternity protection debate" (*bosei-hogo ronsō*) that began in 1918, between the famous poet Yosano Akiko and the writer Hiratsuka Raicho, and later was joined by Yamada Waka and Yamakawa Kikue (see, e.g., Imai 2002; Nishikawa 1985; Nozawa 1990). The issue reemerged after World War II in several "housewife debates" (*shufu ronsō*) and has continued to the present in different forms. The heart of the controversy was whether housewives in Japanese society should be considered oppressed through their containment in the domestic realm, or if instead housewives have certain power and authority because they are in charge of households as chief managers. In the 1980s, the debate between ecofeminist Aoki Yayoi and post-Marxist feminist Ueno Chizuko further highlighted modern industrialization as the center of the gender issue. Aoki (1986), influenced by Ivan Illich's view of antimodern industrial society, argues that technological development in modern industrialized society was the source of alienation of the body from nature, which led to women's oppression. From this perspective, the increase of women's work outside the home cannot be simply celebrated as liberation because it could instead be a sign of further oppression of the female body by modern industry. Ueno points out that ecofeminism romanticizes premodern society and essentializes gender difference in premodern communal social relationships. Instead of simply attributing problems to industrial society, Ueno argues that feminists need to examine critically how the system of difference is constructed through modern industrialization (Ueno 1986, 1994; see also Ehara 1985, 1990).

4. It would be too simplistic to label the "opening" of outdoor guide opportunities for females as a sign of the "liberation" of women. In the year 2000, some female guides took advantage and identified themselves as feminine so as not to be assigned work that involved the additional responsibility of driving and providing outdoor first aid. Because the company paid the same, or sometimes even more, to lead a bus tour (during which the guides could even take a rest on the way back if the situation allowed), some female guides were not enthusiastic about leading outdoor tours even though they enjoyed mountaineering or trekking on their time off. Each female guide's strategy for getting assigned or not getting assigned to outdoor activity tours suggests the complex negotiation of associating gender and work.

5. This specific subculture in the Japanese girl's school has recently gained academic attention. See for example, Kawamura Kunimitsu's pioneering work (1993, 1994, 2003) and the extensive discussion on the formation of this subculture in relation to "modernity." His materials suggest that this subculture emerged in the process of translating the gendered norms developed in the modern Western industrial societies when Japan followed the similar path of modernizing the country through the development of

industrial capitalism, which required solidifying the gender categorization and placing the uniformity in the family structure. The notion of "girl" as an adolescent, somewhere between childhood and adulthood, was introduced and institutionalized through the newly adopted modern school system. See also Imada (2007), Inagaki (2007), Pflugfelder (2005) Robertson (2002) and Shamoon (2012).

6. The word "oyaji" originally means "father" in colloquial Japanese. It turned out to be used to indicate a father-like figure, especially in the workplace. While traditionally used to express the intimacy and respect with the man, the term has gained more delogatory nuance and often used to identify the unfavored characteristics of middle-aged and old men in general.

7. The sexuality of the students in homosocial intimacy, historically identified as a particular form of "sisterhood," or "S" (esu), relationships is hard to identify and raises an interesting debates among scholars. The S relationship became the topic of public debate especially when, in 1911, two students committed double suicide in order to eternally maintain their "pure" platonic love relations, which was sensationally covered by the media (Inagaki 2007, 105). Inagaki Kyōko, scholar of education, argues that the S relationship has come to be gradually tolerated among educators, journalists and sexologists, as long as the relationship remains platonic, and allowed the interpretation that it was a benign temporary phenomenon in adolescence and served as a rehearsal for the heterosexual relationships that would replace them as the girls grew up (111–113). In contrast, anthropologist Jennifer Robertson (2002) points out that how to control shōjo (girls), the ambiguous figure of "not-yet-female female," was a great concern at the turn of the twentieth century and the same-sex love of girl's school students invoked the "deviant" sexual desires in the media (158–159). Robertson also argues, although sexologists found it difficult to distinguish friendship and homosexuality, public figures like Yoshiya Nobuko—a novelist known as a lesbian and for her contribution to the development of the genre of shōjo shosetsu, or girl's novel—helped to create the space for women to express same-sex relationships by eschewing a conventional notion of shōjo and "effectively expanded the dimensions of the shōjo period so that it defined not a phase of life, but an actual lifestyle and subculture as well" (159). Furthermore, historian, Gregory Pflugfelder (2005) suggests that the significance of the debates around the S relationship in the early twentieth century was not so much about forming a public consensus about the nature of the S relationship itself, as the discourses on schoolgirl intimacy contain "both a regulatory and a contestational aspect" (176). Rather, the debates provided the sites for professionals, such as sexologists and journalists, as well as feminists to assert their authority on girls' sexuality. He points out that while young women have been always developing the ways in which they interact with each other in their

own terms, the figure of school girl continue to "function as an emblem of worrisome sexuality" in contemporary Japan (177).

8. Miyazaki Hayao is an internationally known animation director who also made *Princess Mononoke* and *Spirited Away*. The common theme of these films is the conflict between the natural and human worlds. Princess Mononoke, a girl who was raised by a wolf spirit and fights against humans, is an ambiguous character who is a human being but possessed by an animal spirit. She represents the rage of the natural world against humans' environmental destruction and lack of respect for the natural world (see Napier 2001). *Spirited Away* is the story of a young girl who slips into the world of spirits when she and her parents are on the way to a new house in a newly developed suburban bedroom community. The girl is captivated by the spirit world and tries to save her parents, who have been turned into pigs because of their greediness. Through her eyes, the story depicts the forgotten world of natural spirits suffering as a result of human development, now invisible to the eyes of adults (see Kiridōshi 2001). The main characters in Miyazaki's animation are often young girls, who mediate between the mundane everyday world and the spirited natural world. Female characters in Miyazaki's anime are strong, reflecting his interpretation of Japanese ancient history. Miyazaki, influenced by the historical arguments raised by Amino Yoshihiko (1991), argues that until the medieval period, Japanese women maintained a strong power backed by a belief in women's ability to communicate with supernatural powers (Miyazaki 2002).

9. In the anime, while other humans are busy fighting back against the attack of giant mutant insects that represent the anger of the natural world, Nausicaä alone tries to listen to the voices of the natural world and fights to save the monster insects from the pollution that caused their violent attack on humans. She is not an antitechnology figure, but, as a member of the generation after the apocalyptic destruction of the earth, she utilizes simpler technology, such as a whistling instrument and a glider, to redress the consequences of the greedy overuse of industrial technology. Miyazaki (1983) explains in the endpaper of his comic book version of Nausicaä that he developed the story by combining Princess Nausicaa from Homer's *Odyssey* and Mushimezuruhime, the princess who loves insects in a Japanese anonymous classic. Miyazaki describes Nausicaa as someone who "has a superior sensibility" and who "found a greater pleasure in interacting with nature, harp and songs than in the mundane happiness and suitors." Nausicaa was not frightened by the bloodstained Odysseus and helped him when he was cast to the shores of her land. After Odysseus left, Nausicaa remained unmarried, traveled as the first female minstrel, and sang about Odysseus's adventurous sea voyage. Miyazaki interprets that Mushim- ezuruhime, whose name means "Insect-Loving Princess," also did not care

about social conventions and had a free mind. She loved to walk around in the mountains and fields and was moved by the metamorphosis of insects. He explains that Nausicaa and Mushimezuruhime became the same person in his mind, and he wanted the girl to recover her peaceful days after her long battle and struggle.

10. I use "performance" and "performativity" following Judith Butler's (1993) critique of the subject "I." Instead of presupposing a voluntarist subject, by reformulating performativity in speech act theory, Butler argues that "I" as an enunciating subject was produced by the discursive practices of citation. The subject "I" is the product of the enactment of discourses that enable its appearance as an individual human being. In this sense, my usage of "performance" differs from Goffman's (1959) notion of social performance, in which the presupposed "I" with autonomous agency voluntarily and intentionally performs a social role as if he or she takes on a mask.

11. Yoshiko's experience uncannily coincided with that of Nagata Minako, a female journalist who accompanied the Japanese army when it invaded Manchuria in 1932. In her book *Dansō Jūgunki* (Battlefield reports in male clothes), Nagata explains that in order to report the army's activities closely, she decided to wear male clothes and accompany the troops. In her first nights in Manchuria, in a Japanese-style inn, a maid insisted on calling her *danna-sama*, or "sir." even though the maid knew that Nagata was a woman (Nagata 1932, 14–17).

12. The discrepant usage of gendered vocabulary was also commonly observable in contemporary Japanese language use. Among white-collar workers, a hardworking female would be praised by her colleagues for her *otoko-mae* (manly) work attitude. Similarly, there is a common expression for a hardworking woman, *onna ni shite oku no wa mottainai* (you deserve more than being placed as a woman). In contrast, a beautiful-looking man is described as *otoko ni shite oku no wa mottainai* (you deserve more than being placed as a man). These popular colloquial expressions suggest the clear gendered division of aesthetic realms—the physical beauty of a person is considered to be the female realm, and the beauty of work attitude is considered to be the male realm. However, these expressions also indicate the discrepancy between recognition of a sexed body and gender categorization based on social positioning. The verb *shite oku*, or "to place," suggests that the gender/sex category indicates socially placed positions instead of biologically fixed categories.

13. Butler (1993, 15–16) further argues that the "naturalness" of gender is not a performance played onto the biological sex, but the very idea that "an original and true sex" exists under the surface expression of gender itself is constructed through performative acts. In other words, the materiality of sex is the product of performative acts.

14. The two different systems of gender categorizations seem to coincide with what Oyeronke Oyewumi (1997, ix) calls "somatocentric" or "bio-logic"

human categorization in the modern Western epistemology and the other schemes based on social relations rather than "objective" anatomical differences. Oyewumi argues that in her research on Yoruba gender discourse, the category of "woman," a preexisting group characterized by shared interests, desires, or social position, "simply did not exist in Yoruba prior to its sustained contact with the West" (1997, ix). She claims that "the biologization inherent in the Western articulation of social difference is, however, by no means universal" (9). Oyewumi's critique of the universality of the "somatocentric" assumption coincides with Timon Screech's (2001) analysis of premodern Japanese human categorization. He argues that before the Meiji period, the Japanese did not share the unitary categories of "man" or "woman" based on anatomical difference. The central criteria for human categorization were occupation and age, which locate a person in a web of social relations rather than evaluating him or her on the basis of an observable bodily feature. While I greatly appreciate Oyewumi's insightful critique of "somatocentricity," instead of emphasizing the difference between "Western" and "non-Western" epistemologies, I would highlight the particularity of this epistemology in Western history, constructed as a part of modernity. This allows us to situate how the somatocentric perception of gender was constructed in relation to other social realms, such as the development of industrial society, the nation-state, scientific knowledge, and racial discourses. It also enables us to examine how this perception was transmitted and appropriated to other societies outside the West through the aspiration of being modern.

Chapter 5. The Interpretation of Nature

1. MPHIA was transformed into a new organization, the Interpretive Guides Association (IGA), in 2008 and has gone through new program development.
2. The ACMG mountain guides had a good reputation in the international mountaineering community and were highly respected by local hiking guides and outdoor enthusiasts. To acquire a level of skill high enough to take the mountain guide exam required a substantial investment of time and money.
3. James's critical reflections echo William Cronon's (1995) argument about "wilderness."
4. Japanese participants' acts of hugging the Douglas fir present a similar effect to what Homi Bhabha (1994) describes as the "double articulation" of mimicry. The Japanese participants in James's ecology class had a strong desire to reform their knowledge and become recognizable members of the guide community. Yet, in the very act of mimicking James, the Japanese presented themselves as subjects of difference, who were "almost the same, but not quite." In contrast to colonial India, where mimicry as a sign of the

inappropriate further intensified the surveillance and disciplinary powers, in twenty-first-century Canada, where accepting cultural diversity was part of normative practice, the Japanese participants' mimicry turned its disciplinary gaze toward the constitution of dominant knowledge. The presence of the Japanese as subjects of indeterminacy led a conscientious person like James to reflect on the assumptions of "normalized" knowledge.

5. This definition was offered by Freeman Tilden, who first used the term "interpretation" in the park setting in 1957.

6. I thank Grant Otsuki, who helped me to make this translation flow well in English while maintaining the original nuance of the Japanese.

7. Kimie-san's narrative could sound anthropocentric because she tried to understand animal behavior by using the analogy of human behavior. However, her intention was to encourage humans to stand in the animals' position, rather than imposing a human's point of view on the animals.

8. There is some similarity between the narratives of the Japanese tour guides and Eduardo Viveiros de Castro's (1998) discussion on the "multinatural" perspective that includes nonhuman beings as important actors in Amerindian cosmologies. While Viveiros de Castro focuses on animals as nonhuman actors, I observed that in the Japanese tour guides' narratives, more diverse nonhuman actors were present, including plants, glaciers, and other nonanimated beings.

9. Liu (1995) suggests using "guest language" and "host language"; this usage highlights the more complex power negotiation between languages, instead of relying on traditional translation theory's categories of "source" and "target" languages. She argues that "source" and "target" presuppose and reiterate the contrast between the authentic origin in the source language versus an equivalent substitute and lack thereof in the target language.

10. See Mei Zhan (2011) for more about Heidegger's interest in Eastern philosophy from an anthropological perspective.

Chapter 6. The Allure of Ecology

1. The Banff National Park's management plan justifies its adoption of the concept of ecological integrity by stating that it reflects a number of recent national and international environmental initiatives, such as the UN Biodiversity Convention and the Parks Canada Strategic Framework to Sustain the Integrity of Ecosystems, which highlight the importance of environmental conservation.

2. This definition is cited from Parks Canada's Guiding Principles and Operational Policies. The MPHIA handout also includes a definition of ecological integrity from 2000 Bill C-27, "An Act Respecting the National Parks of Canada": "'ecological integrity' means, with respect to a park, a condition that is determined to be characteristic of its natural region and likely to

persist, including abiotic components and the composition and abundance of native species and biological communities, rates of change and supporting processes."

3. The handout states that the park considers humans a "keystone species" within the ecosystem, "which means . . . the long term role pre-historic and aboriginal peoples played in the landscape must be considered when assessing what an "unimpaired" landscape actually is," and the park undertakes controlled burns to "restore historical fire regimes." However, this kind of explanation puzzled some course participants because if the park set the 'unimpaired' landscape to be restored to the landscape before European settlement and the construction of railways and highways, it was not clear how they should make sense of the co-presence of these land usages.

4. Although concrete plans for a partnership between the national park and First Nations were not addressed publicly during the time of my residence in Banff (2000–2001), in 1999, Parks Canada established the Aboriginal Affairs Secretariat to provide overall leadership with respect to building meaningful relationships with Aboriginal peoples (www.pc.gc.ca/eng/agen /aa/te-wt/tdm-toc.aspx). The Banff National Park later suggested the possibility of permitting traditional hunting "when determined as being necessary for management purposes" and if the animal was culled in a safe and humane manner and used by First Nations groups as the park is planning to reintroduce bison to the park, according to the information sheet "Bison and Banff National Park" (Banff National Parks, n.d.).

5. According to Ben Gadd's *Handbook for the Canadian Rockies*, the book used by many guides and naturalists in Banff, 63 elk were introduced in 1917, and 194 more in 1920 (1995, 704).

6. For the problems of translation of science into bureaucracy, see, e.g., Forsyth and Walker (2008) and Mathews (2011).

7. Robert O'Neill critiques this tendency by emphasizing that "ecosystem is a paradigm" not "an a posteriori, empirical observation about nature" (2001, 3276) and suggests that ecologists should clarify both the spatial and the temporal scale of observation on which they apply the analytic framework of ecosystem. Also, see critiques of the confusion between the ecosystem as conceptual model and empirical observation (Pickett and Cadenasso 2002; Willis 1997; Winterhaider 1984).

8. Similarly, Terao Gorō (2002) forcefully addresses his sense of uneasiness toward the fundamental humanistic ethical grounds in nonanthropocentric claims, and the perception of nature that assumes certain stability. He argues that nature is constantly destroying the current state as a natural process of change, and that it is necessary for humans to admit that all living organisms have to take the life of or put pressure on others—thus inevitably "harming" the others—in order to maintain their own lives. He argues that this recognition of interdependence and relationality based

on this inevitable harm among various life forms is missing in the modern environmental discourse of protection.

9. It is notable that the scientists who explicitly asked this question were studying physics, the discipline that popular imagination assumes to be most unaffected by sociocultural factors due to its highly controlled environment of knowledge production, unlike ecology, whose objects are obviously closely related to the sociocultural aspects of the human relationship with the environment. For example, Morinaga Haruhiko (1976), a physicist who had taught at the Technical University of Munich from 1968 to 1991, explores the question in an essay published in the journal *Shizen* (1976). In the essay, he introduces an anecdote about Nishina Yoshio, who is considered to be the father of modern physics in Japan, and who asked Niels Bohr if it was possible for the Japanese can do science. Morinaga states that he also heard the same question from Sakai Mitsuo, then the director of the Institute for Nuclear Study at the University of Tokyo. Morinaga explains that in the everyday practices of doing schematized experiments and following established protocols, these differences could be ignored, but occasionally he felt discrepancies surface, as if he and his German colleagues were using a "different axis of coordinates" when approaching the same problem, and this led him to consider the question of whether the Japanese can do science.

Epilogue. Found in Translation

1. See Lisa Rofel's (2007) discussion of Chinese cosmopolitan desire and the construction of neoliberal subject. Although the kinds of engagement with the globalizing neoliberal economy differ because the specific social, national, political, and historical situations of her observations and mine, it is striking to see how the similar desire for "entering the world" as an equal member is expressed among our interlocutors.

References

Adams, Vincanne. *Tigers of the Snow and Other Virtual Sherpas: An Ethnography of Himalayan Encounters*. Princeton, NJ: Princeton University Press.

Adams, Vincanne. 2001. "The Sacred in the Scientific Ambiguous Practices of Science in Tibetan Medicine." *Cultural Anthorpology* 16: 542–575.

Albert, Michel. 1993. *Capitalism vs. Capitalism: How America's Obsession with Individual Achievement and Short-Term Profit Has Led It to the Brink of Collapse*. New York: Four Walls Eight Windows.

Allison, Anne. 2009. "The Cool Brand, Affective Activism and Japanese Youth." *Theory, Culture and Society* 26: 89–111.

Allison, Anne. 2012. "Ordinary Refugees: Social Precarity and Soul in 21st Century Japan." *Anthropological Quarterly* 85: 345–370.

Althusser, Louis. 1972. *Lenin and Philosophy and Other Essays*. New York: Monthly Review Press.

Amino, Yoshihiko. 1991. *Nihon no Rekishi o Yominaosu* [Rereading Japanese history]. Tokyo: Chikuma Shobō.

Anagnost, Ann. 2008. "From 'Class' to 'Social Strata': Grasping the Social Totality in Reform-Era China." *Third World Quarterly* 29: 497–519.

Aoki, Yayoi. 1986. *Feminizumu to Ekorojī* [Ecological feminism]. Tokyo: Shinhyōsha.

Archibugi, Daniele, ed. 2003. *Debating Cosmopolitics*. London: Verso.

Arendt, Hannah. [1958] 1998. *The Human Condition*. 2nd ed. Chicago: University of Chicago Press.

Asad, Talal. 1986. "The Concept of Cultural Translation in British Social Anthropology." In *Writing Cultures: The Politics and Poetics of Ethnography*, edited by James Clifford and George E. Marcus, 141–164. Berkeley: University of California Press.

Asad, Talal. 1993. *Genealogies of Religion: Discipline and Reasons of Power in Christianity and Islam*. Baltimore: Johns Hopkins University Press.

Banff National Park. n.d. "Bison and Banff National Park."

Barthes, Roland. [1970] 1982. *Empire of Signs*. Translated by Richard Howard. New York: Hill and Wang.

Bella, Leslie. 1987. *Parks for Profit*. Montreal: Harvest House.

Benjamin, Walter. 1968. *Illuminations: Essays and Reflections*. Edited by Hannah Arendt. Translated by Harry Zohn. New York: Schocken Books.

Bhabha, Homi K. 1994. *The Location of Culture*. London: Routledge.

Biehl, João, Byron Good, and Arthur Kleinman. 2007. "Introduction: Rethinking Subjectivity." In *Subjectivity: Ethnographic Investigations*, edited by João Biehl, Byron Good and Arthur Kleinman, 1–23. Berkeley: University of California Press.

Breckenridge, Carol A., Sheldon Pollock, Homi K. Bhabha, and Dipesh Chakrabarty, eds. 2002. *Cosmopolitanism*. Durham, NC: Duke University Press.

Brinton, Mary C. 2008. *Ushinawareta Ba o Sagashite: Rosuto Jenerēshon no Shakaigaku* [Lost in transition: Youth, education, and work in postindustrial Japan]. Translated by Chiaki Ikemura. Tokyo: NTT Publishing.

Bruner, Edward M. 1994. "Abraham Lincoln as Authentic Reproduction: A Critique of Postmodernism." *American Anthropologist* 96: 397–415.

Burns, Robert J. 2000. *Guardians of the Wild: A History of the Warden Service of Canada's National Parks*. Calgary, AB: University of Calgary Press.

Butler, Judith. 1990. *Gender Trouble: Feminism and the Subversion of Identity*. New York: Routledge.

Butler, Judith. 1993. *Bodies That Matter: On the Discursive Limits of "Sex."* New York: Routledge.

Butler, Judith. 2000. "Restaging the Universal: Hegemony and the Limits of Formalism." In *Contingency, Hegemony, Universality: Contemporary Dialogues on the Left*, edited by Judith Butler, Slavoj Žižek, and Ernesto Laclau, 11–43. London: Verso.

Callon, Michel. 1986. "Some Elements of a Sociology of Translation: Domestication of the Scallops and the Fishermen of St. Brieuc Bay." *Sociological Review Monograph* 32: 196–233.

Campbell, Claire Elizabeth, ed. 2011. *A Century of Parks Canada 1911–2011*. Calgary: University of Calgary Press.

Caz Net. 2001. "Onna no Jinsei Wakaremichi Tokushu 5: Jinsei o Risetto! Ichioku Sō Ōhashi Kyosen ka!!" [Crossroads of woman's life special 5: Reset your life! A nation's hundred million population all turning to Ōhashi Kyosen!!]. *Caz Net*, June 27. www.caz.co.jp/voice/jinsei/p4.html.

Cheah, Pheng, and Bruce Robbins, eds. 1998. *Cosmopolitics: Thinking and Feeling beyond the Nation*. Minneapolis: University of Minnesota Press.

Choy, Timothy. 2011. *Ecologies of Comparison: An Ethnography of Endangerment in Hong Kong*. Durham, NC: Duke University Press.

Clifford, James. 1997. *Routes: Travel and Translation in the Late Twentieth Century*. Cambridge, MA: Harvard University Press.

Comaroff, Jean, and John L. Comaroff. 2001. "Millennial Capitalism: First Thoughts on a Second Coming." In *Millennial Capitalism and the Culture of Neoliberalism*, edited by Jean Comaroff and John L. Comaroff, 1–56. Durham, NC: Duke University Press.

Cronon, William. 1995. "The Trouble with Wilderness; or, Getting Back to the Wrong Nature." In *Uncommon Ground: Rethinking the Human Place in Nature*, edited by William Cronon, 69–90. New York: Norton.

Cumings, Bruce. 1993. "Japan's Position in the World System." In *Postwar Japan as History*, edited by Andrew Gordon, 34–63. Berkeley: University of California Press.

Dearden, Philip, and Jessica Dempsey. 2004. "Protected Areas in Canada: Decade of Change." *Canadian Geographer* 48: 225–239.

Deleuze, Gilles, and Felix Guattari. 1987. *A Thousand Plateaus: Capitalism and Schizophrenia*. Minneapolis: University of Minnesota Press.

Derrida, Jacques. [1967] 1997. *Of Grammatology*. Baltimore, MD: Johns Hopkins University Press.

Derrida, Jacques. 1983. *Dissemination*. Chicago: University of Chicago Press.

Dore, Ronald. 2000. *Stock Market Capitalism: Welfare Capitalism. Japan and Germany versus the Anglo-Saxons*. Oxford: Oxford University Press.

Dore, Ronald. 2002. "Stock Market Capitalism and Its Diffusion. Debate: Stock Market Capitalism vs. Welfare Capitalism." *New Political Economy* 7: 115–127.

Dower, John W. 1999. *Embracing Defeat: Japan in the Wake of World War II*. New York: Norton.

Ehara, Yumiko. 1985. *Josei Kaihō toiu Shisō* [Thoughts called as women's liberation]. Tokyo: Keisō Shobō.

Ehara, Yumiko, ed. 1990. *Feminizumu Ronso: 70 Nendai kara 90 Nendai e* [Feminism controversies from 1970s to 1990s]. Tokyo: Keisō Shobō.

Evasdottir, Erika E. S. 2004. *Obedient Autonomy: Chinese Intellectuals and the Achievement of Orderly Life*. Vancouver: University of British Columbia Press.

Farquhar, Judith, and Qicheng Zhang. 2005. "Biopolitical Beijing: Pleasure, Sovereignty, and Self-Cultivation in China's Capital." *Cultural Anthropology* 20: 303–327.

Fluker, Shaun. 2010. "Ecological Integrity in Canada's National Parks: The False Promise of Law." *Windsor Review of Legal and Social Issues* 29: 89–123.

Forsyth, Tim, and Andrew Walker. 2008. *Forest Guardians, Forest Destroyers: The Politics of Environmental Knowledge in Northern Thailand*. Seattle: University of Washington Press.

Fujimura, Joan H. 1987. "Constructing 'Doable' Problems in Cancer Research: Articulating Alignment." *Social Studies of Science* 17: 257–293.

Gadd, Ben. 1995. *Handbook of the Canadian Rockies*. 2nd ed. Jasper, AB: Corax Press.

Genda, Yūji. 2001. *Shigoto no Naka no Aimai na Fuan: Yureru Jyakunen no Genzai* [Insecurities and ambiguities in work: The uncertain current situation of youth]. Tokyo: Chuōkōron Shinsha.

Goffman, Erving. 1959. *The Presentation of Self in Everyday Life*. Garden City, NY: Doubleday.

Gordon, Andrew. 1993. "Contests for the Workplace." In *Postwar Japan As History*, edited by Andrew Gordon, 373–394. Berkeley: University of California Press.

Goto-Jones, Christopher. 2005. *Political Philosophy in Japan: Nishida, the Kyoto School, and Co-prosperity*. London: Routledge.

Goto-Jones, Christopher. 2009. *Modern Japan: A Very Short Introduction*. Oxford: Oxford University Press.

Graburn, Nelson H. H. 2001. "Secular Ritual: A General Theory of Tourism." In *Hosts and Guests Revisited: Tourism Issues of the 21st Century*, edited by Valene L. Smith and Maryann Brent, 42–50. Putnam Valley, NY: Cognizant Communication.

Grusin, Richard. 2004. *Culture, Technology, and the Creation of America's National Parks*. Cambridge: Cambridge University Press.

Guattari, Felix. 2008. *The Three Ecologies*. Translated by Ian Pindar and Paul Sutton. London: Continuum.

Guth, Christine. 2004. *Longfellow's Tattoos: Tourism, Collecting and Japan*. Seattle: University of Washington Press.

Haber, Wolfgang. 2011. "An Ecosystem View into the Twenty-First Century." In *Ecology Revisited: Reflecting on Concepts, Advancing Science*, edited by Astrid Schwartz and Kurt Jax, 215–227. Dordrecht: Springer.

Halberstam, Judith. 1998. *Female Masculinity*. Durham, NC: Duke University Press.

Ham, Sam. 1992. *Environmental Interpretation: A Practical Guide for People with Big Ideas and Small Budgets*. Golden, CO: North American Press.

Handler, Richard. 1986. "Authenticity." *Anthropology Today* 2: 2–4.

Haraway, Donna J. 1991. *Simians, Cyborgs, and Women: The Reinvention of Nature*. New York: Routledge.

Hardt, Michael, and Antonio Negri. 2000. *Empire*. Cambridge, MA: Harvard University Press.

Hardt, Michael, and Antonio Negri. 2004. *Multitude: War and Democracy in the Age of Empire*. New York: Penguin.

Hayden, Cori. 2003. *When Nature Goes Public: The Making and Unmaking of Bioprospecting in Mexico*. Princeton, NJ: Princeton University Press.

Hermer, Joe. 2002. *Regulating Eden: The Nature of Order in North American Parks*. Toronto: University of Toronto Press.

Higuchi, Keiko. 1979. *Itoshiki wa Oi—Bungaku no Naka no Rōjin/Hīrō tachi* [To love aging: Seniors/heroes in literature]. Kyoto: PHP Kenkyūsho.

Higuchi, Keiko. 1990. *Onna to Otoko no Rōyūgaku* [Studies of elderly friendship for women and men]. Tokyo: Rōdōjunpōsha.

Ho, Karen. 2009. *Liquidated: An Ethnography of Wall Street*. Durham, NC: Duke University Press.

Hochschild, Arlie Russell. 1983. *The Managed Heart: Commercialization of Human Feeling*. Twentieth anniversary ed. Berkeley: University of California Press, 2003.

Holling, C. S. 1973. "Resilience and Stability of Ecological Systems." *Annual Review of Ecology and Systematics* 4: 1–23.

Imada, Erika. 2007. *Shōjo no Shakaishi* [Social history of *shōjo*]. Tokyo: Keisō Shobō

Imai, Konomi. 2002 "'*Fujin Shinpō*' to Bosei Hogo Ronsō: Kyōfūkai no Fujinkai ni Okeru Ichizuke o Kentō Suru Shihyō to shite" ["Fujin Shinpo" and the debate over protection of motherhood—as an indicator of positioning the Kyōfūkai in the world of women]. *Kirisutokyō Shakaimondai* 51: 63–84.

Imamura, Yōichi. 2001. "'Ōhashi Kyosen' wa Terebi Bunka de Aru!" ["Ōhashi Kyosen" is the television culture!]. *Galac* 3: 28–31.

Inagaki, Kyōko. 2007. *Jogakkō to Jogakusei: Kyoyo · Tashinami · Modan Bunka* [Girl's school and girl students: Liberal arts, refined taste and modern culture.] Tokyo: Chuōkōron Shinsha.

Inagami, Takeshi. 2008. "Kaisha Kyōdōtai no Yukue" [The direction of the community-model company]. *Ōhara Shakai Mondai Kenkyūsho Zasshi* 599/600: 29–49.

Inoue, Miyako. 2002. "Gender, Language, and Modernity: Toward an Effective History of Japanese Women's Language." *American Ethnologist* 29: 392–422.

Inoue, Miyako. 2003. "The Listening Subject of Japanese Modernity and His Auditory Double: Citing, Sighting, and Siting the Modern Japanese Woman." *Cultural Anthropology* 18: 156–193.

Inoue, Miyako. 2007. "Language and Gender in an Age of Neoliberalism." *Gender and Language* 1: 79–91.

Itō, Osamu. 2007. *Nihon no Keizai: Rekishi, Genjō, Ronten* [Japanese economy: History, current situation, issues]. Tokyo: Chuōkōron-shinsha.

Ivy, Marilyn. 1993. "Formation of Mass Culture." In *Postwar Japan as History*, edited by Andrew Gordon, 239–258. Berkeley: University of California Press.

Iwai, Katsuhito. 1997. *Shihonshugi o Kataru* [Talking about Capitalism]. Tokyo: Chikuma Shobō.

Iwai, Katsuhito. 2002. "The Nature of the Business Corporation: Its Legal Structure and Economic Functions." *Japanese Economic Review* 53: 243–273.

Iwai, Katsuhito. 2003. *Kaisha wa Korekara Dōnarunoka* [What will become of the corporation?]. Tokyo: Heibonsha.

Iwai, Katsuhito. 2005. *Kaisha wa Dareno Monoka* [To whom does the corporation belong?]. Tokyo: Heibonsha.

Japan Ministry of Foreign Affairs. 2013. "Visa: Working Holiday System." Accessed May 1, 2014. www.mofa.go.jp/mofaj/toko/visa/working_h.html.

Japan Ministry of Justice. 2003. *Immigration white paper*. Tokyo: Printing Bureau, Ministry of Finance.

Kamei, Shunsuke. 1994. "Nihon no Kindai to Honyaku" [Modernity in Japan and translation]. In *Kindai Nihon no Honyaku Bunka* [Translation culture in modern Japan], edited by Shunsuke Kamei. Tokyo: Chūō Kōronsha.

Kanbayashi, Hiroshi. 2010. "Kōdokeizaiseichōki no Kaisō Kizokuishiki: Sengo Nihon ni Okeru Kaisō Kizoku Ishiki ni Kansuru Nōto 1" [Social stratification consciousness during the high economic growth era: Note on the social stratification identification in postwar Japan 1]. *Tōhokugakuin Daigaku Kyōyōgakubu Ronshū* 156: 25–54.

Kaneko, Masaru. 1999. *Shijō* [Market]. Tokyo: Iwanami Shoten.

Kanetaka, Masao, and Taiki Morohashi. 2001. "Kyosen no Seikō to Intai: Terebiteki Imi no Kōsatsu" [A success and retirement of Kyosen: An inquiry of meaning of television]. *Galac* 3: 35–37.

Kant, Immanuel. 1991. *Political Writings*. Cambridge: Cambridge University Press.

Karatani, Kojin. 1993a. *Kotoba to Higeki* [Language and tragedy]. Tokyo: Kōdansha.

Karatani, Kojin. 1993b. *Origins of Modern Japanese Literature*. Durham, NC: Duke University Press.

Kawahara, Hiroshi. 1998. *"Jizai" ni Ikita Nihonjin* [Japanese who lived "freely"]. Tokyo: Nōsongyoson Bunka Kyōkai.

Kawamura, Kunimitsu. 1993. *Otome no Inori: Kindai Josei Imēji no Tanjō* [The maiden's prayer: The birth of the image of modern women]. Tokyo: Kinokuniya Shoten.

Kawamura, Kunimitsu. 1994. *Otome no Shintai: Onna no Kindai to Sekushuaritī* [The maiden's body: Women's modernity and sexuality]. Tokyo: Kinokuniya Shoten.

Kawamura, Kunimitsu. 2003. *Otome no Yukue: Kindai Josei no Hyōshō to Tatakai* [The maiden's journey: The representations and the struggles of modern women] Tokyo: Kinokuniya Shoten.

Kawashima, Tadashi. 1998. *Shūshoku Saki wa Mori no Naka* [The nature-interpretation adventure]. Tokyo: Shōgakkan.

Kay, James J., Henry A. Regier, Michelle Boyle, and George Francis. 1999. "An Ecosystem Approach to Sustainability: Addressing the Challenge of Complexity." *Futures* 31: 721–742.

Kelly, William. 1993. "Finding a Place in Metropolitan Japan: Ideologies, Institutions, and Everyday Life." In *Postwar Japan as History*, edited by Andrew Gordon, 189–216. Berkeley: University of California Press.

Kelsky, Karen. 2001. *Women on the Verge: Japanese Women, Western Dreams*. Durham, NC: Duke University Press.

Kiridōshi, Risaku. 2001. *Miyazaki Hayao no Sekai* [A world of Miyazaki Hayao]. Tokyo: Chikuma Shinsho.

Kishimoto, Shigenobu. 1979. *Chūryū no Gensō* [Fantasy of middle class]. Tokyo: Kōdansha.

Kitō, Shūichi. 1996. *Shizenhogo o Toinaosu: Kankyō Rinri to Nettowāku* [Rethinking nature conservation: Environmental ethics and networks]. Tokyo: Chikuma Shobō.

Koizumi, Takeei. 2001. *Tozan no Tanjō: Hito wa Naze Yama ni Noboru yō ni natta no ka* [The birth of mountain climbing: How did people come to climb mountains?]. Tokyo: Chūōkōron-shinsha.

Kondo, Dorinne K. 1990. *Crafting Selves: Power, Gender and Discourses of Identity in a Japanese Workplace*. Chicago: University of Chicago Press.

Kondo, Dorinne K. 1997. *About Face: Performing Race in Fashion and Theater*. New York: Routledge.

Koschmann, J. Victor. 2006. "National Subjectivity and the Uses of Atonement in the Age of Recession." In *Japan after Japan: Social and Cultural Life from the Recessionary 1990s to the Present*, edited by Tomiko Yoda and Harry Harootunian, 122–141. Durham, NC: Duke University Press.

Kuwabara, Takeo. 1997. *Tozan no Bunkashi* [Cultural history of mountain climbing]. Tokyo: Heibonsha.

Laclau, Ernesto. 1977. *Politics and Ideology in Marxist Theory: Capitalism-Fascism-Populism*. London: NLB.

Lambek, Michael. 2008. "Value and Virtue." *Anthropological Theory* 8: 133–157.

Latour, Bruno. 1987. *Science in Action: How to Follow Scientists and Engineers through Society*. Cambridge, MA: Harvard University Press.

Latour, Bruno. 1993. *We Have Never Been Modern*. Translated by Catherine Porter. Cambridge, MA: Harvard University Press.

Latour, Bruno. 2005. *Reassembling the Social: An Introduction to Actor-Network-Theory*. Oxford: Oxford University Press.

Lazzarato, Maurizio. 1996. "Immaterial Labour." In *Radical Thought in Italy*, edited by Paolo Virno and Michael Hardt, 132–146. Minneapolis: University of Minnesota Press.

Leheny, David. 2003. *The Rules of Play: National Identity and the Shaping of Japanese Leisure*. Ithaca, NY: Cornell University Press.

Leopold, Aldo. [1949] 1966. *A Sand County Almanac: With Other Essays on Conservation from Round River*. New York: Oxford University Press.

Liu, Lydia H. 1995. *Translingual Practice: Literature, National Culture, and Translated Modernity—China, 1900–1937*. Stanford, CA: Stanford University Press.

Löfgren, Orvar. 1999. *On Holiday: A History of Vacationing*. Berkeley: University of California Press.

Lowe, Celia. 2006. *Wild Profusion: Biodiversity Conservation in an Indonesian Archipelago*. Princeton, NJ: Princeton University Press.

Lowry, William R. 1994. *The Capacity for Wonder: Preserving National Parks*. Washington, DC: Brookings Institution Press.

Luhrmann, T. M. 2006. "Subjectivity." *Anthropological Theory* 6: 345–361.

MacCannell, Dean. [1976] 1999. *The Tourist: A New Theory of the Leisure Class*. Berkeley: University of California Press.

Machida, Sōhō. 2003. *Yama no Reiryoku: Nihonjin wa Soko ni Nani o Mitaka* [The spiritual power of mountains: What did the Japanese see there?]. Tokyo: Kōdansha.

Maki, Yūkō. 1991a. *Maki Yūkō Zenshū 1*. Tokyo: Satsuki Shobō.

Maki, Yūkō. 1991b. *Maki Yūkō Zenshū 3*. Tokyo: Satsuki Shobō.

Manzenreiter, Wolfram. 2011. "Climbing Walls: Dismantling Hegemonic Masculinity in a Japanese Sport Subculture." In *Recreating Japanese Men*, edited by Sabine Frühstück and Anne Walthall, 220–240. Berkeley: University of California Press.

Martin, Emily. 1994. *Flexible Bodies: The Role of Immunity in American Culture from the Days of Polio to the Age of AIDS*. Boston: Beacon Press.

Marty, Sid. 1984. *A Grand and Fabulous Notion: The First Century of Canada's National Parks*. Toronto: NC Press.

Maruyama, Masao. [1952] 1983. *Nihon Seijishisōshi Kenkyū* [Studies in the intellectual history of Tokugawa Japan]. Tokyo: Tokyo Daigaku Shuppankai.

Marx, Karl. 1992. *Capital*. Vol. 1, *Critique of Political Economy*. New York: Penguin.

Masco, Joseph. 2006. *The Nuclear Borderlands: The Manhattan Project in Post–Cold War New Mexico*. Princeton, NJ: Princeton University Press.

Mathews, Andrew. 2011. *Instituting Nature: Authority, Expertise, and Power in Mexican Forests*. Cambridge, MA: MIT Press.

Matthews, Gordon. 1996. *What Makes Life Worth Living? How Japanese and Americans Make Sense of Their Worlds*. Berkeley: University of California Press.

Michishita, Hiroshi. 2001. *Executive Freeter*. Tokyo: Wani Books.

Miller, Peter. 2000. "Approaches to Ecological Integrity: Divergence, Convergence and Implementation." In *Implementing Ecological Integrity: Restoring Regional and Global Environmental and Human Health*, edited by P. Crabbé, A. Holland, L. Ryskowski, and L. Westra, 57–73. Dordrecht: Kluwer Academic Publishers.

Mitchell, Timothy. 1988. *Colonising Egypt*. Berkeley: University of California Press.

Mitsui, Hideko. 2008. "The Politics of National Atonement and Narrations of War." *Inter-Asia Cultural Studies* 9: 47–61.

Miyake, Hitoshi. 2004. *Reizan to Nihonjin* [Spiritual mountains and the Japanese]. Tokyo: Nihon Hōsō Shuppankyōkai.

Miyazaki, Hayao. 1983. *Kaze no Tani no Naushika*. [Nausicaä of the Valley of the Wind]. Tokyo: Tokuma Shoten.

Miyazaki, Hayao. 2002. *Kaze no Kaeru Basho: Naushika kara Chihiro made no Kiseki* [A place where wind comes back: A trajectory from Nausicaä to Chihiro]. Tokyo: Rockin' On.

Miyoshi, Masao. 1991. *Off Center: Power and Culture Relations between Japan and the United States*. Cambridge, MA: Harvard University Press.

Mol, Annemarie. 2008. "I Eat an Apple: On Theorizing Subjectivities." *Subjectivity* 22: 28–37.

Morinaga, Haruhiko. 1976. "Nihonjin nimo Kagaku ga Dekiruka" [Can the Japanese do science?]. *Shizen* 31: 52–58.

Morris-Suzuki, Tessa. 1998. *Re-inventing Japan: Time, Space, Nation*. Armonk, NY: M. E. Sharpe.

Murakami, Yasusuke. 1984. *Shinchūkan Taishū no Jidai: Sengo Nihon no Kaibōgaku* [The Era of new middle mass: The anatomy of the postwar Japan]. Tokyo: Chuōkōronsha.

Murakami, Yōichirō. 1995. "Gendai Kagaku ga Nihonjin no Shizenkan ni Ataeta Eikyō" [The influence of modern science on Japanese views of nature]. In *Nihonjin no Shizenkan* [Japanese perceptions of nature], edited by Ito Shuntaro. 429–444. Tokyo: Kawade Shobō.

Nagata, Minako. 1932. *Dansō Jugunki* [Battlefield reports in male clothes]. Tokyo: Nihon Hyōronsha.

Nakamaki, Hirochika. 2006. *Kaisha no Kami Hotoke: Keiei to Shūkyō no Jinruigaku* [Gods and Buddha in the company: Anthropology of management and religion]. Tokyo: Kōdansha.

Nakamaki, Hirochika, Hiroyama Kensuke, Mitsui Izumi, Shimamoto Midori, Hioki Kōichirō, Sumihara Noriya, Sawano Masahiko, and Tanushi Makoto. 2001. *Kaisha Jinruigaku* [Anthropology of the company]. Osaka: Tōhō Shuppan.

Nakamura, Karen, and Hisako Matsuo. 2003. "Female Masculinity and Fantasy Spaces: Transcending Genders in the Takarazuka Theatre and Japanese Popular Culture." In *Men and Masculinities in Contemporary Japan: Dislocating the Salaryman Doxa*, edited by James E. Roberson and Nobue Suzuki, 59–76. London and New York: Routledge.

Nakano, Mami. 2006. *Rōdō Dunpingu: Koyō no Tayōka no Hate ni* [Labor dumping: Beyond the diversification of employment]. Tokyo: Iwanami Shoten.

Napier, Susan J. 2001. *Anime from* Akira *to* Princess Mononoke*: Experiencing Contemporary Japanese Animation*. New York: Palgrave.

Nishikawa, Yūko. 1985. "Hitotsu no Keifu—Hiratsuka Raichō, Takamure Itsue, Ishimure Michiko" [A genealogy—Hiratsuka Raicho, Takamure Itsue, Ishimure Michiko]. In *Bosei o Tou: Rekishiteki Hensen* [Question to motherhood: A historical perspective], edited by Wakita Haruko and Kagiya Akiko, 158–191. Kyoto: Jinbun Shoin.

Nozawa, Masako. 1990. "Yōiku to Sono Shakaiteki Enjo no Arikata ni tsuite (II): Bosei Hogo Ronsō no Saihyōka e no Kokoromi" [On Child nurturing and its social support (II): Re-evaluation of maternity protection debates]. *Shakai mondai kenkyū* 39 (2): 1–22.

Numata, Makoto. 1994. *Shizenhogo to iu Shisō* [Nature conservation as thought]. Tokyo: Iwanami Shoten.

Nye, Joseph S., Jr. 1990. *Bound to Lead: The Changing Nature of American Power*. New York: Basic Books.

Nyíri, Pál. 2009. "Between Encouragement and Control: Tourism, Modernity and Discipline in China." In *Asia on Tour: Exploring the Rise of Asian*

Tourism, edited by Tim Winter, Peggy Teo, and T. C. Chang, 153–169. London: Routledge.

Ogasawara, Yuko. 1998. *Office Ladies and Salaried Men: Power, Gender, and Work in Japanese Companies*. Berkeley: University of California Press.

Oguma, Eiji. 2002. *Minshu to Aikoku—Sengo Nihon no Nashonarizumu to Kōkyōsei* [Democracy and patriotism: Nationalism and public space in post–World War II Japan]. Tokyo: Shinyōsha.

Ōhashi, Kyosen. 2000a. *Kyosen: Jinsei no sentaku* [Kyosen: A choice in life]. Tokyo: Kōdansha.

Ōhashi, Kyosen. 2000b. *Kyosen Nikki* [Kyosen diary]. Tokyo: Kōdansha.

Ōhashi, Kyosen. 2001. *Shuppatsuten* [Starting point]. Tokyo: Kōdansha.

Ōhashi, Kyosen. 2002a. *Kiro* [A turning point]. Tokyo: Kōdansha.

Ōhashi, Kyosen. 2002b. *Kokkaigiin Shikkaku* [No longer a councillor]. Tokyo: Kōdansha.

Ōhashi, Kyosen. 2003. *Kyosen 2: Jissen Nihon Dasshutsu* [Kyosen 2: Action, escape from Japan]. Tokyo: Kōdansha.

O'Neill, Robert V. 2001. "Is It Time to Bury the Ecosystem Concept? (With Full Military Honors, Of Course!)." *Ecology* 82: 3275–3284.

Ortner, Sherry B. 1999. *Life and Death on Mount Everest: Sherpas and Himalayan Mountaineering*. Princeton, NJ: Princeton University Press.

Ōsaki, Keiji. 1971. "Hokkaido Kaitaku Seisaku to Sapporo Nōgakō no Setsuritsu [Hokkaido development policies and the foundation of the Sapporo Agricultural School]. *Hokkaido Daigaku Nōkyōronsō* 27: 127–149.

Otake, Hideo. 2003. *Nihongata Popyurizumu: Seiji e no Kitai to Genmetsu* [Japanese-style populism: Hope and disillusionment in politics]. Tokyo: Chūōkōronsha.

Oyewumi, Oyeronke. 1997. *The Invention of Women: Making an African Sense of Western Gender Discourses*. Minneapolis: University of Minnesota Press.

Palmer, Howard, and J. Monroe Thorington. 1921. *A Climber's Guide to the Rocky Mountains of Canada*. New York: Knickerbocker Press.

Papastergiadis, Nikos. 2000. *The Turbulence of Migration: Globalization, Deterritorialization, and Hybridity*. Malden, MA: Polity Press.

Parks Canada. n.d. "Fire Management."

Parks Canada. 1997. *Banff National Park Management Plan*. Gatineau, QC: Parks Canada.

Partner, Simon. 1999. *Assembled in Japan: Electrical Goods and the Making of the Japanese Consumer*. Berkeley: University of California Press.

Passmore, John Arthur. 1974. *Man's Responsibility for Nature: Ecological Problems and Western Traditions*. London: Duckworth.

Pflugfelder, Gregory M. 1999. *Cartographies of Desire: Male-Male Sexuality in Japanese Discourse, 1600–1950*. Berkeley: University of California Press.

Pflugfelder, Gregory M. 2005. "'S' is for Sister: Schoolgirl Intimacy and 'Same-Sex Love' in Early Twentieth Century Japan. In *Gendering Modern Japanese*

History, edited by Barbara Molony and Kathleen Uno, 133–190. Cambridge, MA: Harvard University Press.

Pharr, Susan J. 1996. "Media as Trickster in Japan: A Comparative Perspective." In *Media and Politics in Japan*, edited by Susan J. Pharr and Ellis S. Krauus, 19–43. Honolulu: University of Hawai'i Press.

Pickett, S. T. A., and M. L. Cadenasso. 2002. "The Ecosystem as a Multidimensional Concept: Meaning, Model and Metaphor." *Ecosystems* 5: 1–10.

Pigg, Stacey Leigh. 2001. "Languages of Sex and AIDS in Nepal: Notes on the Social Production of Commensurability." *Cultural Anthropology* 16: 481–541.

Pole, Graeme. 1997. *The Canadian Rockies: An Altitude Superguide*. 2nd rev. ed. Canmore, AB: Altitude Publishing Canada.

Robertson, Jennifer. 1998. *Takarazuka: Sexual Politics and Popular Culture in Modern Japan*. Berkeley: University of California Press.

Robertson, Jennifer. 2002. "Yoshiya Nobuko Out and Outspoken in Practice and Prose." In *The Human Tradition in Modern Japan*, edited by Anne Wathall, 155–174. Oxford, UK: Rowman & Littlefield.

Robinson, Zac. 2004. "The Golden Years of Canadian Mountaineering: Asserted Ethics, Form, and Style, 1886–1925." *Sport History Review* 25: 1–19.

Rofel, Lisa. 2007. *Desiring China: Experiments in Neoliberalism, Sexuality, and Public Culture*. Durham, NC: Duke University Press.

Rorty, Amélie Oksenberg. 2007. "The Vanishing Subject: The Many Faces of Subjectivity." In *Subjectivity: Ethnographic Investigations*, edited by João Biehl, Byron Good, and Arthur Kleinman, 34–51. Berkeley: University of California Press.

Rorty, Richard. 1989. "Review of Gerald J. Larson and Eliot Deutsch, *Interpreting across Boundaries: New Essays in Comparative Philosophy*." *Philosophy East and West* 39: 332–337.

Russ, Ann Julienne. 2005. "Love's Labor Paid For: Gift and Commodity at the Threshold of Death." *Cultural Anthropology* 20: 128–155.

Sakai, Naoki. 1997. *Translation and Subjectivity: On "Japan" and Cultural Nationalism*. Minneapolis: University of Minnesota Press.

Sandford, R. W. 1994. *The Book of Banff: The Insider's Guide to What You Need to Know to Be a Local in Banff and the Bow Valley*. Banff, AB: Friends of Banff National Park.

Sandford, R. W. 2000. *Called by This Mountain: The Legend of the Silver Ice Axe and the Early Climbing History of Mount Alberta*. Canmore, AB: The Alpine Club of Canada and the Japanese Alpine Club.

Satsuka, Shiho. 2009. "Populist Cosmopolitanism: The Predicament of Subjectivity and the Japanese Fascination with Overseas." *Inter-Asia Cultural Studies* 10: 67–82.

Scott, Chic. 2000. *Pushing the Limits: The Story of Canadian Mountaineering*. Calgary: Rocky Mountain Books.

Screech, Timon. 2001. "The Visual Legacy of Dodonaeus in Botanical and Human Categorization." In *Dodonaeus in Japan: Translation and the Scientific*

Mind in the Tokugawa Period, edited by Willy Vande Walle and Kazuhiko Kasaya, 133–143. Leuven, Belgium: Leuven University Press.

Searle, Donald Richard. 2000. *Phantom Parks: The Struggle to Save Canada's National Parks.* Toronto: Key Porter Books.

Sellers, Richard West. 1997. *Preserving Nature in the National Parks: A History.* New Haven, CT: Yale University Press.

Shamoon, Deborah. 2012. *Passionate Friendship: The Aesthetics of Girls' Culture in Japan.* Honolulu: University of Hawai'i Press.

Shiga, Shigetaka. [1894] 1995. *Nihon Fūkeiron* [Japanese landscape]. Edited by Nobuyuki Kondo. Tokyo: Iwanami Shoten.

Shincho 45 [New tide 45]. 2000. "Yomazu ni Sumaseru Besuto Serā: Sengo no Nihonjin no Yume wo Taigen Shita 'Idai Naru Zokubutsu,' Kyosen Jinsei no Sentaku" [Cheatsheet for the bestsellers: "The great snoot" who embodies the postwar Japanese dream. Kyosen, a Choice in Life]. August, 268–270.

Shukan Shincho. 2001. "Mōsho Omimai Mōshi Agemasu: 1. Senkyo Undō Hōridashite Kanada e Kaetta Ōhashi Kyosen." [A mid-summer message: 1. Ōhashi Kyosen, who abandoned his election campaign and went back to Canada.] August 2.

Spivak, Gayatri C. 2000. "Translation as Culture." *Parallax* 6: 13–24.

Star, Susan Leigh, and James R. Griesemer. 1989. "Institutional Ecology, 'Translations' and Boundary Objects: Amateurs and Professionals in Berkeley's Museum of Vertebrate Zoology, 1907–39." *Social Studies of Science* 19: 387–420.

Suzuki, Masataka. 2002. *Nyonin Kinsei* [Off-limits to women]. Tokyo: Yoshikawa Kōbunkan.

Taggart, Paul. 2000. *Populism.* Buckingham, UK: Open University Press.

Tagore, Saranindranath. 2006. "The Possibility of Translation." *Theory, Culture and Society* 23: 79–81.

Takanashi, Akira. 2002. Nihonkeizaino Henbō to Jakunensha Koyōseisaku no Kadai [The changes in the Japanese economy and the problems of youth employment policies]. In *Jiyū no Daishō / Furitā: Gendai Wakamono no Shūgyō Ishiki to Kōdō* [Compensation for freedom / Freeter: The work consciousness and behaviors of contemporary youth], edited by Reiko Kosugi. 175–219. Tokyo: Nihon Rōdō Kenkyū Kikō.

Taylor, John P. 2001. "Authenticity and Sincerity in Tourism." *Annals of Tourism Research* 28: 7–26.

Taylor, Peter. 2005. *Unruly Complexity: Ecology, Interpretation, Engagement.* Chicago: University of Chicago Press.

Taylor, Peter. 2011. "Conceptualizing the Heterogeneity, Embeddedness, and Ongoing Restructuring That Make Ecological Complexity 'Unruly.'" In *Ecology Revisited: Reflecting on Concepts, Advancing Science*, edited by Astrid Schwarz and Kurt Jax, 87–95. Dordrecht: Springer.

Terao, Gorō. 2002. *"Shizen" Gainen no Keiseishi: China, Japan, Europe* [The history of the formation of the concept of "Nature": China, Japan, Europe]. Tokyo: Nōsangyoson Bunka Kyōkai.

Thomas, Julia. 2001. *Reconfiguring Modernity: Concepts of Nature in Japanese Political Ideology*. Berkeley: University of California Press.

Tilden, Freeman. 1957. *Interpreting Our Heritage: Principles and Practices for Visitor Services in Parks, Museums, and Historic Places*. Chapel Hill: University of North Carolina Press.

Tōyama, Shigeki, Seiichi Imai, and Akira Fujiwara. [1959] 1989. *Shōwashi* [A history of the Shōwa period]. Tokyo: Iwanami Shoten.

Tsing, Anna L. 1997. "Transitions as Translations." In *Transitions, Environments, Translations: Feminism in International Politics*, edited by Joan W. Scott, Cora Kaplan, and Debra Keates, 253–272. New York: Routledge.

Tsing, Anna L. 2004. *Friction: An Ethnography of Global Connection*. Princeton, NJ: Princeton University Press.

Ueno, Chizuko. 1986. *Onna wa Swkai o Sukueruka* [Can women save the world?]. Tokyo: Keisō Shobō.

Ueno, Chizuko. 1994. *Kindai Kazoku no Seiritsu to Shūen* [The formation and end of modern family]. Tokyo: Iwanami Shoten.

Uno, Kathleen S. 1991. "Women and Changes in the Household Division of Labor." In *Recreating Japanese Women, 1600–1945*, edited by Gail Lee Bernstein, 17–41. Berkeley: University of California Press.

Virno, Paolo. 2004. *A Grammar of the Multitude: For an Analysis of Contemporary Forms of Life*. Translated by Isabella Bertoletti, James Cascaito, and Andrea Casson. Los Angeles: Semiotext(e).

Viveiros de Castro, Eduardo. 1998. "Cosmological Deixis and Amerindian Perspectivism." *Journal of the Royal Anthropological Institute* 4: 469–488.

Voigt, Annette. 2011. "The Rise of Systems Theory in Ecology." In *Ecology Revisited: Reflecting on Concepts, Advancing Science*, edited by Astrid Schwartz and Kurt Jax, 183–194. Dordrecht: Springer.

von Uexkull, Jakob. [1934] 2010. *Foray into the Worlds of Animals and Humans: With a Theory of Meaning*. Minneapolis: University of Minnesota Press.

Wakita, Shigeru. 2010. "Rōdōhō no Kiseikanwa to Koyōhōkai: Rōdōsha Hakenhokaisei o meguru Kadai" [Deregulation of labor law and the deterioration of employment]. *Sōgō Shakaifukushi Kenkyū* 36: 26–36.

Walker, Brian, C. S. Holling, Stephen R. Carpenter, and Ann Kinzig. 2004. "Resilience, Adaptability and Transformability in Social-Ecological Systems." *Ecology and Society* 9, no. 2: 5.

Watanabe, Masao. 1976. *Nihonjin to Kindai Kagaku* [The Japanese and modern science]. Tokyo: Iwanami Shoten.

Westra, Laura. 2000. "The Global Integrity Project and the Ethics of Integrity." In *Implementing Ecological Integrity: Restoring Regional and Global Environmental and Human Health*, edited by P. Crabbé, A. Holland, L. Ryskowski, and L. Westra, 23–36. Dordrecht: Kluwer Academic.

White, Lynn. 1967. "The Historical Roots of Our Ecological Crisis." *Science* 155: 1203–1207.

Wigen, Kären. 2005. "Discovering the Japanese Alps: Meiji Mountaineering and the Quest for Geographical Enlightenment." *Journal of Japanese Studies* 31: 1–26.

Williams, Raymond. 1976. *Keywords: A Vocabulary of Culture and Society*. London: Collins.

Willis, A. J. 1997. "Forum." *Functional Ecology* 11: 268–271.

Winter, Tim. 2009. "Destination Asia: Rethinking Material Culture." In *Asia on Tour: Exploring the Rise of Asian Tourism*, edited by Tim Winter, Peggy Teo, and T. C. Chang, 52–66. New York: Routledge.

Winterhaider, Bruce. 1984. "Reconsidering the Ecosystem Concept." *Reviews in Anthropology* 11: 301–313.

Woodley, Stephen. 2010. "Ecological Integrity and Canada's National Parks." *George Wright Forum* 27: 151–160.

Worrell, Richard, and Michael C. Appleby. 2000. "Stewardship of Natural Resources: Definition, Ethical, and Practical Aspects." *Journal of Agriculture and Environmental Ethics* 12: 263–277.

Yanabu, Akira. 1982. *Honyakugo Seiritsujijō* [How translations were made]. Tokyo: Iwanami Shoten.

Yanagisako, Sylvia. 2002. *Producing Culture and Capital: Family Firms in Italy*. Princeton, NJ: Princeton University Press.

Yoda, Tomiko, and Harry Harootunian, eds. 2006. *Japan after Japan: Social and Cultural Life from the Recessionary 1990s to the Present*. Durham, NC: Duke University Press.

Yoshimi, Shunya. 2001. "'Amerika' o Yokubō/bōkyaku suru Sengo: 'Kichi' to 'Shōhi' no Kussetsu wo Megutte" [The postwar that desires/forgets "America": On "military bases" and "consumption"]. *Gendai Shisō Special Edition* 29: 44–63.

Yoshimi, Shunya. 2007. *Shinbei to Hanbei: Sengo Nihon no Seijiteki Muishiki* [Pro-America and anti-America: Political unconsciousness in postwar Japan]. Tokyo: Iwanami Shoten.

Yoshinaka, Atsuhiro. 1996. "Kōen Kanri Shuhō to shite no Intāpuritēshon" [Interpretation as a park management method]. *Kokuritsu Kōen* 541: 20–31.

Zhan, Mei. 2009. *Other-Worldly: Making Chinese Medicine through Transnational Frames*. Durham, NC: Duke University Press.

Zhan, Mei. 2011. "Worlding Oneness: Daoism, Heidegger, and Possibilities for Treating the Human." *Social Text 109* 29, no. 4: 107–128.

Index

Buddhism, 13, 23, 24, 98, 115, 116, 180, 181, 203, 216–17
Butler, Judith, 141–42, 236n10, 236n13

Canada: as emigration destination, 42–45; as Japanese tourist destination, 2–3, 14, 34–35, 67; multiculturalism in, 27, 185, 208; Ōhashi on, 84–86; spatial imaginary of, 34, 43–45, 66; as utopia/dreamland, 2, 34, 43, 66, 68; working holiday visas to, 45, 144, 227n4
Canadian National Railway, 26
Canadian Pacific Railway, 15, 156, 188, 191
Canadian Rockies: management plan for, 186; natural image of, 66; promotion of, 14, 27, 163; as utopia/dreamland, 120
Canadian Rocky Mountain Parks World Heritage Site, 2, 6, 163
capitalism: gender and the family in, 130; Japanese, 55; labor in, 110–12; millenial, 231n4; and subjectivity, 110–12; value in contemporary, 13
China, 17, 19, 83
choice, individual, 71–76
Christianity, conceptions of nature in, 172–73, 206
chūkan sō/chūkan taishū (middle layer/mass), 33, 67, 82–83, 226n12. See also shomin
citizenship, 68–69, 77–78, 88
Cold War, 81, 83, 173
Columbia Icefield, 14, 25, 99, 100, 103, 126, 157
Comaroff, Jean , 231n4
Comaroff, John, 231n4
commodities, tour guides as, 95–105, 109–15, 118, 121
co-modification, of the self, 112–15, 121
Confucianism: 181; neo-Confucianism, 77
conservation movements, 148
consumer culture, 40, 50, 70, 81

Convention Concerning the Protection of the World Cultural and Natural Heritage, 163
corporations: corporate nominalism, 53–55; corporate realism, 53–56. See also Japanese corporate system
cosmopolitanism: concept of, 68–69; mountaineering and, 26–28; populist, 67–69, 88; of tour guides, 13, 23, 121, 125, 132; women and, 132
cultural translation: concept of, 12–13; guides' practices of, 15–16, 35–36; Japan and, 17–18; mountaineering and, 25–32; by non-Western people, 16–17; Ōhashi and, 69; politics of, 16–18, 208–12; power/knowledge relations in, 175–76; products/outcomes of, 38; science and, 17, 185; translation words, 18–24

Datsua Nyūou (Leaving Asia and Entering Europe), 18
Deleuze, Gilles, 232n5
democracy, 80, 81
detachment. See jizai
dogs, 193–94
Dore, Ronald, 52–53
dreamland. See utopia/dreamland

ecological integrity: change as key element in, 187–92; humans as threat to, 155; importance of, 167, 169, 184; meaning of, 183–84, 187–88, 238n2; nonanthropocentric approach and, 198–203; in park philosophy and management, 185–89; philosophical background of, 194–98; rules of use based on, 190; stability as key element in, 191, 195, 202–3, 239n8
ecology, 183–212; concept of ecosystem, 196–98; guides' attraction to, 36, 149, 180, 203–5; human place in, 187, 190, 192–94, 201–2, 239n3 (see also nature: humans in relation to); human stressors in, 188; nature interpretation based on, 148, 155,

159–63, 178; resilience in, 187; universal applicability of, 148–49, 155, 184–85, 194, 203
ecosophy, 7
ecosystem, concept of, 196–98, 239n7
elites: cosmopolitan, 68–69; emulation of the West by, 18; and mountaineering, 28, 29; opposition to, 68, 69, 79, 84, 230n15; subjectivity of, 78
elk, 192–93
emperor's ice axe, 10, 25–27
Employment Security Law (Japan, 1947), 58
Enlightenment, European, 29, 70, 78, 111, 115, 216
environment, protection of, 66, 148, 158, 172, 181, 183–85, 190–93, 199–202, 239n8. See also environmental stewardship
environmental ethics, 195–96, 199–202
environmentalism, 134
environmental stewardship, 148–51, 167–68, 171–74. See also environment, protection of
epistemology, Western, 223n1
Equal Employment Opportunity Law (Japan, 1986), 42, 59
ethics: environmental, 195–96, 199–202; humanistic, 196, 198–99, 239n8

fire, 160, 187, 191–92
First Nations. See indigenous peoples
flexible laborers, 2, 12, 23, 34, 40–41, 57–58, 65, 97, 120–21, 149
folk knowledge, Japanese, 180–81
freedom: conceptions of, 13, 115–18, 216–17, 219, 232n6; in frontier lands, 43–45; of Japanese workers, 40–41, 59; nature in relation to, 11–12, 23, 116–17; neoliberal discourse of, 216–19; perceived Japanese constraints on, 11, 23, 41–42, 44–47, 51, 71–76; populist cosmopolitanism and, 69; subjectivity in relation to, 23, 69, 71–76, 78, 113, 117–18; tour

guides and, 13, 23, 34, 35, 43, 51, 108, 115–18, 216–19; as translation word, 23, 115–16; travel as indicator of, 37. See also jiyū
frontier lands, 43–45
Fujimura, Joan, 207
Fukuzawa Yukichi, 29–30, 115–16
furītā (freelance part-time workers), 40–41, 226n2. See also flexible laborers; haken

Genda Yuji, 58
gender: ambiguities in, 129–36, 139–42, 145–46; and city vs. nature, 142–46; in Japan, 130–31, 144, 236n12, 237n14; "naturalness" of, 139–43, 236n13; performance of, 134, 135, 141–42, 146; subjectivity in relation to, 142–43; systems of, 142, 236n14; tour guide roles based on, 126–28. See also women
girls' high schools, 129, 131, 233n5, 234n7
Goffman, Erving, 223n1, 236n10
Griesemer, James, 24
Guattari, Felix, 7, 232n5
guides. See tour guides

Haber, Wolfgang, 197
haecceities, 232n5
haken (indirect employment of temporary staff), 58, 97. See also flexible laborers; furītā
Halberstam, Judith, 133
Ham, Sam, Environmental Interpretation, 164–65, 171–72
Haraway, Donna, 200
Hardt, Michael, 112
Heidegger, Martin, 175–76
Heritage Tourism Strategy. See Banff Bow Valley Heritage Tourism Strategy
high schools, for girls, 129, 131, 233n5, 234n7
Higuchi Keiko, 76
Hokkaido, 44, 50–51, 227n3

hon'yakugo. *See* translation words
Horne, Greg, 27
horses, 194
Hosokawa Moritatsu, 26
housewife debates, 233n3
humanistic ethics, 196, 198–99, 239n8
human nature: innate value of, 115;
shizen and, 20. *See also* nature:
humans in relation to

ie (family system), 55–56
Imamura Yōichi, 82
immaterial work, 13, 110–12, 219
indigenous peoples, 156–57, 188, 191,
239n3, 239n4
individual, concept of, 229n9
Inoue, Miyako, 59
interpretation, concept of, 163–64,
174–75, 238n5
Interpretive Guides Association, 237n1
Ivy, Marilyn, 83
Iwai Katsuhito, 53–56, 228n11

Japan: and cultural translation, 17–18;
economic crisis in, 1, 12; female masculinity in, 129; gender in, 130–31,
144, 236n12, 237n14; mountains in,
28–29; nationalism in, 21–22, 29,
70, 77, 80–81; national park concept
in, 16; Ōhashi's critique of, 79–81,
84–85; postwar attitudes in, 80–81;
sociopolitical significance of concepts of nature in, 11–12; translation
words in, 18–24; US cultural influence in, 45, 71, 80–84, 88–94; US
relations with, 35, 83–86; the West
emulated by, 17–18, 22, 205–6; Western values and lifestyle vs. those of,
73–76, 143–44, 206
Japanese Alpine Club, 26, 27, 28
Japanese corporate system: advantages and disadvantages of, 56–57;
Anglo-American vs., 52–53; characteristics of traditional, 33, 39, 53,
54, 61; community model of, 41–42,
52–58; employee role in, 55; family

system as model of, 55–56; minorities in, 57; Ōhashi's critique of,
71–74; origins of, 55; subject status
of, 54–56; transformations in, 1,
12, 34, 41, 65, 117; women's role in,
39–40, 57, 58–60; younger generations' attitudes and experiences in,
11, 23, 34, 42, 49–50, 58, 60–62
*Japanese-Style Management in a New
Era*, 57–58
Japanese tourists: bus tours for, 3–5;
promotion of Canada to, 2–3, 14,
34–35, 67, 163; shaping experiences
of, 16; tour experiences of, 123–25,
128; Western perceptions of, 3, 5
Jasper National Park, 25
Jasper-Yellowhead Museum, 27
jinen, 180
jishu (self-oriented), 115
jishu nin'i (self-determination), 116
jiyū (freedom), 13, 23, 98, 115–18,
216–17, 219
jizai (liberation as self-detachment),
13, 23, 98, 115–17, 216–17

Kanetaka Masao, 79
Kant, Immanuel, 172, 195
Karatani Kojin, 28
karōshi (death by overwork), 56
Kawahara Hiroshi, 116
Kawamura, Kunimitsu, 131
Keidanren (Japan Business Federa-
tion), 57
keiretsu (group corporation system),
54
Kelsky, Karen, 143–44
keystone species, 202, 239n3
Kitō Shūichi, 199–200
knowledge politics, 173, 208–12, 220
Kojima Usui, 29
Kondo, Dorinne, 53
Kyoto School, 22

Lake Louise, 14, 62
landscape, 28–29
language, 101–2, 106–9, 154, 161

Laozi, 19
Latour, Bruno, 181
leisure, 71–79, 82
Leopold, Aldo, 195
liberalism: concept of subjectivity
   grounded in, 69–70, 111–12, 117,
   232n4; environmental stewardship
   as outgrowth of, 172–73
liberalization, 12
linguistic translation, 15, 175–76,
   224n4, 238n9
Liu, Lydia, 175–76, 238n9
loanwords, 18, 104, 106–7

MacCannell, Dean, 223n1
Maki Yūkō, 10, 11, 15, 25–32, 155
male impersonators, 129–30
Maruyama Masao, 22, 77–78, 230n13
Marx, Karl, 41
maternity protection debate, 232n3
Matsuo, Hisako, 130
Michishita Hiroshi, 41
middle layer/mass. *See* chūkan sō/
   chūkan taishū
Mill, John Stuart, 115, 195
Miller, Peter, 196
mimicry, 237n4
Mitchell, Timothy, 223n1
Mittellegi Ridge, Switzerland, 28, 30
Miyazaki Hayao: *Nausicaä of the Valley
   of the Wind*, 135, 235n9; *Princess Mono-
   noke*, 235n8; *Spirited Away*, 235n8
Miyoshi, Masao, 21, 70, 225n5
modernity: Japan and, 22, 205–6;
   and Japanese women's social role,
   233n3, 233n5; nature in relation to,
   78, 145–46
mountaineering, 25–32, 232n1
Mountain Parks Heritage Interpretation Association (MPHIA), 147–55,
   159–71, 173–78, 180–81, 183–85, 189,
   191–95, 204–5, 207–12, 237n1
Mount Alberta, 10, 25–27, 225n9
Mount Rundle, 159, 169, 209
MPHIA. *See* Mountain Parks Heritage
   Interpretation Association

multiculturalism, 27, 185, 208
Murakami Yōichirō, 206–7

Nagano High School Old Boys Alpine
   Club, 27
Nakamura, Karen, 130
Nakamura Masanao, 115
Nakano Mami, 58, 97
nationalism, 21–22, 29, 70, 77, 80–81
national parks: concept of, 16; function
   and use of, 185–86
National Parks Act (Canada), 186
nation-states, 37, 69
natural rights, 115
nature: Canadian vs. Japanese forest
   practices, 4–5; Christian conceptions
   of, 172–73, 206; city vs., 142–46;
   concept of, underlying nature
   interpretation, 171; contemporary problems of, 145–46, 220–21;
   development-oriented approach to,
   188, 195, 201; freedom in relation
   to, 11–12, 23, 116–17; by guides, 4–7;
   humans in relation to, 66, 77, 93,
   149, 172–73, 176, 179–80, 199–202
   (*see also* ecology: human place in);
   intrinsic value of, 195, 200; Japanese, 11; Japanese conceptions
   of, 19–20, 77, 149, 161–65, 174–84,
   207–8; Japanese tourists' perception of, 3–6; magnificent, 1–2, 5, 11,
   24, 43; modernity in relation to, 78,
   145–46; mountains and mountaineering, 25–32; North American, 1–2,
   11; principles underlying concept of,
   1, 6–7; questions raised by, 6; society
   in relation to, 7, 11; stewardship of,
   148–51, 167–68, 171–74; subjectivity
   in relation to, 6, 11–13, 28, 31–32,
   66; supposed universality of, 220;
   as translation word, 19–21; Western
   conceptions of, 20, 149, 161–65,
   174–84, 206–8. *See also* shizen
nature interpretation, 36, 147–81; basic
   principles of, 165; conceptions of,
   180–81; concept of nature

nature interpretation (*continued*)
underlying, 171; cultural differences
in, 149, 161–65, 174–82; educational
purpose of, 164, 167–68, 171–74, 211;
Japanese translation of, 174–76;
science as vehicle for, 155, 158, 164,
171–72, 178; social and intersubjective factors in, 178–81, 211; stewardship as goal of, 148–51, 167–68,
171–74; terminology of, 163–64,
238n5; theme as central element in,
165, 167–69, 171, 177–78; training in,
163–65. *See also* nature translation
nature interpretation accreditation
program, 36, 147–81; cost of, 153,
154, 210; courses in, 151, 154, 159–65,
185; criteria for passing, 151, 152,
165–71; oral examination for, 165–71;
parts of, 152
nature translation: as cultural
translation, 37; familiarization and
identification as goal of, 15; nature
interpretation as, 163–65, 171; politics of, 220–21; social imaginaries
and, 11–12; subjectivity construction
and, 11–12; tour guides and, 4–7,
32–33, 36, 125, 178. *See also* nature
interpretation
Negri, Antonio, 112neoliberalism:
corporate reforms associated with,
1, 34, 41, 57–58, 65, 117; effects
of, 12–13, 33, 57–58; and freedom,
216–19; park management reforms
associated with, 148–49, 153; values
of, and subjectivity, 59–60, 65, 88,
117, 215–16
New Zealand, 45, 51, 84–86
Nikkeiren (Japan Federation of Employers' Associations), 57
nonanthropocentric approach, 195,
198–203, 239n8
nonhuman actors, 198–203, 238n8
Numata Makoto, 201–2

Ōhashi Kyosen, 34–35, 66, 67–88,
94, 144, 145, 230n14; *11 pm*, 78–79,

81–84; *Kyosen: Jinsei no Sentaku*, 69,
71–76, 79; *Kyosen Nikki*, 73; *Kyosen
2: Jissen, Nihon Dasshutsu*, 87; *Sekai
marugoto how much*, 82
Oberlin, John, 26
Ogasawara, Yuko, 226n1
Oguma Eiji, 78, 81
OLs (office ladies), 40, 62, 226n1
O'Neill, Robert, 239n7
ordinary folks. *See* shomin
Orientalism, 73, 87, 143, 220
Ortner, Sherry, 23–24, 225n8
outdoor guiding, 127–28, 134–35,
233n4. *See also* hiking guides
overcoming modernity, 22
Oyeronke Oyewumi, 236n14

park management: changing principles
of, 189, 190–94; ecological integrity
as foundation of, 183–89, 238n1;
environmental ethics and, 195–96;
neoliberal reforms of, 148–49, 153;
science as basis of, 189
Parks Canada, 36, 186, 188, 190;
Strategic Framework to Sustain
the Integrity of Ecosystems,
238n1
Partner, Simon, 82
Passmore, John, 172–73
Paz, Alejandro, 224n4
performance: concept of, 236n10; of
gender, 134, 135, 141–42, 146; of subjectivity, 13, 24, 35, 38, 68, 98, 118,
125, 136; by tour guides, 99, 106
personal satisfaction, 35
Pflugfelder, Gregory, 234n7
pollution, 73–74
populism, 68
populist cosmopolitanism, 67–69, 88

racism, 153
resilience, 187
retirement, 68, 71–76, 84
Robertson, Jennifer, 129–30, 234n7
Rofel, Lisa, 240n1
Romanticism, 29

S (sisterhood) relationships, 234n7
Sakai, Naoki, 21, 22, 74, 225n6
Sakai Mitsuo, 240n9
sakui (invention), 77
Sandford, Robert (Bob), 26–28, 155–58, 209–10; *The Book of Banff*, 156; *Called by This Mountain*, 10–11
sangyō haikibutsu (industrial waste), 57, 76, 78
sararīman (white-collar salaried men), 39, 46, 49, 59, 71–74, 76, 78, 130
sawayaka (refreshing), 108–9
science: guides' attraction to, 203–5, 207; humankind-nature relationship assumed by, 172; Japanese practices of, 205–7, 240n9; nature interpretation based on, 155, 158, 164, 171–72, 178; park management based on, 189; technologization of, 205–8; and translation, 17, 185; universal applicability of, 17, 185, 194, 205, 207, 220
Screech, Timon, 237n14
seishain (full-time, regular employee), 41, 52, 58
Self-Defense Forces, 89
September 11, 2001 attacks, 213
shachiku (domesticated animal of a corporation), 57, 74, 78
shamans, guides as, 179, 209–12
shareholders, 54–56
Sherpa mountain guides, 23–24, 225n8
shigarami (social rules and expectations), 44, 51
Shiga Shigetaka, *Nihon Fūkeiron*, 29
shinjinrui (new Homo sapiens), 49–50
shinjiyūshugi. *See* neoliberalism
shizen (nature), 19–20, 77, 175, 179–80
shōhin. *See* commodities, tour guides as
shokunin (craftsman), 46–47
shomin (ordinary folks), 68–70, 78–84, 87–88. *See also* chūkan sō/chūkan taishū
shugyō (ascetic practice), 46, 49, 107
shutaisei (subjectivity), 21–22, 70, 77–78
Simondson, Gilbert, 219
sincerity, 98–107

skiing, 40, 44–48, 61
social imaginaries, 11–12
soft power, 71, 88–94
standardization, of tour guides, 98–107, 109
Star, Susan, 24
subjectivity: autonomous, 76; capitalism and, 110–12; and choice, 71–76, 78; co-modification and, 112–15; conceptions of, 228n3; cosmopolitan, 68–69; cultivation of, 75–76; fetishism of, 111–12; freedom in relation to, 23, 69, 71–76, 78, 113, 117–18; gender in relation to, 142–43; Japanese conceptions of, 21–22, 70–88; leisure and, 74–79; liberal conception of, 69–70, 111–12, 117, 232n4; and mountains, 28–29; nature in relation to, 6, 11–13, 28, 31–32, 66; nature translation as means of constructing, 11–12; neoliberal values and, 59–60, 65, 88, 117, 215–16; Ōhashi and, 69–88; personal satisfaction and, 35; responsibility as aspect of, 22, 70, 77; retirement and, 74–76; shomin, 68, 81–84, 87–88; social and intersubjective factors in, 69, 112–15, 117, 121, 219, 232n5; of tour guides, 11, 13, 35–36, 43, 97–98, 112, 118–19, 121, 125, 136, 219, 229n3; as translation word, 21–23, 70; universality of, 70; Western, 69–70; of women, 59–66, 132. *See also* shutaisei
subjects, corporations as, 54–56
sunflower life, 72, 74
systems approaches, 196–97

Taishō democracy, 80
Takanashi, Akira, 228n8
Takarazuka theater, 129–30
Taoism, 19–20, 115, 179–81, 203
Taylor, Peter, 196–97
television, social role of, 82–84
Terao Gorō, 239n8
Thomas, Julia, 78
Tilden, Freeman, 164, 238n5

Printed and bound by CPI Group (UK) Ltd, Croydon, CR0 4YY

23/04/2025

14661003-0001